Evaluating Creativity

Many subjects in the school curriculum ask students to make various kinds of practical and arts based productions. These might include: paintings; creative writing; performances; recordings; videos and multimedia digital creations. Within the subject areas many interesting contradictions arise when students are required to be cultural producers in this way, and these contradictions are most acute when teachers and students evaluate media arts work.

By bringing together studies from different arts disciplines this book raises provocative questions about the function of evaluation in general; the role of formal assessment and its relation with informal evaluation; the role of the audience for the creative product; the value of making within the subject discipline and to the learner him or herself; the balance within the subject paid to product and process; as well as pedagogic considerations such as the role of reflection and the place of the student or young person's voice. This book aims to discuss how the various teaching disciplines each draw on different models of teaching and learning as well as possessing different conceptions of cultural production.

This book aims to debate these different conceptions of young people as cultural producers. Each contribution will give examples of practice from a subject discipline including English, Art, Music, Drama, Media Studies, Design and Technology, Gallery Education and Digital Arts. This will enable those involved with primary, secondary, further, higher, gallery and community education to learn from each other and to develop a coherent approach to the range of creative work produced by young people. By focusing on questions of evaluation and containing a range of practical examples the book will set an agenda for creative work by young people in the school curriculum and beyond.

Julian Sefton-Green is Media Education Development Officer at Weekend Arts College (InterChange Trust). **Rebecca Sinker** is Research Fellow in Digital Arts at Middlesex University.

Evaluating Creativity

Making and learning by young people

Edited by
Julian Sefton-Green and Rebecca Sinker

London and New York

First published 2000
by Routledge
11 New Fetter Lane, London EC4P 4EE

Simultaneously published in the USA and Canada
by Routledge
29 West 35th Street, New York, NY 10001

Routledge is an imprint of the Taylor & Francis Group

Typeset in Goudy by RefineCatch Limited, Bungay, Suffolk
Printed and bound in Great Britain by
Biddles Ltd, Guildford and King's Lynn

British Library Cataloguing in Publication Data
A catalogue record for this book is available from the British Library

Library of Congress Cataloging in Publication Data
Sefton-Green, Julian.
    Evaluating creativity : making and learning by young people /
Julian Sefton-Green and Rebecca Sinker.
        p.   cm.
    Includes bibliographical references and index.
    ISBN 0–415–19241–2 (hb : alk. paper). — ISBN 0–415–19242–0
(pb : alk. paper)
    1. Creative thinking—Ability testing.   2. Arts—Ability testing.
    3. Creative ability—Testing.   4. Educational tests and
    measurements.   I. Sinker, Rebecca, 1963– .   II. Title.
    LB1062.S39   2000
    370.15'7—DC21   99–24015
                                                     CIP

ISBN 0–415–19241–2 (hbk)
ISBN 0–415–19242–0 (pbk)

Contents

Illustrations

Contributors

David Buckingham is Reader in Education at the Institute of Education, London University. He has conducted several research projects on media education and on children's relationships with the media. He is the author of several books in these areas, including *Children Talking Television* (1993), *Moving Images* (1996), *The Making of Citizens* (1999) and *After the Death of Childhood* (2000).

Viv Ellis is Lecturer in English in Education at the University of Brighton. Previously he was Curriculum Manager for English and Expressive Arts at an 11–18 community school in the West Midlands.

Pete Fraser is Head of Media Studies at Long Road Sixth Form College Cambridge and has been a senior examiner and moderator with the Cambridge Examination Board for several years. He previously taught at Latymer School in North London, where part of the research for this chapter was undertaken.

John Garvey is course leader for the PGCE Primary award at Brunel University School of Education. He is the joint author (with Robert Fisher) of a series of design and technology books for primary teachers, *Investigating Technology*. He has been a Headteacher and taught in primary schools for ten years. Current research interests include evaluation in design and technology, and the use of databases to promote thinking skills, ICT and literacy.

Lucy Green is Head of the Music and Drama Academic Group at the London University Institute of Education, where she lectures and researches in music education and the sociology and aesthetics of music. Her current research is about how popular musicians learn their skills and how this relates to the changing position of popular music in schools. Her publications include *Music, Gender, Education* (1997).

Roz Hall is a Research Fellow at the University of Central England in Birmingham. Prior to taking up this post in January 1997, she worked at Watershed Media Centre in Bristol for four years, developing and initiating community-based project work and short courses using chemical and digital photography.

Steve Herne is currently Lecturer in Art in Education at Goldsmiths College. He is co-ordinator of the London Association for Art and Design Education. His publications include *Art in the Primary School – Policy and Guidelines for the Art National Curriculum, Learning by Design* (1995).

Howard Hollands is Principal Lecturer of Art and Design Education at Middlesex University and was former Head of Art at Holland Park School. His research interests include the ideologies of published art resources for schools and young children and the development of critical studies in an interdisciplinary context.

Antony Quinlan is a primary teacher currently with responsibility for co-ordinating design and technology at Sudbury Junior school in Wembley, Middlesex.

Karen Raney teaches aesthetics and art theory at the University of East London. From 1996–98 she was a research fellow at Middlesex University's School of Education, working on the 'visual literacy' research project in collaboration with the Arts Council of England.

Alistair Raphael is an artist and educationalist who has worked predominantly in the independent visual arts and gallery sector for the past decade.

Muriel Robinson is Deputy Head of the School of Education at the University of Brighton. She spent ten years as a primary teacher before moving to higher education, initially as a Lecturer in language and literacy. Her main research interest is in media education, specifically children reading print and television.

Julian Sefton-Green is the Media Education Development Officer at Weekend Arts College (InterChange Trust) where he directs a range of digital media activities for young people. He has taught in secondary and Higher Education and has researched and written widely on many aspects of media education and new technologies, including *Cultural Studies Goes to School* with David Buckingham (1994), *Digital Diversions* (1998) and *Creativity, Young People and New Technologies* (1999).

Rebecca Sinker is currently Research Fellow in Digital Arts Education at Middlesex University with the Institute of International Visual Arts (inIVA). Rebecca has previously worked as a photographer in community arts and in independent television as a researcher and producer. She is also a photographic artist making mixed media installations and online digital work.

John Somers is Director of an MA in Applied Drama in the Drama Department at Exeter University. He specialises in Drama and Theatre in

Education and in applying drama in community settings, including alcohol and drug education in schools, tours to France and Slovakia and carries out co-operative work in Turkey, Brazil and Poland. He directs the international conference 'Researching Drama and Theatre in Education' and edits the journal *Research in Drama Education*.

Acknowledgements

The idea for this book came out of a seminar held at Middlesex University in November 1996. We would like to thank all the participants at that meeting and the educational research co-ordinators at Middlesex University, Victoria de Rijke, Howard Hollands and especially, Richard Andrews. Thanks also to Peter Medway for his comments on an early version of the proposal for this book and to Vivienne Reiss, visual arts department, Arts Council of England for her support for this project. The Arts Council provided financial support for the discussion reported in Chapter eight. Pat D'Arcy and Magnus Moar were involved at an earlier stage of the book's production. Jude Bowen and Helen Fairlie from Routledge have also been supportive during the book's gestation. Colleagues at inIVA, Middlesex and Weekend Arts College have been very patient with our absences from work.

Acknowledgements

1 Introduction

Evaluating creativity

Julian Sefton-Green

Creative subjects

In modern industrialised countries a typical week in school is broken down into now traditionally accepted units of time, place and sense. This kind of organisation is so widespread that it almost seems odd to draw attention to it. Students, especially those of secondary school age, experience their formal education in terms of a timetable and the bounded knowledge of *subject disciplines*. At secondary schools they frequently experience different subjects in specialised locations with different teachers, all of whom will have been trained in their own specialised discipline. For younger children, in primary schools, the process of compartmentalisation may not appear so acute – they will not have as many specialised teachers or access to distinct classroom spaces – but they still move between separate kinds of activities, often bounded and named as Art, English and so on.

The origins of this practice lie in a complex history, where the sociology of knowledge, how we come to understand and make sense of the world, has interacted with the social history of mass schooling. A pragmatic and contingent system has developed to allow kinds of knowledge to be managed within the day-to-day concerns of the school. Indeed, the effects of institutionalised schooling are so pervasive that it is very difficult to think of any activity or experience, practice or idea that cannot be categorised as belonging to the body of knowledge or activities we might label as one particular subject or another. This is not to say that the boundaries around subject disciplines are immovable, and there are many examples, especially in higher education where new trans- and interdisciplinary subjects are developed and sanctioned. At the school level, however, there has been a remarkable continuity over the last hundred years in terms of the structure of the curriculum, the use of a timetable and the notion that what is to be taught can best be managed in terms of traditional subjects: the basic building blocks of knowledge itself.

Subjects, especially in schools, however, cannot just be defined in terms of types of knowledge, or even understood in terms of the history of education – how certain kinds of knowledge came to be viewed as belonging to specific subject disciplines. Subjects also include particular practices, activities and experiences as well as their own models of development and progression. Of course, these are not arbitrary: the idea of conducting experiments, in say Chemistry, is inseparable from an empiricist epistemology, where the idea of testing hypotheses is what constitutes the validity of the subject. Similarly, studying Shakespeare is considered more difficult than learning to write your name, for obvious reasons. However, as has been noted by a range of commentators (see, for example, the study of English in Batsleer *et al.* 1985 or Doyle 1989) subjects tend to settle and define themselves as a series of conventional activities and discourses, which often mask the rationales for the activities or progression in the first place. Obviously, good teachers are always happy to go back to first principles, but in the main, the underlying theories behind these conventions are rarely made explicit for students. Thus, students' understanding of their learning is more likely to be in terms of what they *do* in each lesson and how they perceive, or are perceived by the teacher, to demonstrate progress within it, than on any meta-discursive level – analysing why each subject is organised the way it is.

A key element of making sense of our education system then, is how subject disciplines define ability in their subject; that is to say, how a student's progress can be measured and recorded to demonstrate control of any particular field of knowledge. Here the different ways different subjects record or *evaluate* understanding and progress is important and a key theme in this book is to explore the differences and similarities between the descriptive languages or discourses, used by a range of arts subjects in this respect. The use of the term discourse is significant because I am suggesting that different subjects employ distinct repertoires to talk about themselves, not just in terms of specialised vocabularies, but employing different value systems and even drawing on different models of thinking and learning. Again, I would stress this is a process which does not exist in the abstract. Indeed, it is very difficult to separate the wider institutional imperatives of the school system to define or *assess* individuals or groups from any intra-subject evaluative procedures.

The focus of this book is one part of this larger picture. A number of subjects in the school curriculum ask students to make various kinds of practical and arts based productions. Typically these might include: paintings in Art; creative writing in English; performances in Drama; recording in Music; videos in Media Studies; and multimedia 'digital creations' in all or some of these subjects. In addition, students of school age will often produce 'creative work' in the semi-structured environments of Gallery and Community Arts education. Yet even within these discrete subject areas there are a number of contradictions which arise when students are required to be cultural producers in this way, and these contradictions are most acute when teachers and students either choose, or are required, to *evaluate* this kind of creative work. Indeed, considering the various evaluative perspectives operating across these experiences raises a series of questions: about the function of evaluation in general; the role of formal assessment and its relation with informal evaluation; the role of the audience for the creative product; the value of *making* within the subject discipline and to the learner him or herself; the balance within the subject paid to *product* and *process*; as well as pedagogic considerations such as the role of reflection and the place of the student or young person's voice. These questions, amongst others, are continually debated across this range of fields with their varied sets of subject-based criteria.

As I have already suggested, these various subject disciplines each draw on different discursive traditions: they employ a variety of models of teaching and learning as well as possessing different conceptions of cultural production. Here the history of different subjects is important. For example, one strand in the history of English or Art has fetishised an ideal of romantic creativity, with the idea that poets and painters are divinely inspired. By contrast, subjects like Design and Technology or Media Studies have emphasised notions of 'learning a craft' or 'trade skills' and pay attention to the shaping force of the market. Additionally, subjects may have different notions of how to make sense of young people as producers, in that some subjects value the output of children in itself, whilst others view what young people make in terms of defining a stage in the young person's development. For yet others, practical work merely illustrates theoretical understanding. Yet across the school curriculum and between formal and informal sites of education young people are expected to make arts and media within this range of – sometimes contradictory – perspectives.

Of course, discussing the value of creative work in this context raises other sets of issues in addition to the nature of subject disciplines. The nature of artistic creativity and its place in the curriculum (as well as its relationship with established subject disciplines) is itself a topic of discussion, drawing on a range of analytical perspectives from arts education and cultural theory to developmental psychology. There is debate about the value of the arts in education and indeed about the role of creative work both within young people's learning and the school system. And these debates are linked with a wider set of arguments about the role of the arts in society and individual development roughly covering four inter-related areas. First, from psychological perspectives: that creative work is an integral part of children's personal development, that it facilitates particular cognitive skills and that arts work has a general transferable role in helping young people to grow, think and feel. Second, there is a body of writing exploring the cultural dimension to creative activities. Here it is argued the arts perform two kinds of ideological work. First, developing liberal understanding, empathy and insight into people and society. And second, as I discuss below, this perspective also encompasses the ideas of self-expression and imagination including the study of young people's cultures, thus at times, like the first perspective, distinguishing the concept of creativity from the social practice of the arts. Third, and related to this second perspective, creative work is often considered in the context of debate about the cultural transmission role of the curriculum, that is to say, how creative work relates to developing an understanding and appreciation of a society's literary and artistic heritage, The Arts and Literature. Finally, creative work is valued from vocational and training perspectives, in that it produces a skilled workforce for the cultural industries as well as developing more general work related practices such as team building and negotiation skills.

This book tries to explore some of these broader questions about creativity, young people and education through its seemingly narrow attention to the question of how a range of different schools subjects evaluate practical production by young people. Before introducing the individual contributions to this book I want to map out some of the key themes underpinning debates about evaluation and the arts – themes I shall return to in the concluding chapter of this volume.

Making sense of learning: evaluation, assessment and the school system

Many of the contributors to this volume differentiate between evaluation and assessment. On the whole, and this is not a clear-cut distinction, evaluation is the term often used to describe informal judgements made by teachers about individual students or pieces of work. Evaluations will often include an extended or discursive response, but can include a grade or mark. Sometimes evaluation is used as a diagnostic term – to make sense of an individual's progress – although this is also called formative assessment. On the other hand, assessment is used to refer to formal summative assessments, both terminal examinations or teacher-based marking, either required by law or the internal reporting system of a particular school or institution. The difference between the two concepts is sometimes a matter of degree – a sort of hard and soft kind of distinction and sometimes a matter of principle – see the title of Cullingford's (1997) collection, *Assessment versus Evaluation*. It is of course very difficult to make an absolute distinction between the two terms, because in practice evaluation frequently (sometimes only) takes place during assessments and some assessment procedures are fundamentally evaluative in nature. In some discussions, evaluation is used in the sense of 'making a judgement about' and assessment to mean 'quantifying the amount of', but again this is not an absolutely reliable distinction. The terms are frequently blurred together by teachers and students themselves, but despite any confusion, it would seem as if there is a value in being able to make the distinction between the two terms as concepts, even if recognising their common point of origin.

Maintaining a distinction is all more the important in the current educational climate where increasingly centralised control of formal assessment procedures by the State has placed the nature and function of assessment under the spotlight (Broadfoot 1996). Indeed, part of the impetus for this book derives from a tradition of resistance to the recent changes in assessment resulting from the turn to conservative educational policies in the 1980s (Jones 1992). The increased regulation of assessment procedures, most obvious in the publication of competitive league tables listing schools' examination results, has, it is frequently argued, resulted in an education system dominated by anxiety about assessment. It is accepted that changes to the examination system, (including national testing for seven, eleven and thirteen year-olds in addition to the gateway examinations for sixteen and eighteen year-olds), have resulted in an increased awareness by teachers of some of the fundamental principles of assessment – such as the differences between norm and criterion referenced marking systems and the relation between curriculum planning and the assessment cycle. Nevertheless, there has been increased debate about the ownership of the assessment system and especially its relevance to creative activity. In particular, the authority of teachers to make judgements about their students' learning has come under a variety of attacks, and the role of teacher evaluation in this process is under scrutiny. As many of the contributors to this collection discuss, the importance of evaluation in understanding students' learning, and the role of class teachers in this process, is all more significant because it is suggested we are living through an era of direct conflict between the State and other traditional sources of intellectual authority, especially that in the teaching profession (see Bauman 1989; Edwards 1997).

From this perspective, evaluation as a term exceeds its more literal (or ambiguous) meanings, and becomes a battleground where teachers and the traditions of their subject disciplines are fighting for command of the educational high ground. The right to evaluate and above all the importance of evaluation is positioned against the technocratic demands of a crude assessment system. Of course, there is a specific political history to this conflict (Jones and Hatcher 1996) but from our point of view we need to avoid parodying both sides of the argument. Broadfoot's (1996) analysis of the relationship between society and schooling focuses on the role of the assessment system to regulate competition between individuals and social groups for entry into the labour market. Her attention to the macro perspectives surrounding recent changes to the education systems in the UK and France show how changes in the global economy and job patterns are both cause and effect of the changing nature of the State education system in modern social democracies (see also Young 1998). Here, the role of assessment in ensuring the status quo and the maintenance of traditional class boundaries, (see Bourdieu and Passeron 1977), or in controlling and regulating access to elites and social mobility may seem a long way away from how teachers comment on a child's drawing, but it is important to be able to maintain the theoretical connections between such an analysis and the focus of this book. Broadfoot's work, and that of other sociologists of education point to the ways in which assessment functions as a mechanism for social exclusion whereas writers on evaluation tend to come from a tradition which credits individual development. Whilst not denying the absolute points of difference between sociological approaches to the role of assessment and educational analyses of evaluation, the political stand-off between the two traditions has done little to see how attention to the micro process of teaching and learning in specific classrooms may begin to impact on the wider social effects of changes to the educational system as a whole. A focus on evaluation inevitably raises this larger dilemma.

One relatively recent approach which begins to synthesise this tension is the attention to teachers' cultures and the formation of teachers' identities through studying their personal or group biographies (Goodson and Hargreaves 1996). Here the values of different subject traditions are comprehended through an analysis of how teachers perceive themselves and their work as professionals, thus showing how individual judgements articulate with wider political imperatives. Sanderson's (1997) study of how a sociology teacher marked a candidate in a public examination showed how the teacher's use of criteria to evaluate a student was operating on a subjective and cultural level, drawing on a professional discourse of shared values, rather than making any 'scientific' objective judgement about the student's work. Similarly, Richard's (1998) study of how a media studies teacher defined her role as a teacher of that subject through identifying with the broader values and traditions of the subject drew attention to the affective and personal nature of making professional judgements. In both cases, making evaluative judgements can be understood not as the disinterested exercise of objective rational analysis, but as very particular to how individual teachers perceive their social role as teachers (see Tobin 1997 for a parallel cross cultural study). From this perspective, the discrete histories of subject disciplines are highly relevant to any understanding as to why different subjects value young people's creative work in different ways. This perspective also relates to any understanding we might have of how students make sense of evaluations made about them: how learners internalise the values of different subjects (see Williamson 1981–2).

The final issue I wish to consider in this section is the complex relationship *theories of evaluation* have with *methods of evaluation*. On one level all questions about evaluation are methodological: how we make judgements about students or a piece of work; what counts as evidence; how we interpret the data and so on. All judgements involve some element of ordering and understanding: and on a philosophical or epistemological level this process involves some kind of interpretation. I have just suggested that this process is often influenced by cultural and personal factors, but whether one is persuaded by this approach or not, trying to distinguish between a theory of evaluation (what we are evaluating and why) and the mechanisms we might use to carry out the process is extremely difficult. Indeed, many writers about evaluation and assessment frequently elide these two themes. For example, discussion about the value of self-assessment (see Latham 1997 or Tuck 1997) or authentic assessment (see the collection in Torrance 1995) of necessity produces both methodological and philosophical commentary. The extensive debate engendered by the 1988 TGAT report (see Black 1997) was in part a discussion about procedures and methods and in part an attempt to comprehend a model of learning.

Many of the contributions to this book touch on a similar mixture of methodological and conceptual issues and part of the explanation for this lies in the fact that single acts of evaluation are often made to stand for a host of perspectives about learning using crude and simple mechanisms. Concepts are often forcibly elided with one another. For example, there is a considerable amount of attention at the moment being paid to the evaluation of educational practice in general (e.g., Barber 1996). From this perspective the term evaluation is used in the context of evaluating teachers' teaching and not necessarily students' work. However, it should be clear by now that this is not the focus of this book – although both perspectives, can at times be two sides of the same coin.

In general however, both assessment and evaluation are a kind of bottleneck in the educational process; too little data is made to stand for too much interpretation. Without wishing to pre-empt the following chapters, it is fair to say that when subject specialists are invited to consider questions of evaluation, they want to reflect subtleties, shades of development and nuances of learning. Many of the contributors discuss how to teach students to *self-evaluate* as part of the creative process and this adds further complexity to the issue. Inevitably, most evaluation procedures are simply too crude for this and some of the following discussion re-visits a debate between the value of external summative assessments and time-costly complex teacher-based evaluations. There are no simple solutions to such problems but it is important to bear in mind that questions about method, which invoke classic social scientific concepts (validity, reliability, representativeness and so on) are integrally related to questions about resources, especially teacher time, and that both impact on the quality of interpretations we are able to make of young people's creative work in education.

Creativity, the arts, self-expression and taste

The contributors to this book all take as their starting point an interest in discussing what is at stake in evaluating students' creative or practical productions across the range of subjects. Most of these subjects are traditionally arts based (i.e., Music, Drama, Art and so on) but some like Design and Technology or even Media Studies are not. English, it has been argued, can or cannot be considered an arts subject (see Abbs 1994, ch. 8). The implications of defining subjects as part of 'the arts' are frequently taken up by the contributing authors themselves but it is important to be clear at this stage that, in general, notions of creativity, cultural production, 'making', performing and so on, tend to be considered from within, what we might term, 'social' or 'cultural paradigms' rather than from psychological perspectives.

This is not to deny the significance of developmental psychology within this debate, but merely to delimit the discussion contained within this volume.

This distinction is crucial when discussing a complex and opaque term like 'creativity'. It is important to remember that creativity can be used to describe creative thinking, creative work in the physical sciences or even in the field of business – entrepreneur's are often considered 'creative'. The arts have an ambiguous relationship with this extended definition beyond conventional uses of the term to describe imaginative and expressive work. On the one hand, arts education has benefited from those perspectives, most notably represented by the work of Howard Gardner (1983) or nowadays Susan Greenfield (1997), which do not view human abilities in terms of the boundaries subject disciplines have placed around human activities. Thus the claims of arts educators to provide different ways of knowing through aesthetic understanding, or different ways of developing cognitive abilities through creative arts work have been validated by these psychologists who show how the mind itself is not divided into abilities and discrete kinds of knowledge – as the histories of subject disciplines would have us believe. For example, the abstruse relationship between musical ability (listening and performing) and developing an understanding of mathematical relationships (Davidson and Scripp 1989), or drawing and spatial awareness (see Mathews 1993) make the case for arts education from general developmental perspectives. This has proven helpful in the current climate when the arts are being squeezed under the pressure of the competing demands in the national curriculum (see Eisner 1998), but it ignores the fact that the evaluation of creative work tends to come from the traditions established within subject disciplines and, as the following chapters show, these traditions are as concerned to evaluate *what* students make as much as to investigate what they might *learn* from the process.

David J. Hargreaves' collection *Children and the Arts* (1989) discusses both the differences between traditional arts and psychological perspectives and points of mutual commonality. Inevitably his concern leans towards the learning side of the debate whereas arts practitioners stress the opposite. Hargreaves cites Eisner's critique of the tendency in arts education for teachers to become amateur psychologists and to overvalue children's work for its supposed artistic merits at the expense of utilising evaluative criteria developed within the arts (see Eisner 1985). In general Eisner argues that judgements about quality require some 'connoisseurship' from the relevant arts field. This, he argues, has been dissipated by the twentieth century's tendency to romanticise creative production by children – as evidence of their innate spontaneity and fecundity. Indeed, this attitude toward children and child art(s) highly influenced the development of progressivist education. In turn, this has led to the contemporary position where many feel that the arts have been devalued within the curriculum; and one explanation for this is that, as a consequence of the 1960s turn to progressivism, arts activities are viewed by some vocational and academic commentators as sloppy

and sentimental, unmeasurable and self-indulgent, lacking rigour and relevance. Many arts disciplines are still in the process of restating their claims
to be proper subject disciplines in this context.

The difficulty for arts subjects has been to make the case that they are
rigorous without the umbrella of developmental psychology to justify their
case. In other words, making the case that the arts have a cultural validity in
their own right has been seen as an uphill struggle (Abbs 1994) and here
evaluation must be a crucial term in the debate. Part of the problem lies in
the history of arts discourses which have validated creativity from highly
problematic perspectives, in particular those connected with making judgements about quality and taste. These may have served the interests of an
education system which took for granted its cultural role, but recent changes
in society and culture towards a more pluri-cultural environment have actually made those assumptions about value in the arts open to scrutiny.

The most devastating critique of aesthetic judgement has come from the
French sociologist, Pierre Bourdieu (1984). Bourdieu's explicit target is the
aesthetic theory of Kant whose attempts to provide an objective rationale for
judgements about taste, Bourdieu reduces to questions of class. The simple
explanation for all judgement, Bourdieu argues, can be explained by the
desire to maintain social position: 'Taste classifies, and it classifies the classi-
fier' (1984: 6). In other words, judgements about art and the arts are meaningful in the context in which the judgements are made. From this perspective,
the literary critic F. R. Leavis' famous dictum about literature, 'This is so, is it
not?' (Mulhern 1979) which Leavis apparently used in a frightening manner –
if you understood what he was getting at, you passed the test, if you didn't
you failed – can be interpreted as a means to maintain and police taste
cultures. Passing judgements becomes a way of self-defining membership of
elites. Of course, Leavis was merely continuing in the tradition of Matthew
Arnold, of distinguishing between the philistines and the cognoscenti, but
Bourdieu's analysis points to the ways in which traditional certainties about
value, quality and taste, about what is good and poor in art are not absolute
judgements but socially contingent: that they are a struggle for control over
meaning. This analysis has important ramifications for this book – where
attempts to evaluate evaluation have to move beyond any simple notion of
class conflict if we are to provide a meaningful role for making art work
within the curriculum. It is also possible to view this challenge as part of a
larger project – to define aesthetic value in the postmodern era – where it has
been argued the whole edifice of aesthetics has itself been overturned (see
Frith 1996, ch. 1). I shall return to this problem in the final chapter.

The second area of difficulty for arts education is suggested by the work of
Eisner above, that is, to reconcile the values of arts subjects with their effect
on individual students. By this, I mean that the discourse of self-expression
has so permeated the value of creative activities, that it has become unclear
whether we are evaluating the makers or their products. If a primary value of
arts work is to facilitate personal growth and individual developments, what

is left for the teacher to evaluate, other than the moral worth of the students themselves? And can, or should, that be the role of the teacher? Post-structuralist theory, in particular, has been helpful in explaining how essentialist ideas about the self and identity are socially constructed and it has been especially severe on the discourse of self and identity – critiquing how the 'self' in self-expressive projects are produced and manufactured for the classroom (Gilbert 1989). On the other hand, these critiques have failed to really account for the pleasure and personal investment students derive from creative projects. The motivational power of such work also seems to fly in the face of such criticism. Some subjects have resolved this problem through a recourse to the technical languages of their subject disciplines – paying attention to the craft traditions of their subject. Here ideas about artistic skills and abilities come back into the frame.

Other writers have argued that because of the personal nature of arts work and the implicit nature of the learning experienced through creative production, it is inappropriate to evaluate creativity – as much because it is unknowable as because evaluation is an inappropriate response to creative production (see Ross *et al.* 1993). Ross's earlier work (e.g., 1983) along with that of Peter Abbs (1994), as I have suggested above, treads a difficult line between arguing for the validity of arts in education whilst simultaneously employing a language of transcendence and cultural value which appears to make to make the activities of arts education almost beyond understanding. Abbs, for example employs a fabulous rhetoric , thundering against the tech-nicist instrumentalism in the national curriculum, but ultimately this trad-ition of writing ends up appealing to the kinds of cultural values Bourdieu undermines. This is not to say that we have to account for the unknowable or that there may well be aspects of creative work which it is extremely difficult to make sense of, but appealing to a view of the arts which stresses its privileged discourse, its special way of being and knowing will always be open to the simple accusation of cultural snobbery. Again, we have to note the strong tradition of transcendence in Western aesthetic discourse, but, as many of the contributors to this book suggest, that discourse has lost in dominance in British society today. Equally, it is important not to confuse the language of transcendence with attempts, particularly in the visual arts, to move beyond the linguistic domain, without losing precision or communicative accuracy and I shall return to this dilemma in the final chapter.

An outline of the book

Except for Chapters eight and nine the contributors to this book are all based within conventional subject disciplines. Karen Raney and Howard Hollands explore the role of talk in the evaluation of Art. However, their analysis is not just concerned with how talk might be used as a means of evaluation. The focus in their discussion is the limits and advantages of *language* as a medium for describing the visual domain. This, they suggest, creates a profoundly creative tension which can develop students' learning in Art. What is more, they suggest that strategies which develop confidence in talk within the 'making' environment can assist pupils learn how to self-evaluate. This is, of course, crucial to the making process and the *reflexive* role they ascribe to talk sets up an agenda which other subjects pick up in later chapters. Raney and Hollands' account also establishes some of the historical context for the evaluation of art. Their description of how some of the hidden assumptions about valuing young people's artwork came about also has shared ground with other subjects. In common with most of the following chapters, their account draws on specific examples from classroom practice.

In Chapter two, John Garvey and Antony Quinlan describe the introduction of Design and Technology as a National Curriculum subject within the broader context of vocational influences on education in the 1980s. Evaluation is highlighted as a process central to effective designing and making and is discussed in relation to cultural values and developing pupils' self esteem. Drawing upon case study evidence from work with pupils in primary schools and students on initial teacher training courses, the authors propose a range of strategies for pupils to develop a critical awareness of products and through this, a more confident approach to evaluating their own designing and making. These include a graduation from evaluating familiar products made by others to evaluation of their own designing and making through the support of 'critical friends' within a group context. This emphasis on the social context of evaluation is again a shared theme in the book.

As Muriel Robinson and Viv Ellis note in the opening to their chapter, English is slightly different from the other subjects considered in this book because children need to learn to write for a number of reasons beyond the production of creative writing. The authors outline the three main paradigms of writing which influence writing pedagogy today and discuss why the notion of 'creative writing' is not as popular as it once was. The schools of writing theory, 'skills-based', 'genre' and 'process' may be specific to English, but they all encapsulate fundamental principles of how all texts are constructed and meanings made. Whilst their discussion of each model is subject-specific the models of learning underpinning these three approaches can also be found in the evaluative criteria of other subjects and it is important in the present climate not to separate writing off from other creative arts activities. The authors focus on developing strategies for teachers to become effective readers of pupils' writing beyond simply marking it for accuracy. This involves the development of 'response protocols' and again, both how teachers respond to pupils work' and how real audiences can be mobilised within the evaluation process are themes which resonate through the other chapters. Robinson and Ellis also touch on ways in which digital media may offer opportunities for changing writing practice.

Lucy Green's critique starts from the position that many musical theorists are still wedded to an out-and-out cultural and aesthetic relativism which suggests that any piece of music should be judged only within its own terms, and cannot legitimately be said to be better or worse than any other piece. Green's chapter suggests that not only does this position suffer from relativism *per se*, but also from a tendency to keep secret exactly what the said terms consist of. More realistically, she suggests, is the idea that we judge individual pieces equally in terms of their musical style, and by comparison with other pieces that go together to make up that style. However, musical evaluation is by no means only a scholarly activity, but an informal part of people's everyday assumptions and even unconscious judgements about music. It is something which has been implicitly engrained into the very interstices of the school music curriculum for decades. The chapter considers the evaluation and assessment of pupils' musical performance and composition, in terms of historical changes in assessment techniques, the use of graded exams and difficulty multipliers. It argues that in the present day situation of musical diversity, we cannot adequately assess pupils' work unless we first establish criteria for evaluating not only individual pieces, but styles of music. Green explicitly addresses the relevance of the traditional musical canon and argues that in an era of postmodern pluralism, Music needs to adapt to take into account the significance of music in young people's lives.

Drama has been the arts subject most bitterly riven between competing claims for its essence in recent years. John Somers begins his chapter by reviewing the different models of Drama in education describing how the subject has been divided between those who value drama as a ubiquitous learning process and those who argue that it should focus on teaching the skills of the Theatre. He particularly concentrates on the value of drama as a learning medium. Somers explores drama making and performing in relation to the makers and receivers, drawing on the relationship of form to material – especially attempting to balance an evaluation of the use of the medium in relation to the human issues being carried within it. This 'balancing act' is examined from the different perspectives of the parties involved; teachers, pupils, schools etc. It argues for a synthesis in the divide between drama 'as a learning medium' and theatre education showing how students' exploration of social issues in their drama is fundamentally inseparable from their conceptualisation of those issues through dramatic form.

The chapter on media education explains the very different model of production peculiar to that subject. Media Studies is the subject most likely to justify practical production in terms of how such work demonstrates understanding of critical or theoretical concepts. The authors argue that in some ways the concept of a product in Media Studies is at odds with the notions of creativity in other subjects. This can lead to differing perspectives being held by students, teachers, the peer audience and the formal requirements of public examination – all of which may blur the evaluation of practical media production. The chapter then goes on to consider the different discourses of assessment held by students and teachers in the evaluation of practical work at Media Studies A-level. Although students' practical work gets assessed on a regular basis at this level, the precise basis of how judgements get made within this process is profoundly ambiguous. The chapter argues that different discourses about what counts as valid media knowledge is confused with atavistic discourses of taste and quality, clearly appropriated from other subject disciplines. This is evidenced through an unusual case study of students' talk about their work and teachers discussing the same piece at an examiners' trial marking meeting.

Chapter eight is slightly different from the rest of this collection in that it is a discussion between Rebecca Sinker and three arts educators, all of whom have worked, or are still working, in the informal arts education sector. As a whole, this book does not consider creative production by young people as part of their leisure or general cultural activity, though the connections between arts education and these sites is frequently noted. The arts education represented here is related to the formal educational system in that students will often experience organised arts education beyond the classroom and such experiences can often result in tensions between the expectations of the National Curriculum and the artist in residence or gallery educators who see their work quite differently from teachers in schools. The chapter then tries to explore the dialogue between formal arts educationalists and these practitioners. Inevitably, the discussion format has its own idiosyncrasies and the artists here are interesting not just because of their arguments but also because they embody established positions within the discursive field of arts education. How they speak and represent themselves and their work is part of their position. The artists here also make a slightly different case for foregrounding the voices of young people themselves. Representing this constituency provides a valuable insight into a huge range of arts projects, undertaken by young people, at the margins of the formal curriculum.

The penultimate chapter by Rebecca Sinker discusses the emerging practice of multimedia and digital arts within schools. Basing her argument on three case studies in three very different kinds of school settings, Sinker argues that the emergence of multimedia, almost as a distinct media in its own right is useful because it acts as a vehicle for challenging unstated assumptions about how we evaluate creative production in general. Her chapter engages with *avant garde* practice as digital technologies are exploited by artists trying to find new ways to represent identity, place and difference in the postmodern era. This chapter points to the ways in which multimedia, as a medium, and as a creative activity, acts in cross-curricula ways and because of its hybridity as a cultural form, draws across the other subjects represented in this book. It offers a unique opportunity to break down the boundaries between subject disciplines. However, the difficulties of developing ICT (Information Communication Technology) work with digital media in schools shows the extent of this challenge.

The final chapter revisits the argument of this one: that the histories of subject disciplines means that common 'making' activities may be evaluated through different perspectives within the school system. It argues that in fact, there is a significant amount of shared practice between subjects and that similar models of learning and creativity may well be in use within the different 'arts' disciplines. The chapter tries to disentangle the multiplicity of aspirations which seem to coalesce during the evaluation process concluding that we need to reconceptualise creative activity itself and cultural production by young people if we are to make schools vibrant and purposeful educational environments. The argument of this book points in two directions. First, towards practitioners and educationalists who need to find ways of connecting the everyday processes of evaluation with the aims of their subjects; and second, at the policy implications for teacher evaluation in general. At the heart to both these aims is the need to review students' learning through creative production.

This book aims to stimulate debate within and across creative or 'arts' subjects. It does not pretend to be an exhaustive review of the issues involved. However, by constructing a dialogue around shared concerns, we hope that teachers can be encouraged to look above the battlements surrounding both their subject disciplines and their professional competence to place the importance of cultural production in young peoples' lives in its proper place within the educational system.

References

Abbs, P. (1994) *The Educational Imperative: A Defence of Socratic and Aesthetic Learning*, London: Falmer Press.

Barber, M. (1996) *The Learning Game: Arguments for an Education Revolution*, London: Victor Gollancz.

Batsleer, J., Davies, T., O'Rourke, R. and Weedon, C. (1985) *Rewriting English: Cultural Politics of Gender and Class*, London: Methuen.

Bauman, Z. (1989) *Legislators and Interpreters*, Cambridge: Polity Press.

Black, P. (1997) 'Whatever happened to TGAT?' in Cullingford, C. (ed.) *Assessment versus Evaluation*, London: Cassell.

Bourdieu, P. and Passeron, J. (1977) *Reproduction*, London: Sage.

Bourdieu, P. (1984) *Distinction. A Social Critique of the Judgement of Taste* (trans. Nice, R.), London: Routledge.

Broadfoot, P. (1996) *Education, Assessment and Society*, Buckingham: Open University Press.

Cullingford, C. (ed.) (1997) *Assessment versus Evaluation*, London: Cassell.

Davidson, L. and Scripp, L. (1989) 'Education and development in music from a cognitive perspective' in Hargreaves, D. (ed.) *Children and the Arts*, Buckingham: Open University Press.

Doyle, B. (1989) *English and Englishness*, London: Routledge.

Edwards, R. (1997) *Changing Places: Flexibility, Lifelong Learning and a Learning Society*, London: Routledge.

Eisner, E. (1985) *The Art of Educational Evaluation*, Brighton: The Falmer Press.

Eisner E. (1998) 'Does experience in the arts boost academic achievement?' *Journal of Arts and Design Education* vol. 17, no. 2, pp. 51–60.

Frith, S. (1996) *Performing Rites: On the Value of Popular Music*, Oxford: Oxford University Press.

Gardner, H. (1983) *Frames of Mind: The Theory of Multiple Intelligences*, London: Paladin.

Gilbert, P. (1989) *Writing, Schooling and Deconstruction: From Voice to Text in the Class-room*, London: Routledge.

Goodson, I. and Hargreaves, A. (1996) *Teachers' Professional Lives*, London: Falmer Press.

Greenfield, S. (1997) *The Human Brain: A Guided Tour*, New York: Basic Books.

Hargreaves, D. (ed.) (1989) *Children and the Arts*, Buckingham: Open University Press.

Jones, K. (ed.) (1992) *English and the National Curriculum: Cox's Revolution?*, London: Kogan Page.

Jones, K. and Hatcher, R. (eds) (1996) *Education After the Conservatives: The Response to the New Agenda of Reform*, Stoke-on-Trent: Trentham Books.

Latham, A-M. (1997) 'Profiling and self-assessment; an evaluation of their contribution to the learning process' in Cullingford, C. (ed.) *Assessment versus Evaluation*, London: Cassell.

Mathews, J. (1993) *Helping Children to Draw and Paint in Early Childhood: Children and Visual Representation*, London: Hodder and Stoughton.

Mulhern, F. (1979) *The Moment of 'Scrutiny'*, London: New Left Books.

Richards, C. (1998) 'Teaching media studies; the cool thing to do?' *Changing English* vol. 5, no. 2, pp. 175–88.

Ross, M. (ed.) (1983) *The Arts in Education*, London: Falmer Press.

Ross, M., Radnor, H., Mitchell, S. and Bierton, C. (1993) *Assessing Achievement in the Arts*, Buckingham: Open University Press.

Sanderson, P. (1997) 'Culture and "subjectivity" in the discourse of assessment: a case study' in Cullingford, C. (ed.) *Assessment versus Evaluation*, London: Cassell.

Tobin, J. (1997) 'Playing doctor in two cultures: the United States and Ireland' in Tobin, J. (ed.) *Making a Place for Pleasure in Early Childhood Education*, New Haven: Yale University Press.

Torrance, H. (ed.) (1995) *Evaluating Authentic Assessment*, Buckingham: Open University Press.

Tuck, R. (1997) 'Is self-assessment a valid concept?' in Cullingford, C. (ed.) *Assessment versus Evaluation*, London: Cassell.

Williamson, J. (1981/2) 'How does girl number 20 understand ideology?' *Screen Education* 40, pp. 80–7.

Young, M. (1998) *The Curriculum of the Future: from the 'New Sociology of Education' to a Critical Theory of Learning*, London: Falmer Press.

2 Art education and talk

From modernist silence to postmodern chatter

Karen Raney and Howard Hollands

Introduction

Before the 1980s, talking had a low priority in art education. This fact can be traced to the belief that visual art should 'speak for itself' and not need to be justified in words. Analysis gets in the way of feeling, which was the presumed driving force for creativity. Talk might help to create a relaxed atmosphere in the art classroom, but if talk was considered at all, at best it was thought to be incidental to learning, and at worst, obstructive. If visual art is *visual*, why spend time talking about it?

This disregard of talk was reversed during the 'critical decade' of the 1980s, which instituted the GCSE in schools. Rod Taylor's *Educating for Art* (1986) focused the debate about how to revamp art education. More value began to be placed on discussion in the art classroom, pupil self-assessment was started, and it was recognised that talk itself could count as evidence in the appraisal of practical work. For those pushing for change in this direction, the National Curriculum of 1992 was a dispiriting step backward. The driving force of the Orders for Art was cost-efficiency, accountability and the government's back-to-basics agenda; educational outcomes had to be measurable. It is not surprising, then, that the National Curriculum ignored the results of the GCSE experiment, nor did it draw upon the findings of large scale national research like the 'Arts in Schools' project of the late 1980s. Nowhere in the documents was a specific role was given to talk.

This chapter explores the role of talking in art education, which we see as an under-researched area in need of scrutiny. We proceed from the general to the specific. First, there is discussion of the broad cultural backdrop against which the shift toward talk in art education must be seen. One pertinent change has been from 'modernist' to 'postmodernist' ways of thinking, in which the visual and the verbal are conceived in a very different relationship; another is the move in art practice from a 'skills-based' approach toward one based on concepts, themes and issues. These shifts carry implications for the way practical work can be judged, and even for the notion of judging or evaluation itself. From there we move on to argue what exactly talking *does* in visual arts education. Talking signals and elaborates particular discourses, talking translates from one medium to another, talking creates conceptual frameworks, and talking acts as a means of negotiation between different domains – in particular the visual cultures of home and school. Finally, we use three examples to look at the role of talk in the evaluation of student artwork.

Backdrops

From modernist silence to postmodernist chatter

One branch of criticism in the visual arts began in the early twentieth century and reached its extreme in the theorising about Abstract Expressionism of the 1950s. This line of thinking – and making – stressed the purity of 'the visual' which had to be walled off from contamination by words. Early Modernist theorists, Roger Fry and Clive Bell, (1914: 115) wrote that 'to appreciate a work of art we need bring with us nothing but a sense of form and colour and a knowledge of three-dimensional space'. The High Modernist critics of the 1950s and 1960s, Michael Fried and Clement Greenberg, had a similar commitment to form and to the priority of aesthetic qualities of art over its social relevance.

The idea that the art object was autonomous from its cultural milieu meant that it was – or ought to be – unreachable by words. The viewer needs to be in a speechless, contemplative state in order to have an aesthetic experience. This idea was part of the longstanding Romantic tradition in which feeling, expression and intuition were opposed to thinking, rational analysis and verbalisation. It traded as well on ideas about contemplation going back to Aristotle, and Kantian ideas about the practical uselessness of art and the universal nature of aesthetic judgements. This century, the split between the visual and the verbal was further buttressed by Freud's ideas about two kinds of representation in the unconscious: the mostly visual 'thing-presentation', which was primary, and the secondary 'word presentation' which gets attached to it. As John Berger famously stated in 1972: 'seeing comes before words' (1972: 7).

Art education has registered the impact of these ideas in various ways. In the 1950s and 1960s it was a point of honour for artists not to be willing – or even able – to talk about their work. Silence amounted to a badge of authenticity. If an artist had to explain a work, it wasn't doing its job visually. In schools one of the manifestations of this line of thinking was the so-called 'child-centred' teaching of the 1960s, which was based on the assumption that creativity is a spontaneous outpouring of feelings and children need only paint and paper to develop their artistic selves. Another manifestation was the focus on formal visual elements – line, pattern, tone – rather than on the larger cultural forces at work within and upon art.

However, alongside these prominent discourses was another branch of modern thinking which called into question the supposed purity of the visual, and the separation of art from the rest of society. This line of thought is most often identified with the so-called 'postmodern' theorising of the last thirty years. However, its roots are in the early part of the century, when the work of the 'structural' thinkers – Saussure, Levi-Strauss, Jakobson – began to develop an understanding of culture not as collections of great works, but as language-like systems of meaning. In this anthropological definition, culture is the means by which everyone classifies and represents their world; we 'speak' to one another and think for ourselves through the signs and symbols that our culture makes available to us. These include visual sign systems such as film narratives, clothes, hairstyles, computer games, advertising, art and architecture, as well as speech and writing. In fact, far from being impermeable to words, visual sign systems may themselves be conceived of as a kind of speech or writing – as complex, and culture-bound as language. The New Art History and the Alternative English, which emerged in the 1970s, showed the impact of structuralism and semiotics on enquiry in two already established fields. At the same time, Cultural Studies and Media Studies emerged on the scene as new broad-based subject areas designed to suspend the usual hierarchies of value and to apply the tools of various disciplines to the study of all of a culture's signs and products. In a sense these new subject areas started where art education stopped.

In art practice, the postmodern impulse is rooted in the irreverent work of Duchamp, the Dadaists, aspects of Cubism and Surrealism, which erupted again in the Pop Art of the 1960s and conceptual and feminist work in the 1970s. It is characterised, among other things, by the intrusion of the written word into visual art. For example, in Richard Hamilton's seminal collage of 1956, 'What makes the modern home so, so appealing?', the tone is one of irony rather than earnestness, and subject matter draws from mass culture and the everyday – the very domain which 'high' modernist art had worked so hard to separate itself from. In the 1980s, feminist artist Barbara Kruger combined stereotypical advertising images with a cryptic and challenging phrase and displayed these on billboards, matchboxes and T-shirts as well as in art galleries.

Rather than shoring up the wall between the visual, the verbal, the theoretical and the theatrical, the sacred and the profane, 'postmodern' artists are intent on exploring the overlap of all these phenomena – through work consisting entirely of written words, through 'scripto-visual' work, performances, installations and sound pieces. What these artists share, and what their theorists emphasise, is the belief that visual art is shaped by, and part of, social discourse. A work of art, as *art*, consists not just of what is presented to the eyes, but the kind of space it's displayed in, what is said and written about it, what is *not* said about it – in short, what at any given time the work is understood to mean, or is capable of meaning.

How are we to conceive of meaning? One problem with trying to keep visual and verbal experience apart is that although a medium may be visual, the process by which we recover meaning is one that language participates in, consciously and unconsciously. In accounting for the nature of the 'image itself' or the 'purely visual', one is already embroiled in linguistic structures. This doesn't mean that images and words are the same kind of sign, or that there is no such thing as 'non-verbal experience'. What it means is that, once we learn to speak, there is a deep and unavoidable symbiosis between verbal and visual meanings. Any attempt to account for meaning in the one always appeals to the other. Linguistic metaphors make use of the visual, and supposedly 'pure' visual images are created to some degree by language.

Because of this symbiosis between image and word, talk 'lives within' visual art in a deep, if invisible, way. W. J. T. Mitchell goes so far as to call abstract painting 'a visual machine for the generation of language', in that the more painting tried to purge itself of verbal or literary references, the more reliant it became on talking and theorising (1994: 234). This irony has been expressed in the art cartoons popular between 1920 and 1960, in which there is as much sarcasm about the language used to justify or evaluate modern art as about the art itself.[1] It is notable that now, rather than being praised for their silence, artists are expected to talk, write and theorise about their work – in exhibition catalogues, on television, or when applying for funding, courses and prizes.

The balance between making art and reflecting about what one has done or wants to do, is not an easy one to strike. At the degree level, theorising may have become so dominant that students feel impelled to justify their work with half-digested ideas from Lacan or Foucault. On the other hand, in school art departments a suspicion of theory and verbalising may keep art education from developing as it could.

From craft skill to themes and issues

Craft skill – in particular drawing – has long been the cornerstone of art education. A vocational and functional rationale for art education preceded the more recent 'expressive' rationale, and craft skill still has a high profile in art education debates (Carline 1968; MacDonald 1970). In the National Curriculum for Art, particularly Attainment Target 1 – Investigating and Making – technical skill is given a central place in aesthetic development. Although it is recognised that in practice 'Investigation and Making' is integrated with 'Knowledge and Understanding', it was decided to divide the two areas into separate attainment targets in an attempt to make assessment easier. Many teachers feel this divide is artificial and unhelpful in teaching and in assessment as well.

Craft skill is involved in music and sport, as well as in art, craft and design, but what exactly is it? Dormer (1994) outlines some of its characteristics: craft skill is not easily recovered or described by language; it has structure and rules which are not imposed from the outside but come from the internal logic of an activity and are difficult to translate into theory; it becomes invisible or taken for granted the more expert one becomes; it takes time to acquire. Craft skill is individually held but communal in nature, in that it is learned from another person and linked to a body of common standards against which a product can be judged.

In the visual arts the concept of medium and craft skill are closely connected. The old idea of medium was based on the physical properties of materials – paint, steel, bronze, chalk. Each material was seen to have certain potentials, and the meaning of a work came from the elaboration or stretching of these potentials. The emphasis on craft skill and on medium-specificity led to an approach in art education which is based on showing rather than explaining, 'getting on with it' in a practical sense rather than talking about it. In this discourse, evaluation may be seen as a relatively objective matter of comparing a work to existing standards. Portfolios can be taken home in the boot of the teacher's car, or studied by A-level exam boards in another city and judgements reached about the quality of a student's work.

Much of contemporary art practice, however, is characterised by a lack of allegiance to a particular medium and a turning away from, or a mistrust of, craft skill. Artists turn their hand to film, object-making, painting or written text as the need arises, and as the ideas they want to explore demand. Art practice now is organised more by issues and themes than by a medium and its tradition. In fact, the very notion of 'medium' has changed, as evidenced by, for instance Rosalind Krauss' recent statement that art practice is now defined in relation to 'logical operations on a set of terms for which any medium might be used'. Bruce Ferguson recently defined a medium as a 'communicative network of meanings' (1996: 176). When the sculptor Richard Wentworth was asked in an interview what his medium was, he replied 'thinking'.[2]

In spite of these quite profound changes in the outside art world, art and design teaching experienced by many school children is still based on older pedagogies, in which activities like drawing the cheese plant – or its pop version, drawing the crushed Coke can – have a central place. The Interim report of the National Curriculum working group recorded that in 'approximately' two thirds of secondary schools, drawing from direct observation predominates' (quoted in Allen 1992: 24). This may point to the fact that many people – teachers included – find issue-based or conceptual approaches difficult. If a piece of work is technically accomplished, it may be easier to find a common ground on which to discuss it, and perhaps to measure its worth. Whether observational drawing is still an essential core skill for visual education remains a point for debate. If art education is to adopt postmodern or contemporary approaches, must we first teach the traditional skills? It is important that the skills approach not be jettisoned as uncritically as it was accepted. However, in a rapidly changing, computerised world, the question of drawing and other craft skills needs to be researched and defended rather than taken for granted.

Judging art

The moves sketched out above – from culture seen as 'great works' to culture seen as 'language-like systems', from craft skills to themes and issues – have significant consequences for art education and the role of evaluation within it. One consequence is that ideas of quality and judgement become suspect. An obvious source of discomfort about 'quality judgement' is that this concept seems to fling us backwards – to the high art / popular culture divide, to an unassailable canon of excellence in opposition to sexism, racism, bombast and bigotry. The word 'quality' has a high profile in the National Curriculum whenever it refers to English or Art, and this, as well as the troubled notion of 'heritage', has generated much debate. What standards of quality are being used and *whose* heritage is to be confirmed and valued?

Yet judgement is an idea in need of scrutiny, not only because it finds its way into any educational project, but because of the high profile arenas of judgement that exist everywhere in the art world – prizes, funding decisions, admissions boards, art criticism. Every step of individual and collaborative making involves judgements based on intuitions of excellence, rightness, success. Painters, designers, filmmakers, media producers all make these quality judgements, sometimes while professing not to believe in them.

Why is making and defending quality judgements an important dimension of visual education? For one thing, it is unavoidable: people judge things – as one art educator put it:

> I don't think in the end it's a question of whether you teach it or not [aesthetic judgement]. It's the easiest thing in the world to get kids to make aesthetic judgements. They do it all the time. The hardest thing in the world is to stop them. Oasis are better than Blur, EastEnders is better than Brookside. The question is how well they can articulate it . . . and distinguish between those things which are personal and those things which are not necessarily universal or transcendental but are shared.
>
> (Quoted in Raney 1997: 44)

Reflecting on something, then, and coming to conclusions about its worth and success, is part of any intellectual process. The point is not to ban the idea of judgement but rather to deepen and complicate our discussions about it. Schools need to be environments where pupils are allowed to disagree with received judgements and to develop their own criteria. In such an environment, talking will have a high profile. Michael Buchanan, a former OFSTED inspector for art feels that the main indicator of a dynamic art classroom is the quality of the talking that goes on:

> I place a lot of importance on talk, on dialogue, on the amount of time

allocated to discussion, comparison, analysis and research and thinking
. . . where children are in the habit of having to explain their intentions.

(Quoted in Raney 1997: 27)

If talking is so important in art education, we need to look more closely at
what exactly it might do.

What does talking do for visual art education?

Talking signals a discourse

One of the most basic things that talk can do is to signal and elaborate the
discourse in which someone is operating. Every activity develops its own
vocabulary. These vocabularies allow some things to be thought, valued and
seen, and others to be unthinkable and invisible. A discourse with its special
words thus provides the channels along which our thoughts can run. For
example, a formalist discourse might use a lot of 'effect' words, suggesting a
belief in aesthetic experience, or favour the term 'visual language' because it
implies belief in visual purity or artistic genius. An anti-aesthetic discourse
might tend to use words from other bodies of theory like psychoanalysis,
anthropology or semiotics.

Specialised words emerge along with changes in thinking. New words
might make fresh distinctions or remove old distinctions felt to be no longer
warranted. 'Inscription', for instance, does away with the divide between the
purely visual and the linguistic, by stating that what all forms of cultural
expression do, images as well as words, is to inscribe. 'Installation' gives
name to a new kind of art object. A word like 'subjectivity' signals a different
set of beliefs about human experience than 'individuality' does, and so forth.

The words we use to describe the nature of our enquiry also change. Prior
to the advent of GCSE it was common for schools to use the term 'art
appreciation' which suggests an essentially passive acquisition of knowledge,
mostly in relation to the Western European tradition. Art appreciation did
not include the understanding of a pupil's own work. The phrase 'contextual
studies' has a different spin altogether. It was developed in relation to GCSE
Art and Design during the 1980s when all subject areas were becoming more
interactive and resource-based. Contextual studies drew from a wider range
of visual artefacts and, like 'visual culture', signals a change in the scope of
an enquiry, away from an elevated art history to a more anthropological
study in which art becomes a subcategory. However, just because students are
looking at artwork 'in context' it does not necessarily mean that critical
skills are being used. One of the more unfortunate outcomes of a weakly
applied 'contextual approach' has been pastiches of the work of other artists,
usually Van Gogh's sunflowers and Monet's waterlillies.

The prolonged battles over terms testifies to the power of words and the
baggage they acquire. During the 1980s even the introduction of the term

'critical' was contentious. Some felt that it made an inappropriate literary analogy, or was an attempt artificially to raise the status of art and design education to that of other disciplines. Educationalists have sometimes used all three terms – 'critical, contextual and historical studies' – either to play safe, or else to indicate the range and complexity of the subject at hand.

What are the problems with specialised words? For one thing, they can imply scientific precision and fine distinctions that are not really there. The seeming exactitude of a term might not match the scope or the speculative nature of what it refers to, such as 'The Imaginary' or 'The Gaze', terms derived from Lacanian psychoanalysis. In this sense, the naming function of words may get confused with their abstract reach. Moreover, if terms are borrowed from other disciplines, this often assumes a stability of meaning in the foreign discipline that is not necessarily there. The term 'visual literacy' is a case in point. Its inclusion in the National Curriculum as a goal of art education – without being defined – has generated much debate about what the term might mean and how to best go about achieving it. Those against the term visual literacy often object to its implication that there is a single, fixed code to be learnt, an idea which is itself under threat in the world of print literacy where the term came from (see Raney 1997; 1998).

Another problem with the proliferation of terms is that they usually need to be explained back into experiential language anyway to have a rich meaning. Used habitually without explanation, such terms can create an exclusive in-group. They can also impede communication. It may be easier to fall back on a familiar word, rather than thinking exactly what it is one wants to say. The historian, Ludmilla Jordanova, has pointed out that words like 'power' or 'feminism' have come to have a status and a seemingly obvious meaning, which can lead to imprecision, or it can fix discussion about art and not allow it to evolve (1991).

An exchange between two educationalists, Miranda Cox and Alison Cox, with Karen Raney at Walsall Museum and Gallery highlights the problems and possibilities of specialised words in that setting.[3]

MC: We had big debates a while ago about the word 'installation' and whether we should use that word on an information panel. But we've decided now to use the jargon, but always qualify it with something that explains what the word is. Because we do believe in giving people the tools, the words which the art world uses. It breaks down that exclusivity about the language of art. Once they've seen the word 'installation' four times in Walsall, then they may have a greater awareness of what we mean by 'Installation Art', which may actually affect the way they look at it.

KR: So what was the argument against using the word 'installation'? .

MC: Well, installation standing on its own in a sentence without being qualified is quite a confusing term. It is a jargon term. We still fall foul of this. An instance happened only last week. We tend to refer to art works as 'works'. And within the 'Imagined Communities' Exhibition and the Video Box, we'd put a line, a prompter, to ask people to talk about their experiences. And we'd put a list of possibilities that they might want to talk about. One of them was, 'What is your favourite work?' The majority of visitors took this to mean . . .

AC: Doing the washing up?

MC: Yes, they literally interpret it as a task rather than the art work. So that was a classic example of how we in effect had misled our audience. We didn't think about it. We are so used to saying 'this work, that work', it really hit home. It served us right. We got some very interesting results out of that question, actually, in terms of finding out about people's interests, and what they considered to be work, and what they considered to be leisure.

KR: So that just underscores the need to look at all the specialist words that you use. Or even words that don't seem to be specialist?

AC: Or even the way that you put two simple words together and the person reads something completely different.

MC: Once we used the word 'gungy' to describe a particularly heavy piece of oil painting, we described it as 'gungy paint'. And whilst the younger audience that it was aimed at found it incredibly descriptive and enjoyed that use of the word, a few of the more specialist people that visited complained that we should have used the technical term 'impasto'. .

AC: Perhaps it depends on what means of communication you are using in the first place. Are you using a wall panel? Are you talking face to face? Somebody has described installation as 'art that surrounds you', which I think is a wonderful description. In fact it's better than 'installation'.

'Ordinary' words – as opposed to jargon – are themselves by no means unambiguous. One advantage of ordinary words is that they are felt to be owned by the person using them. Another is that simple language engages more parts of the personality, especially the childlike parts. If everyday vocabulary has a range and precision to be tapped, it is certainly important as well to acquaint pupils with the languages of art and art history which they will hear around them. What is essential is to do this in a way that allows pupils to be critical of these languages and not to treat them as given. The National Curriculum is not particularly helpful on this point. At Key Stage 3 (7–11 years), Attainment Target 2 – Knowledge and Understanding – requires pupils to 'analyse images and artefacts using an appropriate art craft and design vocabulary', and to 'express ideas and opinions and justify preferences, using knowledge and an art, craft and design vocabulary.' Both statements imply that there is a fixed lexicon to be learnt and used, but not necessarily to be questioned.

Not only the vocabulary, but also the form a verbal account takes will signal a discourse, and allow for some kinds of meaning while blocking others. One example observed by Hollands is of two students giving verbal presentations for a GCSE Critical Studies assessment. One student gave a slide lecture on the subject of Monet's paintings, in the mode of an orthodox art history lecture. Another student described her visit to London and the Royal Academy's 'Sensations' exhibition in 1997. This student spent as much time talking about the journey, her expectations of the show, the bag search on the door, as she did talking about the work itself. These 'extraneous' experiences all became associated with the work she was looking at, and the presentation was about how she herself was changed in the process. The change became visible during the course of her spoken account – visible in her manner of speaking, her involvement with the subject, and her confidence and animation. How we evaluate those two very different forms of verbalisation about art will depend on the purpose of such verbalisations. Is it to display knowledge of facts? Is it to demonstrate one's developing ideas and attitudes about art? Some combination of the two? The fact is that talking about art will take different shapes for different purposes and its diverse functions must be respected.

Talking translates from one medium to another

One reason to mix talk with visual making is that words and images may compensate for one another's deficiencies. A picture might vividly present a state of affairs – the way things are or look – while talking might be able to make generalisations and establish the conditions under which that state of affairs occurs.

The idea that words and images are different kinds of sign systems each with their own strengths and weaknesses, has a long history in philosophy, and more recently, semiotics. Verbal language is considered to be made up of discrete, identifiable parts combined according to rules, whereas the visual world and its representations are not. This kind of distinction has been expressed as the difference between motivated and non-motivated signs (de Saussure 1974), discursive and presentational symbols (Langer 1957) or differentiated and dense systems (Goodman 1968). Goodman makes another distinction between notational symbol systems like musical scores which can be broken down into elements, and non-notational symbols, like paintings which cannot, although to Goodman, verbal language lies in between the two. Such distinctions hinge on the idea of resemblance: visual images share structural features with what they stand for, whereas words for the most part do not. Words have a linear structure, spoken or read one after the other, as opposed to vision's 'all at once' grasp. In this view, words deal best with narrative and action, while pictures deal best with states of being in space (see Kress and van Leeuwen 1996).

In Medway's (1996) study of the working habits of architects, visual or verbal communication is chosen because, for a particular purpose, one is more explicit, reliable, quick, economical or eloquent than the other. For instance, drawing is permanent and takes a material form; it can be passed around, signed, owned. It represents non-discursively and spatially. Architects take a ruler to a drawing to find out some hitherto unknown dimension of the building, whereas if a written account did not state that dimension, there is no way to ascertain it by study of the words. But where drawings will not suffice, architects use words – to promise, to gather separate items under an abstract class, to fit 'drawn realities into structures of significance' (Medway 1996: 24). Architects draw, speak, write and gesture according to what each does best for a specific project.

This model of the complementarity of word and image is relevant to the making that goes on in art classrooms. On a practical level, when a craft skill such as drawing is creating anxiety for pupils, talking may open up alternative avenues to explore and thus help to build confidence. But the traffic between word and image may go deeper than a matter of choosing the best means to an end. If images and words are considered to be two different modes of thought, then when one talks about things visual, what is being attempted is something like an act of translation. And the very attempt to translate from one medium to another can be a powerful spur for creativity. Trying to express space in a time-based medium like words, or to express time with a still image, can create a productive tension. So can trying to weave words around an object that seems to defy or elude words, or trying to create a visual equivalent of a literary idea.

Many dynamic educational projects refuse to partition visual art from words, but instead make use of the productive tensions between them. One of these is an after school workshop entitled 'Art and Knowledge' run by Tim Rollins in New York's South Bronx, with a group of urban youths who call themselves 'Kids of Survival'. The starting point is a literary work chosen by Rollins because he thinks it might interest the students. During and after readings of the book the kids make hundreds of small drawings that link its themes with their own lives. They call this process 'jamming', as musicians improvise with their instruments, and they use various modes of expression to unpack the ideas – text and voice as well as visual images. Eventually the drawings are collated and the most 'sincere and moving' ones are selected to be transferred to transparencies. The images then might be projected or painted onto the pages of the book, leading to a large scale collaborative work (see Paley 1995).

One of the most well-known results of this process came from a study of Franz Kafka's *Amerika* in 1985. This book spoke to the experience of the Kids of Survival, many of whom were recent immigrants, or belonged to marginalised sections of American society. 'This is Amerika, where everyone has a voice and everyone can say what they want' was a line in Kafka's story. Rollins said to the Kids of Survival, 'Now look, you all have your own taste and you have different voices. If you could be a golden instrument, if you could play a song of your freedom and dignity and your future and everything you feel about Amerika and this country, what would your horn look like?'

The kids responded enthusiastically to this challenge. The result was 'Amerika I', a six foot by fifteen foot painting of every conceivable kind of golden horn tangled together and superimposed onto all 298 pages of Kafka's book. According to Nick Paley, the painting 'pulses with multiple meaning that shuttle across category and time'. Not only did the work engage with the experiences of the Kids of Survival, but it seemed to capture something of Kafka's literary style – his cramped, obsessively crafted sentences, his depiction of a fantastic reality – as well as evoking a variety of visual art traditions (Paley 1995: 30). The following is a dialogue between Rollins and some of the students who had worked on *Amerika*, about their older and more recent work.

TR: Is there any unity in our work?
GEORGE (GARCES): I think all the pieces look different.
TR: But what about a meaning or mood that connects all this new work?
RICHARD (CRUZ): Well, I know it's not a happy mood!
GEORGE: When we started, it was real important to make beautiful things like the golden horns in the Amerika paintings, the Scarlet Letter works, but these new things don't get lost in beauty.
RICHARD: We're not making the paintings that people want us to.
NELSON (MONTES): We can't be making those golden horns forever!
TR: We could be millionaires! (Laughter)
NELSON: The way I see it, the older work was more about freedom. The new work is about being trapped.

Dialogue is central in this workshop. It is used to generate ideas, find visual equivalents, and reflect on what has taken place in order to move on. This example might suggest as well a more far-reaching value of exploring the interplay between the visual and the verbal. Inhabiting the gap between word and image can bring us up against the gap between the self and various kinds of 'otherness'. The collaborative nature of this project is significant, not only in that it resists the stereotype of the 'lone' artist, but also because by its very nature, collaboration compels us to see ourselves through others.

W. J. T. Mitchell's work on iconology (1986) is relevant in this context. He asks not what is the difference between words and images, or how their sign systems mix and overlap. Instead he asks what interests are served by the claims made on behalf of words and images. Images in this view are not just a particular kind of sign, but something like an actor on the historical stage. The idea of imagery, or the visual sign, acts as a kind of 'relay' connecting theories of art, language and the mind with social and political values. The relation between the visual and the verbal, then, absorbs into it many of the important conflicts of a particular culture.

Another example of an education project intentionally crossing the visual–verbal divide is Sarat Maharaj's 'Monkeydoodle' project at Goldsmith's College, University of London (1997). Maharaj encourages his students to inhabit the 'foggy' space between word and image by pushing words to the point where the 'brute presence of an object' is necessary and conversely pushing visual articulation to the point where words have to be brought into play.

> They're constantly trying out things noting all the time 'this isn't the image, this isn't exactly the word'. The sentence they might have chanced upon sounds like poeticising – that's not what they want. They attempt to put what they're up to into reflective, explanatory gear. I find it inter-esting that they are groping towards what they want to say or picture by means of negative, 'that's not what I want to say or that's not the image I wish to make. . . '. If language is seen to fall short, then much the same with the object.[4]

In a sense, the students are testing the boundaries between word and image, the boundaries of what is 'sayable' and what is 'imaginable'. The limits of both word and image are continually experienced as a no-man's-land of 'in-between-ness'. And for Maharaj, the final destination of questions about the word–image relationship is other kinds of in-between-ness – cultural, sexual or political in-between-ness. Thus, trying to translate between word and image brings us up against various forms of the opposition between self and other.

Talking makes conceptual frameworks

If talking can be a spur for visual creativity and leads to questions about the self and other, it does this in part by making conceptual frameworks, by drawing upon the superior capacity of language to abstract, to generalise, to connect events causally. According to Rudolf Arnheim, (1969, ch. 13), think-ing takes place mostly in the realm of the senses, but words support this visual–spatial thinking in numerous ways. For instance, language helps to 'fortify the observer's urge to discriminate' and thus stabilises and classifies the raw material of visual experience which is presented to us in subtle shades of difference. Naming things might help to identify the level of abstractness which is appropriate to a given situation, something which it is harder for visual perception to do on its own, and so on.

In terms of visual art, it is interesting to consider what we are doing when we try to describe a visual work in words. Michael Baxandall writes that when we follow our instinct to try to describe a visual work we are 'represent-ing our thoughts about having seen it' (1985: 5). Talking about a work thus addresses the relationship between the work and concepts. Verbal descrip-tion involves various kinds of indirectness. There are cause words which infer the action of an agent, such as 'tentative', 'calculated' or 'agitated'. Comparison words compare a work or a part of it to something else, such as 'resonance', 'grid-like' or 'brooding'. Effect words like 'unexpected', 'striking', or 'poignant' describe the response of a beholder.

Baxandall favours cause words, which he considers the most precise and active kind of words in art criticism. Cause words are *active* in two senses: first, they deal in inferred actions, and second, they involve the speaker in the activity of inferring, and the viewer in the activity of reconstructing a pattern of implications. Not only does inferring cause something that deeply penetrates our modes of thinking, but it is sociable and conversable. It 'restores the authority of a common visual experience' rather than a special authority of a professional elite.

If we want to restore the authority of a common visual experience, then the *kind* of verbalising we do about visual art is crucial – in the art classroom no less that in art criticism. In education, what may be most important is the nature and scope of the questioning students are encouraged to do. A project undertaken with children in a primary school in north London called 'This is not the National Curriculum for Art' explored some of the discourses of art, and in particular the role of questioning, through child-centred discussions (see De Rijke and Cox 1994). It was observed that questions posed to children about art can be closed or open. Closed questions might ask for recall of facts, naming of elements ('what is the centre of interest in this painting?'), or they might lead the child to a 'right' answer ('these sculptures are not very lifelike are they?'). The facilitators note that the National Curriculum tends to use closed questioning.

Open questions, in contrast, do not have one right answer. Open questions might ask for observations, measurements, speculations or evaluations, or raise a problem to be pondered. The following excerpt from a class discussion, with the facilitator's questions in italics is from 'Not the National Curriculum for Art':

Can children be artists?
No and yes.

OK some people think no, some people think yes. (General noise of disagreement). Wait a minute. Can you tell me why you think so?
Um, because they're so littler than men they can't lift the . . . they might not let the children . . . the children can't paint so good as grown-ups.

I think the children can't draw so good they have to do it for years and years.

Why? Why can't they? They can, that's not true.

OK Hang on. Someone doesn't agree. What did you say?
I said they can. I'm an artist now and I've sold ten paintings and I'm a child.

And who did you sell your paintings to?
They're all the same person actually. She's the only one that would buy them.

No. She sells them to herself.

It is not. To my friend.

Right. What about you?
I think children can. Maybe they can, maybe they couldn't do a proper picture, but they can do good scribbles and stuff, also they, even if it's not good, even it might be good. Like a baby can do a scribble and it might go in a museum.

Yeah, I've seen a whole load of scribbles in a museum. Children can, grown-ups can, adults can, anyone can really. Art isn't just for adults, it can be for babies or anyone. Anyway we can all be artists.

Open questioning shows an interest in what children feel, know and think, and challenges a belief in fixed answers. During the 'philosophical playful-ness' which such questioning encourages, pupils are allowed to invert the norms, play with the facts and come up with their own questions. Thus open questioning leads to the kind of talking in which conceptual frameworks are created, stretched and remade.

However, the facilitators, Victoria de Rijke and Geoff Cox, point out that this kind of teaching involves a surrender of power. Thus, it may pose a threat either to the authority of individual teachers, or to the back to basics agenda of the National Curriculum as a whole. 'Given the act of teaching itself is closed, it may be something of an impossibility to ask an open question (without an ulterior educational motive) yet if any curriculum area had potential for more openness, it must be art' (1994 Section 5).

Talking can bridge different domains of communication and production

Art departments have many different levels of communication. Teachers may use a different language with pupils, parents and OFSTED inspectors. Talking may take place on a one-to-one or a one-to-many basis; it may take the form of a formal lecture, a chatty 'crit', or an *ad hoc* interaction between pupil and teacher, or between pupils. In each instance, critical language may be used differently and there may be different levels of comfort with it. Pupils may talk about art in the classroom very differently than they do at home. In terms of what children produce, there is a well-discussed and sharp divide between 'home art' and 'school art'. For instance, at school a child may be producing copies of Van Gogh's sunflowers or Monet's lily-pads, while at home she may be experimenting with computer graphics. Can talk-ing of the right kind act as a bridge between these different domains of communication and production?

Rod Taylor (1986) suggests that the divide between school art and home art in the eyes of the child is often based on the unwillingness or the inability of the teacher to discuss the child's ideas, seeing themselves as mainly a technical support. He describes his meeting with Lara, a year 10 pupil in a south east secondary school. Lara had insisted on talking to Taylor despite her teacher's assumption that she would have nothing to say because she had not contributed before. The interview showed someone deeply involved in art and struggling with the words to express what things meant to her.

TAYLOR: Do you look at art books generally?

LARA: Yes. my dad has a whole set of different painters – Seurat, Van Gogh and people.

TAYLOR: Oh, so your dad is interested?

LARA: Yes, up to a point. I'm not sure that he's really interested. He just likes looking at them. It's more me who's really sort of interested. He was given the books. He doesn't really sort of feel it he just looks at it and says, 'Oh, that's quite good', but he doesn't really – he wouldn't try and get any other books and read up on it or go to galleries or anything.

TAYLOR: You said, 'He doesn't feel it'?

LARA: Yes, he doesn't really. I sort of look at a picture and I can sort of see what is happening, and then you look at it for longer and it just becomes something else.

At the end of this interview Taylor reflects:

> How many pupils like Lara remain unidentified, and with them their specific needs, in art rooms? . . . She is already quite critically conscious. On occasions she might struggle for words, leaving a sentence incomplete and an idea floating without being fully resolved, 'oh it's so difficult to describe!'. Nevertheless, she perceptively relates her attitudes to those of her father; she can distinguish her needs in her own work from what she discerns as those of her classmates and she enjoys certain art works in their own right. She is clear and analytical in describing the differences in approach between her work done at home and what she produces in school. She sees why it is necessary to go and look at original works in the gallery, and feels the need to read around the subject . . . she beautifully describes what it is that links the work of artists with what she is attempting to do in her own . . . And yet she had hitherto revealed none of this in school!
>
> (1986: 11)

It is significant that some of the more innovative art programmes are located outside of school. The 'Art and Knowledge' project discussed above began as an extracurricular project in the school where Tim Rollins was teaching. Feeling constrained by this setting, he moved it to a neighbourhood community centre and then to an old factory building in the South Bronx. The workshops are held on a voluntary, drop-in basis after school hours. One of the Kids of Survival, Nelson Savinon, who had just started his first year at art college, had this to say about his experience of school and the 'Art and Knowledge' project:

> The teaching and learning in school is so different from how we work in the studio. In public school it's like you're in prison in a room with forty other people and you have to be there. The teachers, after so many years of doing the same thing, you can tell they are really bored. They write the aim of the day's lesson on the board, you copy it down and that's it. I've always felt that I learned more after school when I went to the studio. We have more resources. We have our own library. We learn a lot about historical references that we can put into our paintings. We get into geometry and math by calculating the sizes of the works. There's no boundaries to what we can learn. But school – it's a giant day-care centre. Actually, you feel the real aim of going to school is just getting out.
>
> (Paley 1995: 44)

Outside of formal education it is easier to suspend the usual definitions of the arts, and to stretch or blur the boundaries between them. 'I love what we do with our project,' said Tim Rollins. 'We drive people crazy because they can't figure out what it is. Is it social work? Is it school? Is it an art project? Is it a fraud? Is it socialism? Is it rehabilitation for juvenile delinquents?' (Paley 1995: 61).

Talk and evaluation

We have been arguing that talk functions in various ways in visual art education. In the broadest sense, talking signals and elaborates a discourse about art. It does this by creating conceptual frameworks for what is seen and made. Talking can also be seen as an act of translation from one medium to another – from image to word, from a space-based medium to a time based one; and the inherent misfit can be a spur for creativity. Last, we suggested that talking has a bridging function, helping to tease out and remedy the disparities between different domains and kinds of communication about visual art. When talking is used as a tool for evaluation, these different functions are brought into play.

This section uses three examples to look more closely at the role of talk in evaluating practical work. The first example is taken from research into student 'crits' – critiques – in a university fine art department. Here we can see talk as a way of situating student work conceptually, involving a negotiation between discourses. The second example involves a student teacher's attempt to run a theme-based project in a skills-based secondary school. This example suggests that problems can arise when students with the expectations, habits and vocabulary of one discourse, are exposed to another.

Talking in this case seems to act as a lubricant between the two approaches. The third example looks at an art programme in a secondary school which has an unusual scheme of evaluation. Here, verbalisation is integrated into every stage of planning and making.

Creating identities for artworks and for people – student 'crits'

In 1996, as part of her ongoing research into the nature of argument, Sally Mitchell studied the kind of talking that goes on in cross-section student 'crits' in the fine art department of a university. In these 'crits', a student's working space is visited by student representatives of each year of the degree, along with one or two tutors, and they as a group discuss the work. Through her observations, and using a model of social and personal development adapted from Rom Harre, Mitchell came to understand art as 'a social activity through which meaning is contested and negotiated, and both objects (art works) and persons come to be recognised and have identity' (Mitchell 1996: 143). Art school 'crits' are a main place where this negotiating is staged, where students test their views against those of the teacher and also against the ethos of the art school itself. It is through dialogue that a student's private meanings can be made public, and that the public (sometimes hidden) agendas of the institution are assimilated, whether the student accepts these or rebels against them.

In the three 'crits' which Mitchell discusses we can see where dialogue succeeds and where it seems to fail. In the first 'crit', although teacher and student do not necessarily agree, or share any particular belief, there seems to be relative equality between them, in that they participate in the same discourse about art. This sharing of 'conceptual resources', paradoxically, is what allows the speakers to argue and differ. At one point the tutor seizes upon a comment the student makes (about the rarity of blue pigments in church paintings) in order to reframe the student's rationale for using the colour blue. 'There is that kind of stuff of spirituality' mused the tutor, 'and simultaneously you're taking the piss, which I think is quite interesting, that. So you're actually doing both at once and in that you've succeeded, really.'

Mitchell points out that the tutor attributes an intention to the student, as a way of transforming the student's 'pretty limp' autobiographical or practical reasons for using blue into ones considered to be more interesting, complex or abstract. Mitchell characterises the teacher's role in this 'crit' as 'discourse leader'. This student is articulate and forthcoming about his work, and is prepared both to concede and to argue with the tutor's points. The movement of insights back and forth seems to endow the work with fresh meanings.

What hinders progress in the second 'crit', is that shared ground is assumed rather than established. The student begins with some uncertain, exploratory remarks – 'I've no idea where it came from or why . . .'. When the teacher moves quickly to frame these at an abstract, theoretical level, this does not seem to resonate with the private meanings of the student. The participants in the discussion are not able to 'move into each other's spaces', and the student ends up feeling that his work is being prejudged by standards which have been imposed rather than negotiated. Perhaps what was needed with this student was a keener and more open line of questioning that would draw out and solidify the student's private motivations before situating them in another framework. As it was, the identity and meaning of the work remained unclear, and the student experienced 'an increasing sense of alienation, an increasing sense in which he defined himself in opposition to the institution and its modes of validation' (Mitchell 1996: 150).

In the third 'crit', there appears to be a stand-off between student and tutor. This student resists any verbal exploration of her intentions or possible meanings by saying that anything is art if it is made to be art – 'it just is art'. When the tutors tries get the student to think about her use of colour and texture, or to consider alternatives, the student retorts that that was a waste of time as she already knew what she wanted to do. Here there was no genuinely shared discourse, as in the first 'crit'; nor was it a matter of a failure to explore points of commonality that were there, as in the second 'crit'. This was an outright clash of discourses. The student was operating from an extreme: refusing to verbalise equals artistic integrity.

What is interesting in these three examples are the conflicts between ideas of individual freedom; uniqueness and personal expression on the one hand, and conformity to institutional standards on the other. These conflicts are found not only between students and teachers, but within the discourses of the art department itself. For instance, in 'crit' two, some areas of meaning failed to be explored by the tutors because their assumptions about sculpture determined what aspects of a work could be talked about. The student felt this was because 'sculpture is under-theorised'. In 'crit' three, however, it was the student who was resisting dialogue and calling on notions of personal expression and artistic integrity to justify her refusal. Presumably these notions come in the first place from the discourse of self-expression common to art schools. Thus at different points we can see a tension between the ideals of modernist silence and postmodernist chatter. Sometimes it was the tutors and sometimes the students who closed down dialogue.

These clashes between discourses, and rifts within them, may be inevitable. They may in fact be the very agent of definition and growth, as students struggle to situate themselves in relation to the institution. As Mitchell puts it: 'In fine art, selfhood and disciplinary identity are brought into proximity and as a consequence individuals become part of the collective by a paradoxical process of alienation from it' (Mitchell 1996: 152). Dialogue is crucial in this process, involving as it does both a reiteration of old ideas and a creation of new contexts for them. If, as Bakhtin (1981) says, 'The word in language is half someone else's', it is also half ours. Every utterance is 'dialogic', that is, rooted in other utterances and oriented to a response. We do not speak into thin air; we imagine an audience, we anticipate an answer, and this anticipation structures in advance what we say. In this sense, evaluating art through talk can be a way of negotiating between different frames of reference – those of students and teachers, institutions and other thinkers, thereby creating identities for artworks and for people.

Integrating process and product – a student teaching experience

The next example describes a project undertaken in a secondary school by a student teacher, Kevin McSharry, in 1998. Kevin was a PGCE (Postgraduate Certificate of Education) student at the time, at Middlesex University. The project's theme was 'Environment and Identity' which tied in closely with the concerns of his own artwork. As part of his university-based course, he had carried out a half hour 'micro' version of the project with his fellow students. This trial run had generated an enthusiastic response and Kevin was keen to apply the ideas in the mixed secondary school where he was to do his placement.

The pupils he worked with were year eight (12–13 years old). The project ran for six hour-long lessons. As the art department of this school operated a traditional programme which was largely skills-based, Kevin's 'Environment and Identity' project was new to these pupils in three ways: the content was new, it involved working as a group, and it introduced new combinations of media.

The pupils had been exploring line in still life with their usual art teacher. From this starting point, Kevin introduced the more abstract idea of line as a journey – their journey from home to school. The pupils were to think of ways in which this journey could be articulated as a linear visual narrative, a process of personal mapping, which brought local history and environment, as well as autobiographical material, into play. The group also looked at paintings by Piet Mondrian as forms of mapping, and they constructed Mondrian-like paintings based on their journeys.

The next stage was to move from linear mapping to more multi-modal assemblages of images. Collage and mixed media were introduced through the tradition of the Dadaists, Kurt Schwitters in particular, and the later work of Robert Rauschenberg and the Pop Artists. This stage involved collaboration. The class was divided into five groups each of which was to produce a collage. The starting point on each group's sheet of paper was a central cluster of spray printed images of local scenes chosen by the pupils themselves from local history archives. The pupils were encouraged by the student teacher to combine images, text and media, and to keep the collage moving by not being afraid to paint or collage over sections already completed.

As the project unfolded, there were several indicators that it was developing differently than it had in the micro-teaching version of it at university. For one thing, the pupils had been asked to bring in images about themselves or their environment to use in the collage, but many failed to do this. They did not seem to be used to this approach in an art lesson. Second, although there was enthusiasm for the project, and the pupils continued into break-times, they did not seem to be sure why they were doing it or how to reflect on what had taken place.

Howard Hollands had observed one of the group lessons, and afterwards raised the question: can the outcome of the project be evaluated – by pupils or teachers – simply by looking at the completed collages? It was decided that it could not, as the project was about process rather than product. The nature of the collaged images reflected this: they were evolving rather than finished, full of disparate images rather than one integrated image. The student's work had been exemplary in terms of lesson planning, resources, timing, progression from stage to stage and classroom management. What seemed to be missing was a framework for the pupils to evaluate all of this. In addition, the role of talk in the evaluative process had been missed. The students did throw out a few superficial responses to the displayed collages, such as 'I like the woman with naked breasts', but this still left the process they had experienced and the issues raised by the images as unresolved questions.

Following the de-briefing, it was agreed that the next and final lesson would be devoted to talking about the experience of making the collages. Through a facilitated discussion, the pupils were able to make judgements about what had worked and what had not, about what the project meant to them and about the experience of working in a group. They were also able to refer back to the work of the artists they had studied earlier and make links to their own collages.

Several points are raised by this example. One is that evaluation needs to be in keeping with the nature of the work. Exploratory, 'process' work demands an evaluation procedure which is exploratory and process-based. Second, critical reflection is something that develops over time and this is not easy to do in an hour's art lesson per week. And finally, student-teachers have to fit their projects into an ongoing programme that is not of their own making. They often have to overcome, or chip away at, fixed ideas. In this case, a varied and concept-rich lesson was being introduced to pupils used to a fairly narrow, skills-based agenda. Kevin's fellow university students may have engaged so quickly with the project because they were already primed for it – that is, they were familiar with its ideas, its terminology and its methods. In the school, where this was not the case, talking at each stage of the project was probably crucial in order to bridge the gap, and to develop the critical thinking skills that may have been lacking. Students need to learn, and be taught, how to participate in this process.

Sketchbooks, self-assessment, and fleeting insights – Crofton School

Crofton School is a mixed secondary school in the London Borough of Lewisham with pupils from diverse cultural backgrounds. The art department has a long history of theme-driven teaching, and Martin Kennedy, who became head in 1987, developed the programme into one that is regarded as exemplary in its inventiveness, its ability to engage students, and the range and high quality of the work that is produced. (For full description and discussion of the Crofton School programme, with illustrations of student work, see Binch and Robertson 1994, Kennedy 1995 and Newbury 1994.)

Each year pupils work on a theme such as metamorphosis, revolution, journey, taboo, witness, or fear. The theme is introduced by way of printed and visual 'trigger' material' which is devised collaboratively. During an induction period, pupils collect material relevant to the theme and this is put together to make a 'theme wall', or what Kennedy calls an 'annotated visual flow chart' which is displayed in the studio. Trigger material is also collated in video form. Students then make a presentation to the group, describing three of their own ideas for projects about the theme, and backing them up with their sketchbooks. These presentations involve a rigorous question and answer period in which ideas are challenged or further information is requested.

About six classroom hours are devoted to this theme induction stage, which is largely teacher-driven. 'The emphasis is on active investigation centred around key teacher generated inputs' (Kennedy 1995: 10). However, pupils have full responsibility for the planning and assessment document which follows. This document, 'the snail', is discussed below.

After induction and inauguration of the snail, pupils start work on their projects, under the banner of three words 'what?' 'how?' and 'why?'. 'Why?' is the most important, as it encourages students to have a personal stake in what they do. The goal of passing an examination is downplayed in favour of the larger and more personal answers to the 'why?' question. The following is an example of a school student talking about her work and how it developed.

> We went to the National Gallery to find a piece of work that we found interesting and I chose the 'Rokeby Venus' by Velasquez. First I was thinking about things like admiring, admiration, vanity – you know, like young women's self-discovery, discovering your beauty and things like that. Then I was talking to my teacher and I was thinking about the function of art in those times and maybe it's like an old version of what we have today, top shelf magazines . . . you know, a bit of an excuse for a dirty old man to look at a woman.

The student ended up making a painting called 'Shop Window' which depicts a naked woman in the pose of the Rokeby Venus, in a cake shop window in Catford, being ogled by passing shoppers. The student took photographs of passers-by from inside a shop window which she used as source material, and in her sketchbook she explored notions of voyeurism, power and integrity. Particularly important to this work was the issue of eye contact and the exchange of looks which paintings and photographs stage with the viewer.

At Crofton, students are encouraged to be interested in each others' work. Kennedy describes an instance in which two white boys started their investigation of the theme 'Black' by videotaping interviews with black students talking about their lives. One of the students talked about the racial threats which she and her family had endured which led to them being re-housed. The students' final piece consisted of a collection of still photographs taken from the interview with the interview transcript superimposed on top of it. The outline of the girl's face was then painted on top in order to 'bring the work together' and to allude to her 'great dignity in the face of disgusting behaviour'. The girl who was the subject of this work then went on to make her own painting about the experience of being at the receiving end of racial abuse.

The theme-based approach taken by this art department does not preclude or denigrate technical prowess, but instead places it at the service of the drive to say something. It also forges natural links with other subject areas like sociology, history and english. Most importantly, perhaps, the theme approach connects visual art to the students' social environments and their private experiences. Significant to our subject here is the fact that a thematic approach requires a lot of talking.

Evaluation of student work at Crofton School happens at many points. Three main forms of assessment are: the sketchbook, including the snail; the finished work; and students' verbal insights during formal or informal class discussions. In Kennedy's view, the sketchbook is the key document for assessment:

> It is within the sketchbook and the accompanying body of realised work that the degree of student ownership of process and course content can be determined. It is within the sketchbook that questions are asked and matters of ethical, moral, and social and political importance are addressed.
>
> (Kennedy 1995: 11)

In addition to all the material made and collected over the course of the unit to support their project, student sketchbooks contain a planning and assessment form called 'the snail'. It has the look of a board game, and was given this name because of its uncurling shape. The starting point is at the centre of the snail which names the theme and describes the *Trigger Material*. This moves into *Research*, which includes 'work by other artists', 'connections made' and 'social/historical references'. *Planning* includes the three ideas and the final choice of project, with an explanation of why it was chosen. This is followed by *Experimentation* and *Making the Realised Work*, in which the student describes how the work developed, any problems encountered and how they were solved. The final sections are *Review*, which is a self-assessment, and *Springboard*, which encourages thoughts about future projects or ideas to be explored. In *Review*, students are asked: How well do you think you researched? How well did you develop your ideas? Do you think you chose the right medium/art form? Do you think you improved your skills? How? Are you satisfied with the finished piece?

The snail acts both as a guide or map for the pupils, and as a record of achievement as their work progresses. Students can annotate the form, colour code it, or otherwise alter it to suit their learning style and the needs of their particular project. It is emphasised that there is no fixed order of progression through a unit.

Assessment of the finished work, then, will be inextricable from assessment of the conception, planning, development, problem shooting and self-reflectiveness of the student as evidenced in the snail and sketchbook. But there is another kind of evidence of learning which is harder to record. That is the spoken insights which crop up in classroom discussions. Crofton teachers are aware of this and have devised a way to capture some of these telling verbal moments and use them in assessment. Kennedy describes this method in an interview with Karen Raney.

MK: A few years ago we were doing some work on movement and we were looking at some Muybridge photographs. The next week, it was a year 8 class, I showed this particular class Duchamp's 'Nude Descending a Staircase.' This kid put his hand up and said; 'You know, if you took those photographs that you showed us last week and you put them on top of each other rather than side by side, it would look like this painting that we're looking at now.' Which is quite an astute comment. Now, I would say that's a piece of evidence. It's not a drawing, it's not a piece of sculpture, it's not a piece of writing in a sketch book, but it's nevertheless evidence of something having made an impression, and a pupil making his own connections in a way that was original within the context of that group.

KR: And it's a visual connection.

MK: A visual connection, which is then expressed in words. Now, that comment and others like it led to a group of teachers devising a system whereby we can record those moments of achievement which can otherwise just go. It's a grid system. For example, critical contextual understanding would be one column, and then we use a system of arrows going up, across and down. If somebody made an outstanding verbal contribution within a certain context, you would just quickly pick the register up, find their name and put three arrows pointing up, and the date. You don't record the exact comment, but what you do have is a fairly accurate measure of specific blocks of achievement. Some of them are practically biased, but a lot of them are geared to those ephemeral moments where things happen and if you're not careful you forget them and when you come to write your end of key stage statement, how do you justify these comments that you're going to make? Or how do you justify the collaged statement bank that you're likely to produce for parents when these kids are fourteen? And it seemed to us that it was a good idea to have some specific evidence, not only about levels of skill and control of basic elements, not even about levels of competence in terms of investigational research, which one would hope to find in a sketch book, but just those moments where you think 'that's such an interesting connection'.

KR: It's trying to capture in a non-formal way moments of visual insight.

MK: It's also to do with empowerment and with the fact that we automatically miss so much. We can't ever be privy to all the conversations going on in an art studio.

Conclusion

The kinds of evaluation procedures used in a particular institution are normally consistent with the discourses about visual art that are in place. If an art department is mainly craft skills-based, evaluation will stress technical prowess, and teachers might see evaluation as something that can be done *to* a student's work from the outside. This approach may take different forms. To someone with an apprenticeship understanding of craft, as described by Peter Dormer (1994) on p. 19, evaluation would be an intuitive process whereby those who have internalised the knowledge and skills can discern quality, though not necessarily explain it. A more rigid, and in our view inappropriate, approach to 'evaluation from above' would be to hold rules and checklists against which a work is judged. Sadly, with the demands for accountability and measurability that are being placed upon art education, this checklist approach is the direction in which assessment seems to be moving.

A teacher who considers art as a value-laden social practice, and puts a premium on ideas as well as execution, might see evaluation more in the spirit of negotiation. If choices about value are made not in an aesthetic limbo, but in relation to what a piece can do and who it is for, then 'aesthetic judgements' can unpack a whole series of questions about personal, class and cultural history. Assessment here might be seen to spring in the first instance from the student. It would necessarily entail dialogue, as all negotiation does. This is the kind of evaluation which we feel is most revealing, stimulating to students and the most appropriate to what visual arts education is – or needs to be – evolving into.

Although we have been arguing in favour of more and better talking in the art classroom, we want to conclude by saying that our intention is not to reinstate a hierarchy in which verbal expression is valued above visual expression. Students come with different aptitudes, and those who speak more eloquently with their hands than with words should not be penalised for this in a visual art department. What we are trying to do is to underscore the ways talking might assist reflection and hence *development* – of our critical faculties, perceptual awareness, or visual ideas. By inhabiting the space between word and image, we may also, potentially, find out something about the boundaries between ourselves and others. At its most useful, talking about art has an integrating action, ushering into living awareness more of the visual world and illuminating our relationship to it.

What kind of research needs to be done into talking and art education? One area that is ripe for investigation is the kind of talking that goes on informally and formally between pupils, and between pupils and teachers, in light of the kinds of work that an art department produces. More comprehensively, we would recommend an analysis of the entire 'semiotic landscape' of art classrooms. What is written, spoken, fashioned, drawn, painted, photographed, and otherwise displayed – how, why, when and where? The point of this kind of overarching approach would be to give equal weight to image and word, and to see how they interact. What mixtures of 'making' and 'discussing', of visual display and verbal reasoning, are most promising? An enquiry of this kind would have to take into account the very real practical constraints that exist in schools such as the problem of time – time to reflect and discuss and revisit things. However, the fact that some schools have managed to create exciting art programmes with limited time and resources is a source of optimism that it can be done.

Art teaching in the end relies on the commitment, enthusiasm and inventiveness of art teachers. Therein lies another implication of an art education that gives talking a high profile. Particularly if talk is going to form part of assessment, teachers need to be skilled enough to tailor their discussion style to the different needs of each student. Although it is a skill that many develop on their own, art teachers are not currently being trained in this. At the heart of good art teaching is the ability to recognise when talking helps, and when it is distracting, beside the point or obstructive. At times such as those, silence may, after all, be golden.

Notes

1 For a collection of these cartoons, see Melly, G. (1973) *A child of six could do it*, London, Tate Gallery.
2 From an unpublished interview with Karen Raney on 15 July, 1998.
3 Unpublished interview with Karen Raney on 23 August, 1996.
4 Unpublished interview with Karen Raney, 1 October 1996. For further information about the 'Monkeydoodle' see Maharaj (1997).

References

Allen, D. (1992) 'Production in art education' unpublished paper.
Arnheim, R. (1969) *Visual Thinking*, Berkeley, California: University of California Press.
Bakhtin, M. (1981) *The Dialogic Imagination*, Austin: University of Texas Press.

Baxandall, M. (1985) *Patterns of Intention: On the Historical Explanation of Pictures*, New Haven: Yale University Press.

Bell, C. (1914) 'The aesthetic hypothesis' reprinted in Harrison, C. and Wood, P. [eds] (1992) *Art in Theory: 1900–1990: An Anthology of Changing Ideas*, Oxford: Blackwell.

Berger, J. (1972) *Ways of Seeing*, London: BBC and Penguin Books.

Binch, N. and Robertson, L. (1994) *Resourcing and Assessing Art, Craft and Design: Critical Studies in Art at Key Stage 4*, Corsham: National Society for Education in Art and Design.

Carline, R. (1968) *Draw They Must*, London: Edward Arnold.

De Rijke, V. and Cox, G. (1994) *This is not the National Curriculum for Art: A Collaborative Project with Children on the Discourses of Art and Education*, London: Middlesex University Press.

De Saussure, F. (1974) *Course in General Linguistics*, (trans. Bally, C.), Bungay: Fontana.

Dormer, P. (1994) *The Art of the Maker*, London: Thames and Hudson.

Ferguson, B., Greenberg, R., and Nairne, S. (1996) *Thinking about Exhibitions*, London: Routledge.

Goodman, N. (1968) *Languages of Art: an Approach to a Theory of Symbols*, New York: Bobbs-Merrill Co.

Jordanova, L. (1991) 'Linda Nochlin's lecture "women, art, and power"' in Bryson, N., Holly, M. and Moxey, K. (eds) *Visual Theory*, London: Polity Press.

Kennedy, M. (1995) 'Issue based work at Key Stage 4: Crofton School – a case study', *Journal of Art and Design Education*, vol. 14, no. 1, pp. 7–20.

Kress, G. and van Leeuwen, T. (1996) *Reading Images: the Grammar of Visual Design*, London: Routledge.

Langer, S. (1957) *Philosophy in a New Key*, Cambridge, Mass.: Harvard University Press.

MacDonald, S. (1970) *History and Philosophy of Art Education*, London: University of London.

Maharaj, S. (1997). 'Monkeydoodle: annotating the anti-essay "after history"', *Art Journal*, Spring 1997, pp. 65–71.

Medway, P. (1996) 'Writing, speaking, drawing: the distribution of meaning in architects' communication', in Sharples, M. and van der Geest, T. (eds), *The New Writing Environment: Writers at Work in a World of Technology*, London: Springer Verlag.

Mitchell, S. (1996) 'Institutions, individuals and talk: the construction of identity in fine art', *Journal of Art and Design Education*, vol. 15, no. 2, pp. 143–53.

Mitchell, W. J. T. (1986) *Iconology: Image, Text, Ideology*, Chicago: University of Chicago Press.

Mitchell, W. J. T. (1994) *Picture Theory: Essays on Verbal and Visual Representation*, Chicago: University of Chicago Press.

Newbury, D. (1994) *Photography, Art and Media: New Directions in the Teaching of Visual Culture*, Birmingham: University of Central England.

Paley, N. (1995) *Finding Art's Place: Experiments in Contemporary Education and Culture*, London: Routledge.

Raney, K. (1998) 'A matter of survival: being visually literate', *The English and Media Magazine*, no. 39, Autumn 1998, pp. 37–42.

Raney, K. (1997) *Visual literacy: Issues and Debates*, London: Middlesex University.

Taylor, R. (1986) *Educating for Art: Critical Response and Development*, London: Longman.

3　Evaluation and Design and Technology

John Garvey and Antony Quinlan

The development of Design and Technology as a subject within the National Curriculum

The introduction of Design and Technology as a curriculum subject had its roots in the perception that in a highly competitive world economic market, the education of young people in technology and design is critical for the future prosperity of the country. The upheaval inherent in the reform of the British economy in the 1980s proved to be a portent for a radical transformation of the education system, heralded by the introduction of the National Curriculum in 1990.

The seeds of development and change for technology and design were already being sown in 1982, when the Prime Minister, Margaret Thatcher, held a seminar at 10 Downing Street aimed at transforming design at secondary school level from being taught as an art-based subject to, 'a practical, problem-solving discipline that is ideal for preparing young people for work within the constraints of user need and the market' (Thatcher 1983: 22). This controversial interpretation of design education gained further credence in 1987 when it became evident that the Engineering Council and Design Council had been collaborating in an effort to promote design education as part of technology in the school curriculum.

The importance of technology had been recognised by Her Majesty's Inspectorate (DES 1985a) when it formally acknowledged a ninth area of learning and experience to complement the aesthetic and creative, ethical, linguistic, mathematical, physical, scientific, social and political and spiritual areas – that of the technological. Establishing links between the subjects of Craft Design and Technology (CDT) and science were perceived as vital at secondary level. In addition, primary schools were encouraged to develop CDT as a means of enhancing the understanding of scientific concepts.

In March of the same year the White Paper, 'Better Schools' (DES 1985b) stressed the need for schools to respond to the rapidly changing needs of the labour market and for the curriculum at 14 to 16 to prepare pupils for employment. The paper gave particular consideration to the role of technology within the government's Technical and Vocational Educational Initiative

(TVEI). This had been introduced in November 1982, under the auspices of the Manpower Services Commission, an agency of the Department of Education. It was aimed at developing the provision of vocational and technical education for 14 to 18 year-olds. The initial funding for fourteen local education authorities was expanded in 1987 to a national scheme involving all state maintained schools and colleges.

The avowed aims of the TVEI included the need for 'pupils to use their skills and knowledge to solve the real world problems they will meet at work' and the need for a greater emphasis on 'developing initiative, motivation and problem solving skills'. These aims were widely interpreted by teachers and local education authorities as a context for the introduction of a variety of technologically based courses at secondary level under the umbrella of CDT. A tension soon developed between an interpretation of TVEI as a pretext for practically based work with its roots in a narrow definition of technological capability and that of a cross-curricular approach, often characterised by collaborative projects aimed at simulating mini-business enterprises. The success of such ventures heavily influenced the TVEI Unit when in 1988 it sought to refocus the aims of the initiative to spread across the whole curriculum.

The Engineering Council's Standing Conference on School Science and Technology (SCSST 1985) had already promoted a model of problem solving in science and technology heavily geared towards the successful design, manufacture and promotion of new products. This was based on a linear model of designing and making, incorporating such elements as identifying and specifying a market need, research and development, design and material selection from a number of options, manufacture and evaluation.

This approach was criticised by the Assessment of Performance Unit (APU 1987), which had been set up by the Department for Education to identify strategies for assessing pupil capability and progression in a range of curriculum areas. The APU had taken on as part of its brief the task of analysing the process of design and technology with a view to effective assessment of pupil capability. It expressed concern over product-driven, linear models of the design process, arguing that they 'can reveal a greater concern for "doing" all stages of the process, than for combining a growing range of capabilities in a way which reflects individual creativity and confident and effective working methods' (APU 1987, section 2, point 12).

The recognition of designing and making as a complex, and at times confusing, process led to the proposal of an iterative model which recognised the centrality of the interaction of mind and hand. The model described an innovative way of looking at the process of design and technology with its stress on recursive movement between thinking and doing, with products seen as part of, but essentially subservient to the process.

A driving force behind this model was the perceived need to assess design and technology capability in a holistic manner in order to reflect the complexity and richness of the process, rather than as the sum of individual

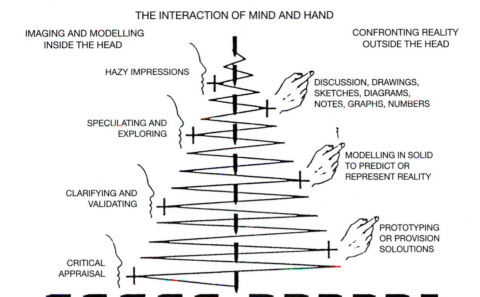

Figure 3.1 APU model of interaction between mind and hand (Kimbell *et al.* 1991: 22)

parts. There was a clear emphasis on the cognitive benefits of pupils engaging in a process described as 'thought in action'.

The influence of these diverse strands of thinking and action were clearly evident in the final report of National Curriculum Working Group for Design and Technology, published in June 1989 (NCC 1989). This heralded the introduction of the new subject of Technology at primary and secondary school level, distinguished by its inclusion of two components – Design and Technology and Information Technology. The design and technology group had worked under the terms of reference that technology should be viewed as 'that area of the curriculum in which pupils design and make useful objects or systems, thus developing their ability to solve practical problems' (NCC 1989). The report was greeted with a mixture of concern and relief from school-based representatives of the historically diverse subject areas incorporated into the new subject – business studies, home economics and CDT. There were fears for the future of the integrity of these areas within the structure of the National Curriculum, which were partially allayed by significant elements of each of them appearing within Design and Technology.

The final Orders for Design and Technology (NCC 1990) did not explicitly state in concise terms the nature of Design and Technology. The curriculum did, however, represent a challenging cross-curricular approach which was embodied by the four attainment targets of:

AT 1   Identifying needs and opportunities:
Pupils should be able to identify and state clearly needs and opportunities for design and technological activities through investigation of contexts of home, school, recreation, community, business and industry.

AT 2   Generating a design:
Pupils should be able to generate a design specification, explore ideas to produce a design proposal and develop it into a realistic, appropriate and achievable design.

AT 3   Planning and making:
Pupils should be able to make artefacts, systems and environments, preparing and working to a plan and identifying, managing and using appropriate resources, including knowledge and processes.

AT 4   Evaluating:
Pupils should be able to develop, communicate and act upon an evaluation of the processes, products and effects of their design and technological activities and those of others, including those from other times and cultures.

Evaluation then, is not just part of the assessment process, but part of the very content of the subject itself.

Implementation of the National Curriculum for Design and Technology

The implementation of the Design and Technology component in schools proved to be problematic, for a number of reasons. The timing of the introduction of the new subject was particularly unfortunate. At primary level, where staff were expected to teach all subjects, teachers were reeling from the introduction of the core and foundation subjects, all of which were presented in weighty A4 folders, representing levels of prescription and challenge in terms of subject knowledge never before encountered. Many were baffled by the complexity of the Design and Technology Programmes of Study and concerned about resourcing and issues pertaining to health and safety. The expectation that pupils were to identify their own needs and opportunities for designing and making a range of 'artefacts, systems and environments' generated a great deal of anxiety with regard to managing the diverse design-and-make projects undertaken.

Understanding and managing evaluation proved to be particularly challenging. Bloom *et al.*'s *Taxonomy of Educational Objectives* (1956) identifies evaluation as a key thinking skill. While this was, on occasion, recognised in an implicit manner by teachers as a desirable skill for pupils to develop, it was not until the introduction of the National Curriculum that widespread explicit reference was made to the importance of pupils being encouraged to evaluate their own work and that of others. This was evident not only in design and technology but in a range of other subject areas. Pupils were encouraged to examine primary and secondary sources of evidence in a critical manner to assess their historical relevance and veracity. In Religious Education artefacts from a variety of religions were evaluated with a view to discovering their symbolic and spiritual significance. Pupils were expected to draft and edit their writing in English with regard to the purpose and audience for their work. The emergence of the word processor and desk top publishing helped to support such evaluative strategies in the form of publication of pupils' own writing in the form of wall mounted work and publicly displayed books. There were many occasions when, upon entry to primary schools, visitors were confronted by pupils' own vivid attempts at painting their own interpretations of the work of famous artists.

While the recognition of the importance of pupils evaluating their own designing and making and that of others was to be applauded, the identification of evaluation as an attainment target within Design and Technology was not without its drawbacks. The act of designing and making was perceived by the National Curriculum Council in the Design and Technology Non Statutory Guidance (National Curriculum Council 1990) as an interactive model whereby the processes identified as attainment targets would feed off each other, allowing pupils to explore and develop a range of capabilities within a variety of contexts. Within such a model, evaluation was identified not only as an attainment target but as integral to every stage of designing and making. However, the timing of, and haste with which the Design and Technology curriculum was introduced into primary classrooms (with little preparatory in-service provision), meant that few teachers had opportunities to fully analyse and understand the process of designing and making. This led, in many cases, to the adoption of a rigid linear model of designing and making, which was exacerbated by the numbering of the attainment targets which seemed to implicitly suggest such an approach. The concerns of the APU (1987) that, within such an approach, the 'process of design and technology can become a series of products' proved to be well founded. Typically at primary level, pupils were initially encouraged to identify what they were going to make, then draw a design, make their product and then complete a final evaluation of their product, often based upon a few simplistic questions from teachers. Much of the work took place in a vacuum with little consideration of the designed work of others in informing the design process. Indeed, evaluation was often perceived as a bolt-on task which was often conspicuous by its absence.

At secondary level, the challenge of cross-curricular planning proved to be particularly difficult with entrenched departmental cultures expressing particular concern about the 'deskilling and redundancy of hard won expertise' (Layton 1995). Her Majesty's Inspectorate (1992) commented on a decline in making activities and expressed concern over low standards of work.

An influential report by Smithers and Robinson (1992), commissioned by the Engineering Council, concluded that 'technology in the National Curriculum is a mess', lacking in progression and identity, with an over-concentration on aspects of designing at the expense of making. The report was flawed with regard to focusing almost exclusively on Key Stages 3 and 4, drawing upon a very limited evidence base of six school visits and seventeen interviews with interested parties, including teachers and parents. Nevertheless, it triggered a sense of alarm in the media that Design and Technology was not preparing pupils for the world of work and had degenerated into little more than a series of 'Blue Peter' style activities. This was exacerbated by criticisms from the National Institute of Economic and Social Research (Prais and Beadle 1991) concerning the displacement of craft-based subjects from the secondary curriculum. The criticisms were based on invidious comparisons with vocational and craft training in the rest of Western Europe, which was claimed to underpin manufacturing productivity.

The National Curriculum for Design and Technology was not without its supporters. Eggleston (1992) acknowledged that the introduction of the subject had been accompanied by significant teething problems, but supported the radical nature of the curriculum and its concentration on the expressive and intellectual aspects of technology. He warned that, 'We are in great danger of diluting or abandoning one of the country's most ambitious and well thought out innovations' (1992: 4).

However, the writing was clearly on the wall for the original orders and in 1993 a consultation exercise was carried out by the National Curriculum Council resulting in the publication of a revised set of proposals for Design and Technology. It should be noted that things got worse before they got better – the National Curriculum Council consultation document was subjected to a number of published revisions. At one stage in 1994 there were four published variations of the Design and Technology National Curriculum. The confusion was finally resolved by the adoption of the Dearing Proposals (1993) for a slimmed down National Curriculum leading to the current Design and Technology curriculum, introduced into primary schools in 1995.

At the heart of the new curriculum was the requirement that 'pupils should be taught to develop their design and technology capability through combining their designing and making skills with knowledge and understanding in order to design and make products.' (DfEE 1995: 4). It was clear that there was a heavy vocational influence in the reformulation of the curriculum. The emphasis on the centrality of 'products' was reinforced in the requirement that pupils should engage in three key activities:

'Pupils should be given opportunities to develop their design and technology capability through:

• assignments in which they design and make products;

- focused practical tasks in which they develop and practise particular skill and knowledge;
- activities in which they investigate, disassemble and evaluate different products.'

(DfEE 1995: 4)

While the requirement that pupils engage in these activities was implicit in the original orders, they were lost within the mass of documentation that made up the programmes of study. One clear benefit of the new curriculum was the prominence given to these activities in helping to structure the development of pupil capability.

The first of these activities requires that pupils engage in design and make assignments which give full rein to the exploration and realisation of their own ideas for the making of products. Such work should take place within a range of contexts using a variety of materials including textiles, food, construction kits, reclaimed (junk) materials, mouldable materials, sheet materials such as card and materials suitable for making frameworks, including wood. As a precursor to this, pupils are expected to engage in focused tasks aimed at the development of knowledge and particular skills relevant to the manipulation of the materials being used. Throughout these activities, subject knowledge is developed through practical activities involving mechanisms and motion, control, structures, health and safety and what makes for a quality product. One key innovation was the importance attached to children evaluating products and applications in order to develop an understanding of the designed world with a view to using this understanding to inform their own designing and making of products.

Evaluation

There is an explicit recognition throughout the Design and Technology curriculum that evaluation is central to the process of designing and making. A major step forward with regard to this has been the requirement that pupils evaluate products designed and made by others through investigating and disassembling products and applications. While there is little doubt that the introduction of this strand of evaluation had its roots in a drive to relate design and technology to the world of work, there are strong educational reasons for pupils to investigate the designed work of others. Martin (1995) asserts that through such activities pupils can learn about;

- how things work;
- how their own work relates to the world around them;
- developing critical judgements;
- improving their observation, discussion, questioning and evaluative skills;
- the values associated with products and applications.

Evaluation, investigation and disassembly is often carried out as a precursor to designing and making and is based upon Baynes' (1992: 40) assertion that evaluation has two distinct elements:

> There is first the ability to appreciate, analyse and debate what others have done . . . the second is the ability to analyse, criticise and learn from the child's own activity.

Johnsey (1995) has expressed concerns about the second of these two facets of evaluation, stating that there is a danger of confusing the evaluation of the learning process with the evaluation of the design process. He proposed that it might be more useful for pupils to make evaluations of four different aspects of design and technology:

- their own design and technology work as it proceeds – ongoing evaluation;
- their own work when it is finished – summary evaluation;
- their own procedures – procedural evaluation;
- the designed work of others.

He proposed a range of very useful strategies for teachers to help pupils evaluate, some of which will be discussed in this chapter. His central argument was that it is essential that pupils 'specify the purpose of the product', as a key element of 'making good quality products fit for their intended purpose' (DoE 1992). In order to achieve this pupils should be asked to set out criteria for products that they are about to design and make. These criteria should be informed by evaluation of the designed work of others and an awareness of their own designing and making capabilities. Once criteria have been established they can act as a set of benchmarks against which evaluative comments or changes can be made throughout the process of designing and making.

Johnsey's proposals form a valuable starting point in developing the skills of evaluation. However there is a fundamental area of concern which needs to be addressed if effective evaluation is to take place within design and technology – that of self-esteem.

The problem of self-esteem

Riggs and Conway (1991: 32) have argued that:

> any education should involve critical reflection and evaluation. This involves not just cognitive and physical skills but should include those aspects of experience that take feeling, believing and trusting seriously. This is especially true when reflecting upon the roots of value judgements.

The challenge of evaluation should not be underestimated. Personal experience of working with adults on initial teacher education and in-service
courses has highlighted the extent to which many people are likely to down-
grade the results of their work in design and technology. This lack of
confidence is even more striking when working with pupils. Witness the
following observation from a teacher (Nicola Castle) working with year four
pupils on a design and make assignment involving the use of textiles:

> Ashik's stencil (of a mosque) was fairly intricate with many thin cuts. He
> chose to use a pair of scissors to make the cuts. This proved quite
> challenging and the stencil tore easily. He quickly became despondent
> and threatened to throw the stencil away and make something easier. I
> encouraged him to persevere with the stencil as he had already spent so
> much time on it and it looked very effective. Ashik finally decided that it
> was worth pursuing and sellotaped the tears. It made me think of how
> easily pupils reject their work and silently put it in the bin – how many
> times had this happened unnoticed?

Design and technology has enormous educational potential in that, through
evaluation, it can give a unique insight into quality. Boud *et al.* (1985) suggest
that it is the process of reflection and evaluation that turns experience into
learning and provides the capability to transfer the benefit of that experience
to other situations. While such a process is of enormous value, it can be a
two-edged sword. The act of designing and making in the primary classroom
is essentially a public one and as such it can expose pupils' efforts to what
may be perceived to be the cold, hard light of public scrutiny and attendant
possible ridicule from peers. One only has to bear in mind pupils' obsession
with conforming to dress codes to see just how far they will go to prevent
themselves being seen as different from their peers. Covington and Beery
(1976) indicate that 'an overwhelming proportion of students of all ages hold
unrealistically high self-expectations'. How frustrating it must be to be asked
to labour at producing something with limited skills at one's disposal, the
final fruits of which may bear little or no resemblance to the polished manufactured products available in almost any shop one may care to visit. To be
then asked to state publicly how 'it might be improved' may prove for many
to be adding insult to injury. This can be exacerbated by the challenge
of working with peers who may be perceived to be more confident or
competent in their designing and making.

In some cases this lack of confidence in designing, making and evaluating
may be attributed to a lack of self esteem. This problem may not be readily
apparent in the very early years of formal education. Constable (1994) found
that younger pupils in Key Stage 1 found it difficult to find fault with their
own work, rating it as 'very good' regardless of whether it fulfilled the
intended purpose. It was at the age of six or seven that elements of self
criticism began to emerge. It is at this age that pupils are beginning to be

more influenced by their peers. It is possible that a key time in which to intervene in terms of employing strategies for promoting confidence in evaluating is at around the age of six or seven so as to channel emerging self criticism in a constructive manner.

A recent case study undertaken by a PGCE student highlights some of the issues pertaining to evaluation and self-esteem. It is an honest account of the challenge encountered by the student in enabling year three pupils to evaluate process and product as part of their designing and making. The pupils had little previous experience of designing and making within the classroom.

Case Study – 'Mr Mole's Lamp'

The design and make assignment had deliberately been set within a social 'helping' context with an emphasis on reflection and evaluation that research has indicated may be attractive to girls, but with a degree of 'technological tinkering', characteristically appealing to boys (Kimbell *et al.* 1996). The work was rooted in the context of 'Mr Mole's Lamp', a story of a mole who could not see to read his comic. Pupils had been given some experience of working with electrical circuits. To complement this, a range of lighting appliances including torches and ordinary table lamps were investigated and disassembled to see how they worked. Pupils were then invited to find a solution in the form of a product that might help Mr Mole.

Initial designing

Class discussion led to a number of interesting ideas and a variety of proposed solutions ranging from conventional reading lamps to torches. A great number of pupils experienced problems in committing their ideas to paper – Karamjit and Julie were typical (see Figures 3.2 and 3.3). Initially, this was perceived to be through a lack of skill in drawing, but their general art work was good by comparison. This, together with the size of drawing and discussions with the pupils, seemed to indicate that the problem was due to a lack of confidence and an avoidance strategy, their ideas on paper being open to possible criticism.

Informal evaluation in making

Informal ongoing evaluation occurred throughout the activity as the pupils enthusiastically set about making their lamps. However, the end products did not bear much resemblance to their original designs. There were three main reasons for this:

- the work may have been too challenging in terms of making;
- a lack of knowledge and capability, the designs being insufficient for construction purposes;

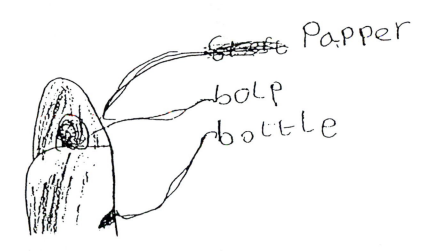

Karamjit had difficulty expressing her ideas on paper. She was hesitant when questioned and required much confidence building. The size and positioning of her design on the paper seems to reflect a lack of confidence, as is the lack of commitment to detail.

Figure 3.2 Karamjit's lack of confidence expressing her ideas on paper

- a number of pupils were unable to relate designing and making and considered them as distinct and unrelated operations.

Both problems could potentially have been overcome through relevant focused tasks and experiences such as the opportunity to handle materials before coming up with their design proposals. This would have given pupils the opportunity to discover the limitations and possibilities of materials at their disposal. Designing is not simply drawing and needs to be practised within the context of the designing and making process.

The pupils continually evaluated their work, made decisions and took appropriate action whilst constructing. However, some pupils became disenchanted by a perceived lack of success of their efforts. An extreme example of this lay in the complete abandonment of the project by some groups of pupils, although generally the process was more subtle, most often evident by a lack of motivation in engaging with the work.

Evaluating as a final stage in the activity

This proved to be more problematic than any other aspect of the process. When asked to indicate an improvement that might be made, the pupils were very reluctant to offer suggestions, many considering the project already complete. Improvement drawings were completely divorced from any

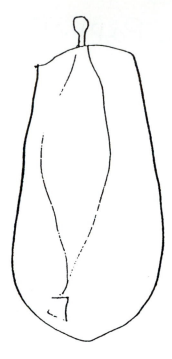

When questioned, Julie came up with a number of improvements on her original design. She was asked to highlight them on her original drawing. When I left her to work independently, she crossed out the orginal and started again. Through discussion with her, it appeared that it was 'wrong' and she 'didn't like it' and was embarrassed by it.

Figure 3.3 Julie's 'crossing out'

outcomes (see Figure 3.4). A number of pupils showed signs of stress in attempting to evaluate their work. They were automatically making judgements and because of low self-esteem, these judgements would often be negative. At one point one child was on the verge of throwing her work in the bin because she 'didn't like it anymore'.

In order to support pupils in their evaluating an alternative strategy was adopted using a simple worksheet. The rationale for this was based on break-

Figure 3.4 Improvement drawing

ing down the process of evaluation into manageable steps, with a view to enabling pupils to draw the outcome as it actually came out, thus making a connection between the physical, the mental imagery and the drawn modelling. Weakness in this aspect of capability had been apparent in earlier design work. This strategy could be developed in future design work and in formulating improvements in future evaluations. In addition, pupils were encouraged to channel judgements into positive statements. Some published materials have provision for enabling pupils to categorise judgements, all categories being positively worded – this was incorporated into the worksheet. To complement the identification of positive elements of their work, the pupils were asked to look for one improvement. As the original designs barely resembled the outcomes, it proved impossible to get the pupils to superimpose their improvements over the original designs – any drawings they attempted were from scratch. In their previous attempt at evaluation, drawing improvements from scratch gave pupils the opportunity to completely ignore the outcome. The pupils were therefore required to express their ideas in words – only then were they allowed to incorporate their ideas into their drawings.

The results of this strategy were interesting in that all drawings related to outcomes. Judgements were varied, with three pupils (including two with special educational needs for learning or behavioural difficulties), judging their work as 'great' – this mirrored a generally positive approach to design and technology as a whole by the three individuals concerned, which was not always evident in other subjects. Interestingly, Lee and Natalie, two of the most able pupils in the class (in other subjects) invented a new category for their work – that of 'bad' (in the pejorative 'non-slang' sense). Suggestions for improvements varied from simple improvements to the physical appearance – 'paint it' (Figure 3.5), to functional improvements – 'putting the lid on top of the bottle to stop light going up where it was not useful' (Figure 3.6). The requirement for the improvements to be written first (with teacher support given through questioning and transcribing, where required) proved to be valuable in developing thinking.

The case study highlights some key issues. Prominent amongst these is the recommendation that the process of evaluation be broken down into manageable steps. Wood *et al.*'s (1976) use of the concept of scaffolding is useful within this context whereby the teacher intervenes in such way as to help a child understand concepts which in the long term can be internalised by the child. It is important to view scaffolding as a construct involving intellectual, social and emotional processes. It also became clear that pupils need to develop a vocabulary relevant to this type of work. This vocabulary might relate to technological aspects concerning circuits, cells and switches, but more importantly might incorporate a bank of evaluative words or phrases to help pupils clarify and extend their thinking. Most importantly, analytical, critical and creative thinking needs to be developed over the long term through the planning of appropriate strategies to support pupils.

In order to address some of these issues, the following range of strategies are recommended to encourage competence and confidence in evaluating.

Developing self-esteem through evaluating

One reason for pupils lacking self esteem in their designing and making is that, from a very early age, they are bombarded with images of products which are presented as 'state of the art' in terms of their potential for providing pleasure for the user. To enable pupils to begin to gain a critical insight into these claims, one can start by looking at the world which pupils inhabit and give them regular practice of verbally articulating their views about products that they know about – for example, by asking about preferences for toys. In the early years one might invite pupils to say why they play with

 <u>My Lamp Design</u>
<u>for Mr. Mole.</u>

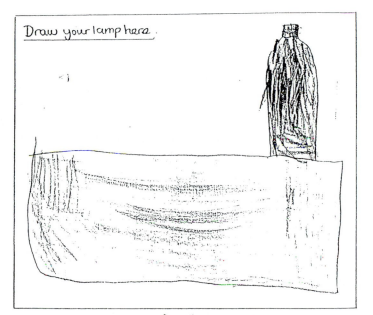

<u>Draw your lamp here</u>.

Was your lamp : {Great}   (nice)   (O.K.)

How can you make it better?

<u>Panit it.</u>

Figure 3.5 'Paint it'

My Lamp Design for Mr. Mole.

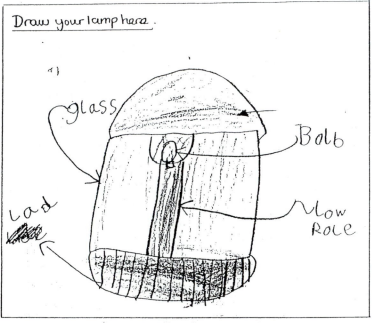

Draw your lamp here.

glass

Bolb

Lad

Low Role

Was your lamp : Great   Nice   OK.

How can you make it better?

I can make it better by
Puting the lide on top of
the boetle.

Figure 3.6 'Putting the lid on'

certain toys, moving from the more generalised and descriptive ('its nice') to the more focused and functional ('I can build lots of different things with it'). Pupils can be given the opportunity to make choices about their work, initially perhaps about such simple, small things as the colour they wish to paint their models. Work with models made from reclaimed materials might be preceded by verbal evaluations of toy vehicles, supported by teacher questioning – 'What colour are fire engines painted and why?' 'Why are police cars painted with bright stripes?' 'What is similar about the way in which tipper trucks and doors work (hinge mechanisms)?'. The play corner can be discussed with regard to what would be needed to turn it into a hospital or what babies might need to keep them happy. Such discussion can form a valuable stimulus for designing and making.

Through such discussion and action, pupils can begin to understand that their opinions and decisions are valued. Evaluating involves the formulating and expressing of ideas and opinions. People, and particularly adults, showing an interest in and valuing of pupils' opinions will have a beneficial effect on self-esteem. Such work can also develop knowledge and understanding about the needs of others and how products can be designed and made to fulfil those needs. However, these kinds of critical dialogues will not emerge naturally or spontaneously: they need deliberate teacher intervention and support. Equally, for such discussions to be valued by the students, they need to have equivalent status to other kinds of traditional educational outcomes – writing – if students can really internalise the value of disinterested evaluation.

Divorcing evaluation from self-criticism

In order to develop confidence in pupils' constructive ability to be critical, there is a need to separate out evaluation and criticism of products from criticism of self. A promising starting point can be the tasting and testing of food. Such work can be particularly revealing in that pupils are used to making choices about food and have strong views on how they want it to taste. What they may lack is the vocabulary for expressing their ideas. Figure 3.7 shows the evaluation of an apple by a seven year-old using a star diagram (Ridgewell 1994). The class had been asked to set criteria by saying what they wanted their apples to be like and recording their tasting (evaluation) of the apples on a star chart.

An alternative way of evaluating the apples might be through tasting charts where each apple is rated according to specific criteria – (see Figure 3.8). It is important that pupils gain experience of setting their own criteria for evaluation and that these criteria are valued. Ollerenshaw and Ritchie (1993) found that pupils tend to evaluate their work according to their perceptions of what the teacher wanted, such as neatness or correct spelling. One implication of this is that teachers should make their own expectations about what they value explicit through the use of specific praise and demonstration, for

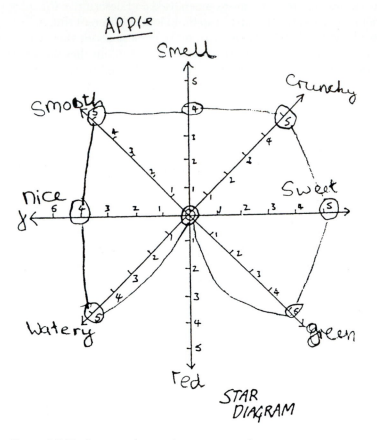

Figure 3.7 Evaluation of an apple using a star diagram

example, in stressing that as consumers and users of products, pupils' own criteria are important.

Knowledge and critical awareness of food products can be developed by other activities such as attempting to distinguish between one cola drink and another through blind-tasting and evaluating snacks such as crisps according to a variety of criteria (e.g., crunchiness, health, saltiness). Such activities and associated discussion can develop critical awareness about how expectations may not always match reality, develop vocabulary for describing and evaluating food and promote independence and confidence in the setting of appropriate criteria. It is important at this early stage that a limited number of products and small range of criteria are considered so as to focus pupils' thinking on key issues.

These activities can be carried out on a whole class basis or through pupils working in groups. Such brief, small-scale evaluation activities should occur on a regular basis, so that such critical awareness of products can become an

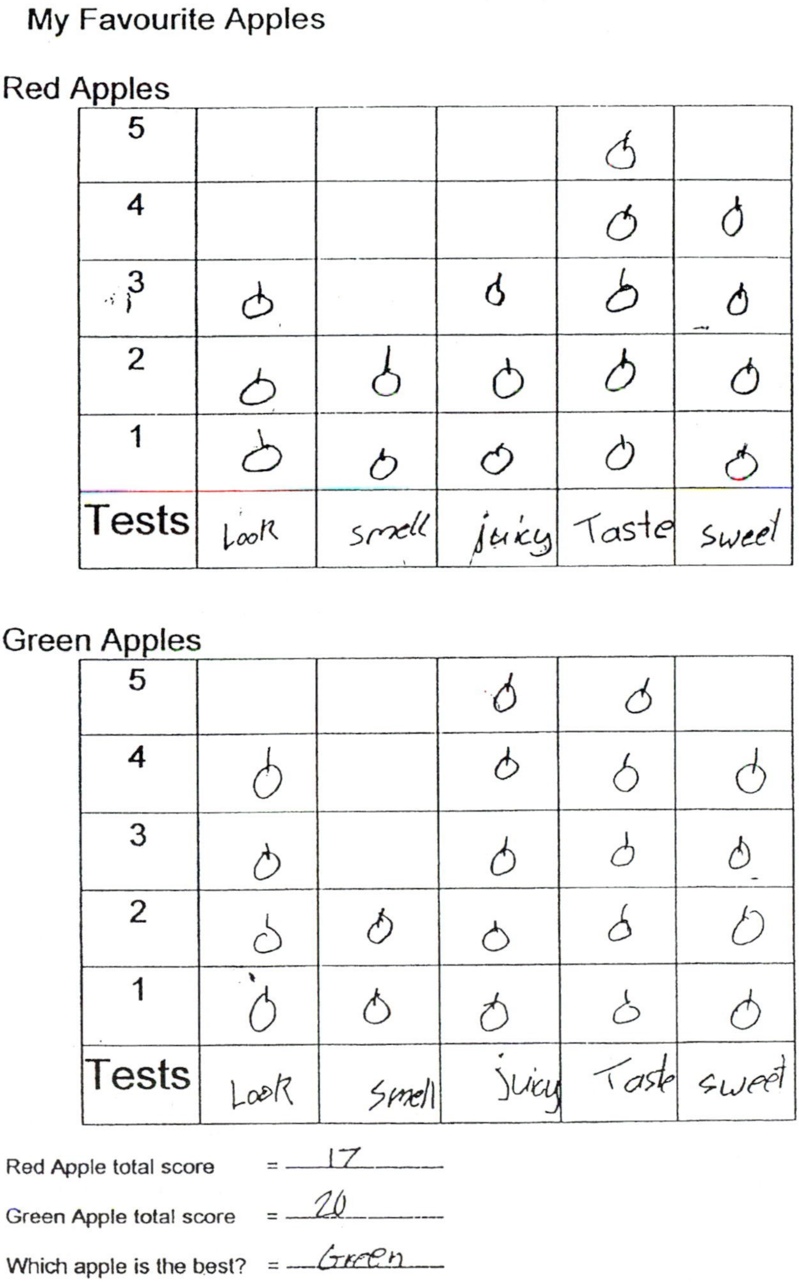

My Favourite Apples

Red Apples

	Look	Smell	Juicy	Taste	Sweet
5				●	
4				●	●
3	●		●	●	●
2	●	●	●	●	●
1	●	●	●	●	●
Tests	Look	Smell	juicy	Taste	sweet

Green Apples

	Look	Smell	Juicy	Taste	Sweet
5			●	●	
4	●		●	●	●
3	●		●	●	●
2	●	●	●	●	●
1	●	●	●	●	●
Tests	Look	Smell	Juicy	Taste	sweet

Red Apple total score = 17

Green Apple total score = 20

Which apple is the best? = Green

Figure 3.8 Rating of apples using criteria

integral part of the fabric of school experience. With regular experience, pupils can begin to internalise some of the intellectual processes that lie behind evaluating. The time spent on such activities can be justified by reference to the fact that evaluating is a key skill that is of value across the curriculum.

From such starting points one can move on to evaluating other products that pupils have in-depth knowledge of. They can be encouraged to think about key characteristics of products. Favourite toys might be revisited: 'What's good about them?; What works?; What doesn't work?; How does it work?; Does it stand up to testing?; Has it lasted?; Could it be improved?'.

Values – developing and extending critical awareness about products

To develop and extend such insights about products, older pupils can be invited to discuss the distinction between needs and wants (Ritchie 1995) through the evaluation of everyday designer products such as trainers and T-shirts. A recent observation of school experience was distinguished by a (very confident) student teacher walking into a year six class wearing a bright yellow baseball cap with the words 'Mothercare' printed prominently on the front. He invited the pupils to comment on how 'cool' he looked, generating a wave of laughter, which was skilfully channelled into a valuable discussion on fashion and the high cost of desirable items of clothing. The issue of self-esteem was apparent in the comments made by pupils – it was evident that some pupils had a high level of insight into how they were being manipulated into wearing certain brand name items but 'couldn't afford' not to wear them for fear of being teased or at worst ostracised by their peers.

From such an example it is clear that there is no such thing as 'value free' technology. There are indications that from a young age pupils have a sophisticated understanding of the values attached to products. Constable (1994) found that the presence of a recognised logo tended to heavily influence pupils at Key Stage 2 in their judgements about products.

A case study in Leeds by Outterside (1995), aimed at revealing the values of nine and ten year-old pupils with regard to everyday products, involved the evaluation of different types of supermarket carrier bags from Marks & Spencer, Morrisons and Netto respectively. When the bags were laid out on a table, they were greeted with stifled laughter, with some pupils refusing to admit that they had ever shopped at Netto, although they later disclosed that they had. Twenty-one out of the twenty-five pupils said that they liked the Marks & Spencer bag the best, because of the colour, whilst three said Morrison and one the Netto bag, because it was strong. The bag liked least was the Netto bag, because it 'wasn't a good shop' with some not liking the colour or logo.

The pupils were then asked to describe people who might use the Marks & Spencer bag . There was unanimous agreement on 'rich and posh' people, with pupils insisting that, although they had all been to Marks & Spencer, they themselves were not 'rich' or 'posh'. The Morrisons shopper was a 'normal person', like themselves. The Netto shopper was characterised as someone who was poor, lived on a council estate, a back-to-back house or even slept rough on the street. Netto shoppers were thought to be mainly old age pensioners, certainly older than those who used Marks & Spencer. These observations were also clearly evident in the pupil's drawings: see Figure 3.9.

When questioned about the origin of these stereotypical observations the pupils were insistent that they came not from adults but from each other, although some pupils openly cited the view of their parents that Netto was 'cheap and crummy'. Such descriptions were, by association, attributed to the people who shopped there. The pupils here clearly understood how products might be seen to define identity (see Kline 1993).

Product evaluation can open up pupils' eyes to stereotypes that exist about products and in so doing may enable them to begin to take more control of their own lives by understanding the forces that shape consumption. It is through the evaluation and investigation of products that pupils can begin to consider a wide range of issues pertaining to economic, social, moral and environmental concerns. One strategy that may be useful in this context is proposed by Barlex (1994) who recommends that the question of 'who wins and who loses' when a product is made should feature highly as stimulus for discussion amongst pupils.

Product evaluation can also be of great value in revealing stereotypical views concerning technology from a range of cultures. Siraj-Blatchford (1995) describes a strategy for eliciting values concerning products citing the use of Kelly's Repertory Grid. This is a technique, initially developed in the 1950s in the field of clinical psychology, designed to reveal how people construe and make sense of the world around them. One aspect of this approach with regard to design and technology involves eliciting the views of participants with regard to three products, asking them to 'think of a way in which two of the products are similar yet different from the third'. In the study, students in an initial teacher training workshop were asked to randomly select three items from a group of seven artefacts drawn from a range of cultures: a home made jumper, pocket computer, a North American Indian bow and arrow, a fluorescent bulb, an electric epilator and a dhava (used for cooking chappatis). A range of descriptive bi-polar constructs were derived from individuals concerning the products:

- modern/advanced – ancient/primitive;
- dependent upon electricity – non electrical;
- clothing – non clothing item;
- environmentally friendly – non environmentally friendly;
- expensive – cheap;
- basic/survival – luxury;
- hand made – machine made.

Marks
und
Spencer

Netto

This lady has
a plain walking
stick to help her
walk. Her coat is
worn, so are
her shoes.
Her dog's coat
is tattord tatty.

This man
has a smart
suit and a posh
walking cane for fun.
He has a bic pen and
shiny shoes.

M.S   M.S

This lady is very rich
lives in a very wealthy neighbourhood

This man is a busker
he lives in a council flat
and is a bit of a punk

Figure 3.9 Stereotypical images of shoppers

These constructs proved to be a fruitful basis for discussion, revealing conflicting value positions within the group which were vigorously challenged and defended. The activity allowed a wide range of issues to be opened up for consideration, including conceptions of technological appropriateness and advancement in relation to concerns for the environment, leading to an in-depth discussion on ecology and the appropriateness of saving labour during periods of unemployment. Such an approach could be adapted for use at primary and secondary school level with due regard for the need for a sensitive, open and tolerant approach on behalf of teachers and pupils.

Alternatively, the evaluation of products made by others can be an excellent platform for the designing, making and evaluation of products by pupils themselves. We have suggested strategies that are of value in these contexts and the reader's attention is drawn to the work of Constable (1994) for a further range of strategies. To complement these, one should not overlook the value of group work and communication in developing capability in evaluation.

Group work

Kimbell *et al.* (1991) indicate the critical role that group work has to play in the development of design and technology capability; 'the pupils response to each other's criticism was a major force in shaping the success or failure of artefact in their own eyes' 1991: 9.1). However, successful group work does not occur spontaneously. It is necessary to structure groups and tasks in such a manner as to foster constructive criticism. Initially, pupils should be placed in pairs with a 'critical friend' working on a highly structured focused task – this can enable them to focus on evaluating in a fairly safe context where the task demand is not too high. Pairs might then be teamed up to make groups of four, again working on highly structured tasks – this can focus pupils' efforts into establishing group cohesion without the distraction of an over-demanding activity. As group cohesion develops, tasks presented can become more open-ended and challenging, enabling frank and open evaluation of process and product to take place in contexts where pupils will feel relatively unthreatened. One has to be aware, however, of the possibility of the group becoming become 'too cosy' and develop and monitor interaction through appropriate questioning and explanation.

Communication – making thinking visible

The value of group work lies in its potential for developing communication – a key element of evaluating is communicating one's thoughts to others. The act of communicating can help to clarify thinking. Communicating in as visual a manner as possible will help to clarify pupils' understanding of concepts.

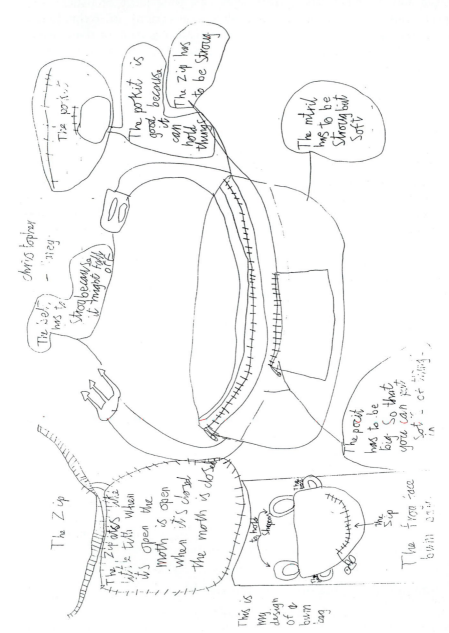

Figure 3.10 Belt bag

One such strategy in the development of ongoing evaluation is for initial ideas to be boldly sketched in one colour of felt tip (removing the temptation to 'rub out' ideas) with subsequent modifications signified by the use of a felt tip of a different colour. By this means one can trace the development of design ideas as they interact with the 'reality' of making. It is important to make one's expectation clear through stressing that design proposals are working diagrams rather than finished products. Pupils should be encouraged to keep all aspects of their work in progress, including prototypes – the use of a process diary can be a valuable means of recording and evaluating ideas as they develop (Djora and Bratt 1994). Such work can form valuable evidence of achievement and capability.

Close observational drawing of products with an emphasis on identifying functional characteristics of an object can help to crystallise understanding and provide a stimulus for ideas. For example, the evaluation of a belt bag by a year three child shows an understanding of the needs of the user in terms of strong, soft materials and the size of pockets (see Figure 3.10). The zip is used as a stimulus for the child's own ideas about designing and making his own bag.

It is important that these strategies are set within a range of contexts in order to give pupils the opportunity to work from and develop strengths within designing and making. In working from strengths, pupils can begin to develop self-esteem through the evaluation process, thus developing confidence and competence in a key area of design and technology. Insights derived from such work might also be significant in fostering a reflective approach to the development of values and technological literacy.

References

Assessment of Performance Unit (1987) *Design and Technological Activity: A Framework for Assessment*, London: APU/DES.

Barlex, D. (1994) 'Winners and losers', *Design and Technology Times*, Cheltenham: Education Development Unit.

Baynes, K. (1992) *Children Designing*, Loughborough: Loughborough University of Technology.

Bloom, B. S., Engelhart, M. D., Furst, E. J., Hill, W. H. and Krathwohl, D. R. (1956) *Taxonomy of Educational Objectives*, London: Longman.

Boud, D., Keogh, R. and Walker, D. (1985) *Reflection: Turning Experience into Learning*, London: Kogan Page

Constable, H. (1994) 'A study of aspects of design and technology capability at Key Stages 1 and 2' in *IDATER 94: International Conference on Design and Technology Educational Research and Curriculum Development*, Loughborough: Loughborough University of Technology.

Constable, H. (1993) 'How do children evaluate?', *Primary DATA*, vol. 3, no. 3, pp. 19–23.

Covington, M. and Beery, R. (1976) *Self Worth and School Learning*, New York: Holt, Rinehart and Winston.

Dearing, R. (1993) *The National Curriculum and its Assessment: Final Report*, London: HMSO.

Department for Education (1992) *Technology for Ages 5 to 16 – Proposals for the Secretary of State for Education*, London: HMSO.

Department for Education and Employment (1995) *Design and Technology in the National Curriculum*, London: HMSO.

Department of Education and Science (1985a) *The Curriculum from 5 to 16. Curriculum Matters 2*, 16, London: HMSO.

Department of Education and Science (1985b) *White Paper: Better Schools*, 23, London: HMSO.

Djora, J. and Bratt, F. (1994) 'Developing Design and Technology capability through the process diary', *Primary DATA*, vol. 4, no 3. pp. 17–21.

Eggleston, J. (1992) 'Editorial' *Design and Technology Teaching*, vol. 24, no. 3, pp. 3–4

Engineering Council, Standing Council on School Science and Technology (1985) *Problem Solving: Science and Technology in Primary Schools*, London: Engineering Council.

Her Majesty's Inspectorate (1992) *Technology, Key Stages 1, 2 and 3. A Report by HM Inspectorate on the First Year, 1990–91*, London: HMSO.

Johnsey, R. (1995) 'Criteria for success', *Design and Technology Teaching*, vol. 27, no. 2. pp. 37–39.

Kimbell, R., Stables, K., Wheeler, T., Wozniak, A. and Kelly, V. (1991) *The Assessment of Performance in Design and Technology: The Final Report of the Design and Technology APU Project*, London: Evaluation and Monitoring Unit. Schools' Examination and Assessment Council.

Kimbell, R., Stables, K. and Green, R. (1996) *Understanding Practice in Design and Technology*, Buckingham: Open University Press.

Kline, S. (1993) *Out of the Garden: Toys and Children's Culture in the Age of TV Marketing*, London: Verso.

Layton, D. (1995) 'Constructing and reconstructing school technology in England and Wales', *International Journal of Technology and Design Education*, vol. 5, no. 2. pp. 89–114.

Martin, M. (1995) 'Perceptions of products and applications' in Smith, J. (ed.) *IDATER 95* Loughborough: Loughborough University of Technology, pp. 58–62.

National Curriculum Council (1989) *Technology 5–16 in the National Curriculum: A Report to the Secretary of State for Education on the Statutory Consultation for Attainment Targets and Programmes of Study in Technology*, London: HMSO.

National Curriculum Council (1990) *Technology in the National Curriculum*, London: HMSO.

Ollerenshaw, C. and Ritchie, R. (1993) *Primary Science: Making it Work*, London: David Fulton.

Outterside, Y. (1995) 'What values do primary children attribute to an everyday product within their experience?', unpublished paper: Leeds Metropolitan University.

Prais, S. and Beadle, E. (1991) *Pre-vocational Training in Europe Today*, London: NIESR

Ridgewell, J. (1994) *Tasting and Testing*, London: Ridgewell Press.

Riggs, A. and Conway, R. (1991) 'Values and Technology Education', *Design and Technology Teaching*, vol. 23, no. 1, pp. 31–3.

Ritchie, R. (1995) *Primary Design and Technology: A Process for Learning*, London: David Fulton.

Schools Curriculum and Assessment Authority (1994) *Design and Technology in the National Curriculum – Draft Proposals, May 1994*, London: HMSO.

Siraj-Blatchford, J. (1995) 'Kelly's repertory grid: a technique for developing evaluation in design and technology' in Smith, J. (ed.) *IDATER 95*, Loughborough: Loughborough University of Technology, pp. 195–200.

Smithers, A. and Robinson, P. (1992) *Technology in the National Curriculum – Getting it Right*, London: Engineering Council.

Thatcher, M. (1983) *The Times Educational Supplement*, 29 April, p. 22.

Wood, D., Bruner, J. and Ross, G. (1976) 'The role of tutoring in problem solving', *Journal of Child Psychology and Psychiatry*, vol. 17, no. 2, pp. 89–100.

4 Writing in English and responding to writing

Muriel Robinson and Viv Ellis

Introduction

English as a school subject has a long history of the production of written texts by pupils, and these texts have always been subject to some form of evaluation or assessment, but the ways in which we as English teachers have conceptualised this process have often been very different from those in other subjects addressed in this volume. This is for a variety of reasons: first, English has a different function in society from the other subjects in this collection. This different function has led to a different emphasis within the evaluative process which in turn has meant that we have become very good at some aspects of evaluation and relatively unpractised in others. This chapter will attempt to explore the ways in which production in English has developed and the resulting problematic nature of evaluation in English before suggesting some examples from recent practice which may offer ways forward.

To begin with, it is important to explore the ways in which English is different from other media arts. These stem from the values placed on this subject in our society. English, alone of the subjects in this book, is not just a curriculum subject, but one of the core three. By labelling it as such the National Curriculum maintains a national belief in the importance of literacy, but it does so in a context which focuses attention on certain aspects of literacy and cultural heritage which have strong social importance and which complicate the creative process involved in the production of a written text. We are used to a view of schooled literacy as something which has a clearly functional purpose. The creative process of the production of written texts in English is much more easily seen as a means to an end of producing functionally literate children. Employers praise or blame schools not for the creative content of students' work but for such surface features as spelling, punctuation and handwriting. Bored academics give their undergraduates spelling tests to show the limitations of A-level education and broadsheet and tabloid papers alike print the results with glee, and with little attention to the contradictions between such commentary on English usage and that found in their book review pages.

That such a view is prevalent not just among traditionalists and 'back to basics' campaigners is shown clearly by the rhetoric around the newly introduced National Literacy Strategy. Of the eleven learning objectives set out in the Framework for Teaching, only the eleventh mentions any creative process in writing (DfEE 1998: 3), with accurate spelling, fluent and legible handwriting, use of a range of genres and re-drafting skills all having their own bullet points higher in the list. This is despite the fact that there is long tradition of creative writing as a part of English teaching: indeed, what teachers understand by such a term will be explored later in this chapter. However, it is important at this point to emphasise the limited importance placed on creativity, in whatever way it is defined. The emphasis is on learning form, structure and technical vocabulary. Spelling, grammar and handwriting are highlighted and foregrounded as the skills to be developed and the product disappears into a tool for the achievement of these aims.

Such a functional view of writing produces a particular evaluative stance, as we shall consider below, but it is important before moving to this to contrast this school approach to writing with the ways we judge published literature in our society. As suggested above, this dualistic view can be seen clearly in media reports on students' literacy and published literature. Both popular literature and more demanding fiction tend to elicit responses which are to do with the *power of the message* and the *enjoyment* of the reader. The features of written language which attract attention in school are more frequently primarily form and structure – spelling, grammar, handwriting, organisational conventions and the like. Whilst the deliberations of the Booker prize judges are confidential, we would be surprised to learn that they dwell overmuch on the technical aspects of a writer's style except insofar as such aspects are related to the meanings offered by the text and the enjoyment afforded to the reader. (Of course, at times, the ability to play with conventions, as opposed to the ability to conform to them, is acknowledged as a valuable attribute, as recent shortlists attest.) Handwriting and spelling become irrelevant, as printing presses and proof-readers intervene to re-code the author's text before we read it. This has created a gap between our perceptions about the written products of school children and commercially available texts which we are only now beginning to address within the education process and which national policy has done little to eradicate or even identify.

What is significant for teachers is the extent to which we have allowed this differential approach to survive, despite our long-held awareness of the importance of what children want to write about and what they have to say. We turn now to consider how the development of our approaches to writing has led to the existence of competing paradigms of writing pedagogy and how this competition has resulted in a failure to shift the evaluative emphasis in the direction of message and meanings.

Form over desire: current models of writing production and pedagogy

There seem to be at least three competing paradigms of the teaching of writing on offer in the current curriculum prescription. The first is the skills paradigm in which writing is seen as an orchestration of discrete language skills which can be taught in an explicit and unproblematic way with communication as the simple outcome. This paradigm is hard to link to any theoretical school but is very prevalent in 'common sense' accounts of literacy of the sort found in politicians' rhetoric. It is manifested in photocopiable worksheets and workbooks which focus on these discrete skills, such as letter formation and spelling patterns, or which require students to follow a formula to produce a piece of writing (letters to an imaginary pen friend, for example, or simple narratives based on sequences of pictures). Many of the English textbooks which are designed to be worked through by students week after week through the year are based on this principle of teaching separate skills, with different sections addressing such components of the writing process as grammar ('using adjectives', for example), spelling patterns (such as 'magic e' or 'i before e') or language structures (for example, paragraphing and key sentences). At first glance this view of learning as something best broken down into manageable chunks can seem very appealing and, as such, has held sway in a large number of classrooms even until now, despite its lack of research evidence, theory or presence in teacher education courses. The everyday support for this view and teachers' own encounters with this approach, coupled with the appeal of something which seems to offer system and order, conspire to maintain it despite its limitations as pointed out by those supporting other paradigms.

The second paradigm which is particularly relevant here is that developed by the genre theorists (see Cope and Kalantzis 1993). This regards literacy as a social practice and suggests the teaching of certain, privileged language structures as a means of enabling and empowering students to make meaning in important, culturally-determined ways. This involves 'modelling' and the provision of 'exemplars' for discussion, imitation or completion and a consideration of the demands made by notions of audience and purpose. At first glance it has many similarities with the traditional skills approach just described, but here the emphasis is on empowerment. For example, the EXEL materials developed by Wray and colleagues in Exeter (Lewis and Wray 1995) offer developing writers supportive structures ('writing frames') which are designed to offer genre models to extend children's familiarity with different language styles and enable them to use a wider range of styles when writing. The emphasis within the genre school has been on non-narrative writing, with this divided into such genres as 'recount', 'comparison', 'argument' and 'persuasion'. However, this paradigm has been criticised for its lack of a subtle categorisation of the many kinds of narrative writing and for its view of genres as fixed and limited; critics have also questioned how far simply learning genre rules is really empowering without some attention to other causes of social inequality. In practice, it is easy for teachers to turn the thoughtful ideas promulgated by Lewis and Wray into a set of exercises to augment or replace those already used as described in the skills paradigm. For a critique of the genre approach see Barrs (1991–2).

The third paradigm, now almost a distant echo in most British schools, is the process writing paradigm which positions the writer as an individual author and theorises writing as a recursive, cognitive process. This is the legacy of Britton *et al.* (1975) and Graves (1983), popularised in a limited but significant way in the UK and partially inscribed into the Cox curriculum. In this view of writing, the emphasis is on the student as writer. A workshop approach encourages the student to reflect carefully on the choice of topic (which should be self-selected rather than imposed) and to develop this topic through successive drafts with the aid of a writing partner, who may be the teacher or a fellow student. Skills of responding to texts are developed within the conferences held with the writing partner and the final product is less significant than the journey towards it. Where there is a final product, though, the emphasis is on sharing this through publishing within the class or school so that the work is read by a real audience, i.e., somebody interested in the message rather than in assessing the product. Much of the work produced by students in writing workshops is highly personal, described by Britton as an 'expressive mode' (Britton *et al.* 1975). There is, at least in early writing on this paradigm , little emphasis on developing a child's repertoire of styles and a view of secretarial skills as subservient to the composition process and only effectively taught within this context. As the opening sentence of this paragraph suggests, despite the enthusiasm of those who have tried this approach and experienced the power of the resulting writing, it has been largely overwhelmed by a return to a more skills-based approach which is at least implicitly encouraged by the National Literacy Strategy, despite its presence within the National Curriculum.

If one looks at the most recent piece of curriculum prescription in this area, *The National Literacy Strategy: Framework for Teaching* (DfEE 1998), these paradigms are all present to the extent that their vocabulary is appropriated. It is, however, the skills and genre paradigms which prevail. Even the notion of audience in writing is used as a rationale for the emphasis on the skills of proof-reading, presentation and layout:

> Pupils need to understand from an early age that much of their writing will be read by other people and therefore needs to be accurate, legible and set out in an appropriate way.
>
> (DfEE 1998: 5)

Composing is just as much a skill here as 'the *skills* of planning, drafting, revising, proof-reading and [. . .] presentation'. Children must be taught to move along this line as quickly and as accurately as they can. Communication skills must be honed to be simple, fast and error-free.

The genre paradigm is evident throughout in the exemplification of 'text-level writing composition' work, subdivided into 'fiction and poetry' and 'non-fiction.' For example, from year one term three, where children are asked to 'use poems or parts of poems as models for own writing, e.g., by *substituting words* or elaborating on the text', to year five term two, where they are asked 'to use the structures of poems read to write extensions based on these, e.g., additional verses, or *substituting own words* and ideas' [our emphasis], there is a repetitive emphasis on the completion of 'frames' or templates and the use of texts that have been read purely as structural or organisational models. The meaning of these texts is something that can be extracted and disposed of as the children attempt to imitate the 'polished forms', to name the structures and commit their names to memory – cinquain, epitaph and rhyming couplet in year four, for example. This is not to say that the *National Literacy Strategy* doesn't take elements from the process-oriented or whole-language approaches to writing. It does, but its momentum is elsewhere. It appropriates the key words into a different discourse dominated by narrowly-defined and conflated ideas of purpose and theme, organisation and structure (which are determined *for* you before you start to write) and accuracy (which you must consider as an aspect of presentation for your audience). This focus on skills and genre in the document is effectively an emphasis on 'form'. The desire to write has been sublimated by an induction into the structures of privileged forms.

It is worth noting that these kinds of distinctions, the sub-divisions between so-called genres are also problematic in terms of improving teachers' ability to respond to creative written work in a variety of ways. It draws unhelpful and inaccurate boundaries between different discourses and assumes simple parallels – narrative and non-narrative texts do not necessarily equate with creative/ fictional work and information. Genres are not fixed in the way some genre writers would have us believe but evolve and blur; crossing the expected boundary may be the most effective way to get the point across (poems to the bank manager etc.). For a fuller discussion of the genre debate see Rosen (1993) or Barrs (1991/2).

Donald Graves' famous first sentence 'Children want to write' (1983) seems utterly irrelevant to the *National Literacy Strategy: Framework for Teaching*. To be fair, the freedom of student writers to choose topic and develop meaning in the way and when they chose has been an alien concept in the context of compulsory schooling in the UK for at least the last ten years. Even the ideas of drafting (in which writing goes through a process of qualitative development) and writing conferences (in which a piece of writing becomes the focus of an extended discussion by a group of readers and or writers) have been shaped differently and with varying degrees of success in our classrooms. Teachers have been able to identify when a writer has found her 'real voice' in a piece of writing but unable to identify how this happened

or their own role, if any, in this event. The failure of drafting and conferencing with writers in many schools arises both from the valuing of these
processes for their own sake (the rush to publication or display and an obsession with correctness) and, more controversially, from the insecurities of
many English teachers. Teachers are commenting on students' work – and
very often encouraging other students to comment on their peers' efforts –
principally from their experience as a reader and not from their experience
of teacher as writer. There are some interesting comparisons to be made here
with teachers in other areas such as Music, Drama, Dance and Art where the
experience and practice of the teacher-as-artist/composer is at the heart of
the pedagogic activity.[1] In English as presently constructed by statute, composing is, at best, just one part of a complex enterprise and one in which an
emphasis on the structure of forms may suffice. Transmission of cultural
heritage, aesthetic valuing and the development of standards of correctness,
however, have always had a major stake in this subject and it has been
relatively easy at times to see the English curriculum as a reading curriculum.

By arguing for the importance of the process writing paradigm, we are not
simply proposing an approach to the teaching and evaluation of writing that
is purely expressive and affective and positions the writer and writing as
almost magical manifestations of an exterior creative urge. We do not seek to
deny the cognitive aspects of the teaching and evaluation of writing. Language and discourse are tools which we share and with which we work,
shaping subjective experiences into performances. In order for students to
know and to be able to critique language and discourse, they need to be able
to realise meanings and develop social relationships. As Pennycook has said,
we need 'to enable students to write (speak, read, listen) back', to support
'voices that speak in opposition to the local and global discourses that limit
and produce the possibilities that frame our students' lives' (1994: 311).

It was Pennycook's description of a 'critical pedagogy' that led Woods *et
al.* to elaborate the metaphor of the English or writing classroom as an
atelier, that is a space where language-users learn and share a craft, a space for
artisanal activity. The notion of atelier:

> invites people to bring in and work with their language rather than store
> it in a locker on entering the school, to be picked up on the way out.
> And to extend that metaphor, we can also see how school can insist on
> language becoming uniform, a uniform, not entirely ours, ill-fitting for
> many of us, one we may or may not grow into.
>
> (Woods, Dias and Ellis, 1996: 7)

The expertise of the teacher is acknowledged as is the expertise of all the
other artisans and their desire to produce meanings. The teacher may be an
'expert craftsperson' and the 'apprentices' may share in this but the expertise
is shared and owned by the atelier in the process of production and shifts
between the artisans. The artisans already know the forms they wish to use to

realise their meanings and they plunder them. This recognises that meaning is partly understood through forms, but only by making the form one's own. The experience of each artisan in the realisation of meaning through self-determined and appropriated forms is at the centre of the work of the atelier. In this model of the English/writing classroom, the teacher begins with the subjectivities of the students and their desire to *realise* (rather than simply produce) meanings and works with them and their language tools allowing feedback and evaluation when it is required as part of a dynamic process. There is a parallel tradition of writing workshops which has emerged over recent years in the adult education world, which at its best brings together published and aspiring writers in a 'master class' situation. This has had little influence on school-based approaches to the teaching of writing in terms of stimulating a similar focus on sharing understandings of the craft of writing, despite the increased numbers of authors visiting schools. In other words, we are suggesting that this idealistic model is not that common at present and is likely to be even less so in the immediate future.

There are many similar models of the 'writing' classroom, in particular, with names such as 'Writers' Workshop' or 'Community of Writers' (see, for example, Elbow and Belanoff 1995). These approaches work particularly well when there is a separate focus on the development and evaluation of writing *per se* rather than viewing writing as one of the three National Curriculum attainment targets which must cross-fertilise each other and as an 'activity' which must be combined with the two other 'activities'. Inevitably this leads to the privileging of some forms over others (ones that have been read and discussed, for example) and institutionalised others (those that are used to test or measure knowledge or skills). Few current teachers of English, however, would say that they felt able to devote much time to an atelier approach to writing, especially in the primary phase. Confronted by the prescription of the National Curriculum and the coercion of the National Literacy Strategy, teachers are anxious that their students would not write in the required range of genre or cover the appropriate range of subject areas or even produce or complete anything at all. Perversely, the prospect of something which 'frames' or limits the possibilities of the desire to write becomes attractive. And teachers of English may not always have the meta-language necessary for the kind of effective teaching of writing Graves envisaged.[2] This metalanguage is partly grammatical (rather than being form or genre-based) but it is also about having words to respond to what another person has just produced and grows out of one's own experience as a writer.

The desire to realise meanings must be limited if issues of entitlement or access and cultural heritage are prioritised. We know we wouldn't enrol in a single history of architecture module if we wanted to build a house yet we are adopting a literacy strategy which places forms and structures and the ability to name these, over the ability to realise meaning. Why this focus on the architectural history of writing? Perhaps for two reasons: this approach is easily measured and monitored by national tests and the Inspectorate and, second, it chimes with the current political rhetoric of entitlement and inclusion. In order to participate in the culture, children must be taught the forms of participation and this is more important than identifying individuals within the culture as authors. Politically, it is problematic to argue for the place of the individual's desire to express meaning over a collective induction into the socially important codes. Culture has become something which is transmitted and given rather than realised.

Freire offered us two competing models of education (1972). In the first, which he calls the banking model, learners are seen as passive receptacles of knowledge, the teacher's role being to deposit the appropriate facts or skills in the learner much as we might deposit cash in a bank account, ready to be drawn out later when needed. The teacher, as the possessor of knowledge, is the only one who can judge relevance and learners are not involved in decisions about their learning. This model was one he found to be particularly prevalent in many of the adult literacy programmes being offered (and failing) in the developing world, often to the extent that even the language used was that of the teachers rather than the students. So, for example, Peruvian Indians were offered literacy programmes in Spanish (which they often could not speak) which taught them to read texts selected by their teachers. Freire's alternative model, which he called *conscientisacao* (usually translated as conscientisation) started instead from the perspective of what the learners might want or need to know. It changed the power base so that learners were consulted about the process and empowered by it. Texts were selected to support this or written by and for those using them. In Freirean terms, a banking model of education is currently prevailing in the UK over the potential conscientising alternative offered by the process writing paradigm, partly because the banking model is the one held by the government of the day and partly because those teachers working for conscientisation and entitlement do not have the necessary response protocols to enable their pupils to make the most of this opportunity.

Mechanics and measurement

Traditional advice on English has placed much emphasis on correctness. This is not only the case for previous generations of pupils but also the stance held by successive waves of 'back to basics' enthusiasts. Surface features such as handwriting, spelling and conventional grammatical structures have been the main foci for praise or blame. Such attention to content as there has been has considered such matters as use of paragraphing and key sentences to make the meaning clear or asked for more use of adjectives as a descriptive device. Response by teachers working in this mindset has focused on proofreading, even when the same teachers have been concerned to develop the child's meaning-making potential. We turn now to show how this emphasis has been maintained through successive moves to improve the quality of the teaching of writing over the last thirty years.

In 1964 an anthology of children's writing was published which was to become a core text for generations of trainee teachers and which celebrated the richness of the products of children in the West Riding of Yorkshire (Clegg 1964). Alongside the children's work were comments from their teachers about their approach and how they evaluated the work. What is striking is that within this commentary there is an unacknowledged tension between the tacit knowledge they are using to inspire their pupils and the explicit strategies they describe for marking work:

> If the child's experience is a rich one, then he is better equipped to write 'freely and willingly' . . . He must at all times be given encouragement and criticism, not only by the teacher and head teacher but also by his fellow pupils . . . Generally in this school work is corrected promptly, the following procedure being current. 'S' in the margin denotes a spelling mistake, 'P' denotes punctuation and 'E' (English) denotes mistakes of usage and expression.
>
> (Clegg 1964: 84–5)

So although there is a tacit understanding of the importance of evaluative response which addresses the message, the explicit features which the child receives as permanent evaluation focus on the surface features. This example may seem very much a relic of the past, yet twenty years later the National Writing Project reports much the same approach:

> I acquired my formal marking style along with my PGCE . . . I became an expert on the field of red pens. No medieval monk lavished more care on his marginalia than I did during my first months.
>
> (NWP 1989: 13)

Again, this teacher goes on to voice views which show a tacit understanding of 'the really important work' of 'building on and delighting in the felicitous phrase, the appropriate tone, the pleasing rhythms' (*ibid.*), but does not make explicit the strategies used to carry out this important work.

Other early moves to develop children's writing, such as Sybil Marshall's work (1963) on creative writing, which did focus on meaning, often ignored, or paid limited attention to surface features and so caused a separation between the messages children received about their writing in 'creative writing' lessons, and the messages they received in other writing situations. Such developments thus proved easy targets for attacks on so-called progressive education by parents and media. Most significantly though, although they did raise teachers' awareness of the importance of what children were trying to say, they still failed to make explicit for teachers ways of responding to texts which would help children move forward, and in practice also failed by paying more attention to form than content or desire as explained below.

Rarely at school level, then, have children received response to the content of their work in such a way as to engage with them in the writing process and enable them to develop their ability to convey their chosen meaning and to reflect on this meaning. Recent whole language trends have attempted to redress the balance. Such researchers as Graves (1983) have championed the idea of writing conferences where children and teachers have written together and discussed the content and meaning of their work. Graves privileges meaning, and in particular the child's own meaning and choice of topic, in his writing workshop approach, yet also through his emphasis on publishing (see below) his approach creates real opportunities for discussion of surface features and form. Yet still teachers find conferencing difficult and re-drafting is all too often an exercise in proof-reading and handwriting. And so we find from Clegg to the Cox report little change – both show an awareness of the problem and an inability to address this:

> It is much easier to recognise a successful piece of writing than to explain what makes it good.
>
> (Clegg 1964: 101)

> The best writing is vigorous, committed, honest and interesting. We have not included these qualities in our statements of attainment because they cannot be mapped onto levels.
>
> (Department of Education and Science 1989: para 17.31)

Why this might be the case is, of course, the significant question. We would argue that it comes from a lack of explicit sophisticated protocols available to teachers to use in their responses to written products and the ready availability of simple protocols such as the red pen and abbreviations for identifying surface feature errors, but the continued lack of procedures for evaluating the strength of a piece of writing in terms of its message and voice and the continued interest in surface features also need investigating.

A protocol is a set of commonly agreed procedures or behaviours which act as a frame for our actions in any situation, as in the sense of diplomatic protocol (see Scholes 1989). In this case, as we have suggested, we mean the particular ways in which teachers respond to students' writing. We have suggested that the traditional response protocols (such as marking spelling mistakes in an agreed way and requiring a set action by the student to address them) are all focused on surface features of language structure. What we are saying here is that there is a need to work out a new set of protocols which get more to the heart of the writing endeavour and which offer students clear support and guidance as to how to improve and develop as writers. We have been evolving our protocols for responding to published writing over the past century, from the early days of the subject English through the era of Leavis to post-structuralism, and teachers are relatively confident in helping students to use these response protocols in their reading. What is lacking in the teaching of writing is a set of protocols which draw on what we know both about the writing process in its entirety and, within that, what we have developed as ways of responding to published writing. For example, it is common to discuss with students the narrative voice of a novel and the effect this may have on readers, and teachers have ways of explaining this concept and helping students to take on this way of thinking about the text. It is less common for the same discussion to take place around a piece of student-produced writing in such a way that the processes involved in creating a narrative effect are made transparent and accessible to the pupil.

As we suggested earlier, teachers' own experiences as learners and writers have often been in situations where teacher response did not offer them a model for responding to meaning and desire. Many teachers are very inexperienced writers in this sense and so they have lacked strategies for introducing conferencing and genuine redrafting. Even the attention paid to this in the work of Graves or through the English National Writing Project only goes a certain way towards offering response protocols, and these have to be taken on by teachers as new behaviour rather than building on patterns they have experienced both as teachers and learners. The researchers and teachers seeking to develop practice have been limited in their ability to turn their own tacit knowledge into explicit guidance which can help teachers develop.

On the one hand, then, teachers often lack response protocols which can help them take on the writing workshop emphasis on children as writers with something to say. At the same time, the whole language movement has had the effect of heightening awareness of the nature of the writing process and of the difference between compositional and secretarial aspects. This in turn has allowed a greater awareness of the developmental nature of spelling and handwriting. This awareness has led many teachers to become fascinated by the development of secretarial aspects revealed by allowing children to write for themselves instead of copying, and this new found confidence in supporting secretarial skills coupled with the lack of strategies for responding to the compositional aspects has led much process writing and redrafting to focus much more on the surface features in conferencing. A recent publication on assessment in the early stages of writing typically explores the fascinating patterns of development in letter formation and spelling knowledge displayed by children working in a whole language environment, but says hardly anything about meaning and offers no guidance at all as to how to use this assessment to offer a useful and constructive response to the children producing these texts (Gorman and Brooks 1996). Although such response has tended to be less judgmental and more encouraging of children's efforts to write, the continued focus on surface features has in many cases led to a continued emphasis on the secretarial aspects as privileged over the compositional. Since all of this development has been taking place in this country against a backdrop of continued concern about standards, it is hardly surprising that teachers have been led to this position.

A clear example of this comes from recent Key Stage 3 national assessments. The 1996 report on National Curriculum Standards in English at Key Stage 3 (SCAA 1997) lists seven 'implications' for teachers based on the marking of the end-of-key-stage tests. Four of these relate explicitly to knowledge of structures and the demonstration of skills in written answers. One comments on the ability of students to use dialogue effectively in narrative and notes regression in the use of this technique from Key Stage 2. The place of dialogue in narrative is regarded as an unproblematic performance indicator and this is reiterated in the 1997 report with regard to Key Stage 3 students who 'use dialogue infrequently in narrative writing' (QCA 1998: 21). It is hardly surprising, then, that children avoid the use of dialogue in examination situations when its 'effectiveness' is measured principally by the test markers in terms of the correct layout and punctuation of direct speech.

Secondary teachers of English acknowledge that the quality of writing at GCSE has diminished since changes in examination regulations require that 60 per cent of the examination must be a terminal sit-down paper, allowing only 40 per cent for coursework (of which just 20 per cent is written coursework). This is shown in Mike Lloyd's survey for the Save English Coursework campaign in which 95 per cent of the respondents were in favour of the restoration of 80 per cent coursework and only 1 per cent approved of the current arrangements (Lloyd 1997: 7). This shows that teachers are committed to quality in student writing. In the US, the pursuit of quality has led to an interest in the 'authentic' assessment of children's work and in terms of writing this means 'portfolios'. However, if the act of producing a written text is to be taken seriously, we will need to consider those aspects of practice which have had an impact on all aspects of children's writing and to disseminate such ideas in a way which makes explicit the tacit knowledge drawn on by those teachers who are enabling their children as writers.

We may wonder how much this emphasis on structure and form at the expense of voice and content matters, since some children do find ways to express themselves powerfully and some continue to grow into the published authors of the next generation, but the evidence is that detailed and thoughtful feedback plays a vital role in the learning process (Black and Wiliam, 1998). What ways are there which can help teachers develop their own confidence and ability in offering such detailed formative feedback, and what evidence do we have that these might work?

Ways forward: some examples from practice

Interestingly, there has been significant progress in helping teachers develop their students' strategies for responding to written text in terms of the teaching of reading and literature. The various groups encouraging response to text, literature circles and group reading and the use of reading journals have all helped teachers to see ways of engaging with texts by published authors which move beyond an examination of the structure to consider how meanings are generated and how the structure works to facilitate or impede the reader's ability to draw a personal meaning from any text. These circles ask members of the group to read a common text, not during their time together, but in preparation for the group meeting. Children in the group then discuss the text in terms of the themes raised, the discourse style and the meanings they take from it, much as avid adult readers share and discuss books with each other (see King and Robinson 1995; MacKenzie 1992). Children who have the experience of working in literature circles are thus given access to a set of protocols for reading which offers a way of moving beyond the simple retelling of a text to a deeper examination of its power for them. This has potential for development into a set of protocols for responding to the children's own texts which uses similar approaches.

The actual development of useful and powerful protocols is dependent on the ways in which the literature circle is set up and run. Too close a control by the teacher may lead to a closing down of the agenda and an emphasis again on form or on simple retelling of the plot, but where teachers have been able to empower groups to take the initiative, children have shown tremendous potential for developing their own ways of exploring a text's potential. In the project reported by King and Robinson, a group of year five children developed to the point where they were able to hold an autonomous and thoughtful conversation lasting over half an hour based around their reading of Anthony Browne's *Gorilla*. This explored not just the events of the story but the themes, the subtext, the polysemic potential of the illustration and the ways the children had empathised with characters and emotions captured in the text.[3] This project was focused on reading, but a similar stance towards a discussion of the children's own texts could lead to the development of a powerful set of protocols for developing writing.

Within the literature circle process, children are usually encouraged not just to discuss but to use written responses to the published text being shared in the form of a journal. They use this to reflect on the reading process and the questions and reactions raised by the text and to prepare for group time. Often these journals are interactive and teachers read and respond to the children's entries. The teacher response is to the content of the child's comment and not to the surface features – often children are told that in their journals they should not worry so much about surface features and there is rarely any redrafting either. What happens when journalling is working well is that a written conversation develops which allows the child to see in writing a way of responding to their product which equates much more closely to the response to the published text (see King and Robinson 1995; MacKenzie 1992). This journalling approach has also been introduced in other subject areas and was one of the ways in which the National Writing Project (1989) worked to help teachers develop ways to respond in a worthwhile way to children's writing.

Publishing children's work also offers potential for changing the nature of teacher and peer response. By publishing, we mean here not making texts commercially available but handmade or computer-generated copies of children's work which are made accessible to other children by simple binding and location within the range of texts available within the class or school library, as recommended by Graves (1983). In our experience as teachers, such published texts are read enthusiastically by children and are treated in a similar way to the commercially available texts alongside which they are located. The discussion in class around these published texts has the potential to draw on the strategies children have been encouraged to develop for discussing commercially published literature, thus bridging the divide identified at the beginning of this chapter.

Publishing itself is changing radically, though, with the increasing availability of electronic texts via the Internet. As more schools come on-line, it seems timely to explore how the potential of Web publishing changes the nature of the writing-response process. One of us has been actively engaged in an electronic writing project which we now consider to explore the possibilities within this new way of working.

Writing and the Internet

As part of the first year undergraduate programme in English in Education at the University of Brighton, students take a module, 'Developing Reading and Writing', which looks at the changes in literacy practices in electronic spaces and the ways these spaces change in response to the literacy processes. They begin by considering writing itself as a technology and then look in some detail at the use of electronic mail and hypertext in a variety of media. The classroom is both real and virtual in that one of the sites of debate is a newsgroup dedicated to the work of the students.

Newsgroups are part of Usenet which is the bulletin board of the Internet. There are tens of thousands of newsgroups of which the university subscribes to about 4,500. Each newsgroup has its own subject and identity and some are more friendly places than others! Participants in the newsgroup access the site through a web browser and publish (or 'post') texts asynchronously. The metaphor of the bulletin board is appropriate in this respect and it is unlike on-line 'chat' in that responses can be more considered and crafted. Our newsgroup was set up by the university's network services officer specifically for this module and, as the assessment task for the students is their contribution to it, the postings are archived for longer than usual (six months rather than several weeks).

Although this is quite a common strategy in US universities, it is still relatively unusual in the UK, particularly in teacher education. The students involved usually don't have any previous experience of newsgroups and many have only used computers before for fairly simple word processing. At the beginning of the module, the tutor takes a relatively didactic approach to the use of the newsgroup, posting a message to which all the students respond, very much like a question with a single 'thread' of replies. Gradually, the students begin to respond to each other's replies and begin to form 'threads' of their own. When this happens, the tutor stands back and the students take control of the newsgroup, posting what and when they like. Occasionally, other readers and writers from other parts of the university will stumble upon this little corner of cyberspace and contribute something themselves. The result is that one text published in this way can lead to multiple 'threads' of meaning and different writers respond in different ways and to different issues. It becomes a writing conference without a teacher, conversations (we think this an appropriate word) that develop according to the desire of the group around a once central, perhaps unwritten or barely legible text.

Students appropriate the forms and conventions of the newsgroup for their own purposes. They learn how to subvert the structures and to irritate the guardians of the system who value architectural precision and correctness. Their meanings are realised in expressive and poetic modes which blur the boundaries of personal and academic, private and public. The atelier model outlined earlier is embodied in this dynamic shifting of expertise between writers and the ways in which feedback and evaluation are almost continuous and continuously sought.

This dynamic process, inherent in this form of on-line writing conference, can be seen in the following thread which grew out of one student's posting on her experience with synchronous computer-mediated communication in chat-rooms and, particularly, in a MUD [multi-user Domain; often used for long-term role-playing games or collaborative story-writing]. We will call her Jenny. She was beginning to see the potential of this technology in her future teaching. The thread was entitled 'Composing Reality':

VICKI D. [in response to Jenny]: I really don't see any potential for these technologies in schools, even where there is plenty of security. This kind of 'role-playing' really does not interest me.

CHRISTY M. [to Vicki]: I'd take an opposing view. This type of activity could really help children who find 'real' social interaction difficult. I know one child who has benefited enormously from learning through role-play. My brother is another example. He has changed his name from Daniel to Anarion Melchelzdeck and is really enjoying playing escapist games!

DAVID R. [in response to Vicki D]: I agree with Vicki. One thing that really threw me during the demonstration was when [our tutor] used particular codes to 'emote' his response. If one is unfamiliar with this kind of technology, how are you supposed to learn what the codes mean and how to respond to them?

JAMES [in response to David]: Every society and subculture has its own language and slang. It's how you keep the outsiders outside :)
Cockney rhyming slang, Polari, IgPay AtinLay . . . all languages of identification and obfuscation. And you learn them by immersing yourself in the culture and seeing the context they're used in and by how

people respond. And then you start using them, and making mistakes and people can identify you as a newbie.

But then, six months later, you're using LOL and IIRC and ROTFLMAO with wild abandon and someone new comes in and asks 'What does that mean?' and you think 'How can they not know that? What are they? Totally new around here?' and then you realise that you've acclimatised, and become part of the culture.

It's not just the Internet. All societies are like that.

The thread continued for some time and was one of the most popular sites for debate. James's comments, in particular, show an acute awareness of his colleagues' knowledge of the social dimensions of language on the Internet. This sharing and shifting of expertise, in a medium that encourages the blurring of traditional boundaries, was a characteristic feature of this group's relationship with the technology. Their writing, in this public space, was both more critical and responsive than when engaged in similar, 'real' conferences which could have been perceived as more private. Over the course of the module, the students themselves came to realise this themselves.

The digital technologies by themselves will not revolutionise the publication of writing or make the mechanism of publishing any more democratic. Old relationships of power and patronage can be reproduced in electronic contexts and new forms and structures are invented to limit the possibilities. There is, however, the potential for different kinds of publishing, something new which is more democratic and more dynamic, something more akin to oral conversation and debate. With the promised investment in Information and Communications Technology infrastructure and the possibilities of the National Grid for Learning, the use of Internet newsgroups and local intranets is gradually developing in schools. More importantly, there is a slow change in orientation to the technology away from the information-retrieval stance to one which can promote and stimulate the realisation of meaning and genuine response.

Conclusion

What we have argued in this chapter is that there has been a tradition (which continues) of emphasis in school approaches to writing on form and structure rather than message and meaning. As a result, teachers have a traditional set of protocols and the accompanying metalanguage to enable them to give children explicit and detailed feedback on these aspects of their writing. Recent developments in our understanding of the nature of the writing process have led to a greater awareness of what these protocols need to be, and they have been refined and developed as a result of the work of whole language research, including the National Writing Project, and of the work of the genre theorists, in particular through the EXEL project in this country.

The development of the National Curriculum and, more recently, of the National Literacy Strategy, has supported these protocols and placed great public value on form and structure in children's writing.

We have also shown how teachers have for many years also been aware of the need to give children space to write about what matters to them and have been excited by the times when children have produced writing which has a real sense of authorial voice and a powerful set of meanings, but that there has been no explicit metalanguage available to most teachers to give children explicit feedback on their work to help them develop this sense of voice and ability to convey their personal meanings more powerfully. In part, this comes from the traditional privileging of reading (reception) over writing (transmission) within English which has made most teachers more confident readers than writers and which has rarely created opportunities for the exploration of a reading-writing continuum. Since most teachers have not been and are not writers they have little personal experience to draw on and this exacerbates the lack of explicit protocols.

We have argued that the process-writing paradigm, which offers the potential for the development of more explicit protocols, has itself had to compete with other paradigms which are more in line with the establishment emphasis on form and structure, and so has largely failed to realise its potential, particularly in England. Paradoxically, its fascination with the developmental nature of spelling and structure has led to this paradigm too helping to develop and extend response protocols which focus extensively on structure.

However, we have also argued that there are ways forward which are already in evidence and which are compatible with current national policy and strategy. We have shown how reading workshops and literature circles have the potential to help children and teachers develop response protocols and mutually supportive strategies which can be translated into the writing situation. We have shown how publishing children's own work has an influence in bridging the reading–writing divide and allowing links to be made between response to commercially-published and classroom-produced texts. We have argued that the new electronic forms of publishing, including newsgroups, have a particular potential to shift the power relationships between teacher and student. Where such developments are included in the initial teacher training experience, they have a particular role in helping future generations of teachers to have a more appropriate metalanguage and an explicit set of protocols for responding to all aspects of their pupils' writing. The responsibility then rests to a large extent to those of us involved in initial and continuing professional development for teachers to continue to re-assess our own practice so that more appropriate ways of facilitating and responding to the production element of English will become regular practice.

Notes

1 The experience of teachers as writers and their teaching of writing is explored in a research project reported in King (1997).
2 'Metalanguage' is a term used for the specialist and general vocabulary used to discuss language – literally, a language about language. So it includes such relatively familiar terms as *word*, *noun*, *paragraph* and *grammar*, as well as more specialist terms such as *metonymy*, *genre*, *discourse* and so on. For a fuller exploration of the metalanguage that teachers use to respond to form and meaning in children's writing see D'Arcy (1989).
3 This discussion, referred to in King and Robinson 1995, can be seen in the video *Creating Communities of Readers* (University of Brighton 1995).

References

Barrs, M. (1991–2) 'Genre theory: what's it all about?' in *Language Matters – Thinking About Writing*, 1991–2, no. 1, pp. 9–16.

Black, P. and Wiliam, D. (1998) *Inside the Black Box: Raising Standards Through Classroom Assessment*, London: King's College London School of Education.

Britton, J., Burgess, T. and Martin, N. (1975) *The Development of Writing Abilities (11–18)*, London: Macmillan.

Clegg, A. (1964) *The Excitement of Writing*, London: Chatto and Windus.

Cope, B. and Kalantzis, M. (ed.) (1993) *The Powers of Literacy: A Genre Approach to the Teaching of Writing*, London: Falmer Press.

Department of Education and Science (1989) *English for Ages 5 to 16* ('The Cox report'), London: HMSO.

Department for Education and Employment (1998) *The National Literacy Strategy: Framework for Teaching*, London: HMSO.

D'Arcy, P. (1989) *Making Sense, Shaping Meaning*, Portsmouth, NH: Boynton/Cook.

Elbow, P. and Belanoff, P. (1995) *Community of Writers*, Portsmouth, NH: Heinemann Educational.

Freire, P. (1972) *Pedagogy of the Oppressed*, Harmondsworth: Penguin.

Gorman, T. and Brooks, G. (1996) *Assessing Young Children's Writing: A Step By Step Guide*, London: NFER/The Basic Skills Agency.

Graves, Donald (1983) *Writing: Teachers and Children at Work*, Portsmouth, NH: Heinemann Educational Books.

King, Carole (1997) 'Writing teachers as teachers of writing', unpublished MPhil thesis at the University of Brighton.

King, C. and Robinson, M. (1995) 'Creating communities of readers' in *English in Education*, Summer 1995, pp. 46–54.

Lewis, M. and Wray, D. (1995) *Developing Children's Non-fiction Writing*, Leamington Spa: Scholastic.

Lloyd, Mike (1997–8) 'Dark before dawn on coursework?' in *NATE News: Autumn 1997*, see also corrections *NATE News: Spring 1998*.

MacKenzie, T. (ed.) (1992) *Readers' Workshops: Bridging Literature and Literacy, Stories From Teachers and Their Classrooms*, Toronto, Canada: Irwin.

Marshall, S. (1963) *An Experiment In Education*, London: Cambridge University Press.

The National Writing Project (1989) *Responding to and Assessing Writing*, Walton-on-Thames: Nelson.

Pennycook, A. (1994) *The Cultural Politics of English as an International Language*, London: Longman.

QCA (1998) *Standards at Key Stage 3: English. Report on the 1997 National Curriculum Assessments for 14 year olds*, London: QCA 1998.

Rosen, H. (1993) 'How many genres in narrative? in *Changing English*, vol. 1, no. 1, pp. 179–91.

SCAA (1997) *Standards at Key Stage 3: English. Report on the 1996 National Curriculum Assessments for 14-year-olds*, London: SCAA 1996.

Scholes, R. (1989) *Protocols of Reading* , New Haven: Yale University Press.

University of Brighton Media Services (1993) *Creating Communities of Readers* (video package), Brighton: University of Brighton.

Woods, Claire, Dias, Patrick and Ellis, Viv (1996) 'English and the World', in *English in Australia*, no. 116, July 1996, pp. 3–14.

5   Music as a media art

Evaluation and assessment in the contemporary classroom

Lucy Green

Nowadays, almost any kind of music is a media art. Even a busker on a street corner is bound to be playing music that people can hear on a radio, CD player, television or some other type of media equipment. Very often music is functionally tied to a media form such as a film, television programme, music-video or advert. There is still a tendency to think that classical music is autonomous and removed from the concerns of everyday life, and by contrast, that popular music is socially determined and tied to the machinations of the mass market. But nearly all music is technologically mediated, and nearly all music both contributes to and survives by virtue of a commercial market. Different styles, sub-styles and genres of music exist only in contra-distinction to each other: without classical music, there would be no popular music, and so on. What is more, almost everyone living in this country, as well as many other countries, is immersed in this musical diversity whether they like it or not, and for pupils in school music classrooms the diversity is particularly poignant. Unlike the normal, everyday relationships that most people have with music, pupils are explicitly required to engage, consciously and practically with whatever music or musical activities are specified by the teacher. Today, most schools include musical diversity within their curricula, some focus on one style to the exclusion of others: but whichever way it is, pupils cross the threshold between the diverse musical world at large and a different musical world of the school, every time they enter the music class-room (for discussions of the pop–classical split in schools, see Vulliamy 1976; 1977a; 1977b, Vulliamy and Lee 1976, Green 1988; 1997). Therefore, whether pupils in schools are listening to, analysing, performing or compos-ing a wide diversity or a narrow range of music, when considering the role of evaluation in music as a media art, we need to take into account the entire musical terrain.

   In this chapter I will organise my discussion around three axes or themes, each of which contains two distinct approaches. These axes are helpful, but of course they are by no means the exclusive means to consider the evalua-tion of music. After discussing each one, I will relate them to the music classroom.

Three evaluative axes

Notes or contexts

In the study of music we can detect two approaches which may be characterised, for the sake of clarity, as 'ideal types': one of these approaches focuses on the organisation and execution of musical 'notes', and the other, on the 'social contexts' of musical production, distribution and reception. In the terms of the former ideal type, there is immanent musicological analysis of parameters such as tonality, modality, melody, harmony, metre, rhythm, texture, form, and so on. This sort of analysis tends to focus on the relationships of notes to other notes within the piece under consideration and within the norms of the appropriate genre and style. Not only do musicologists consider how those norms are articulated, but also in what ways they relate to the norms of previous or contemporaneous genres and styles, and whether they are expanded to open up new musical horizons. This type of work, which is technical, is unfortunately too often disparaged as 'formalist' by some theorists working in other fields. However there is nothing inherently formalist about such work unless explicit claims are made about the untrammelled autonomy or universality of the music in question.

In the other ideal type, there is analysis of the social significance of a piece or pieces of music within the particular contexts of their production, distribution and reception. This analysis might be sociological, anthropological or it might take a cultural studies, or some other approach, often altogether avoiding any mention of notes or related musical technicalities. It, in turn, has initiated criticisms, including the complaint that it leaves out of consideration the very object (i.e., music) which should be at the centre of its project. Again, such criticisms are not pertinent in cases where no claims are being made to discuss the 'music itself' but concentration is instead explicitly focused on the mediation of the music, the organisation of musical practices and the construction of musical values.

In terms of these ideal types, a Beethoven piano sonata for example can be judged, on the one hand, by musicological criteria concerning form, harmony, melody, counterpoint, voice-leading, metre, rhythm, grouping, modulation, development, fragmentation and so on with reference to classical sonata form; or on the other hand it can be judged in terms of the social functions of chamber music at the end of the eighteenth century, Beethoven's position as a composer struggling to escape the fetters of aristocratic patronage, the changing role of the piano solo recital between the salon and the concert platform during the nineteenth and twentieth centuries, and so on. A James Brown single, equally, can be judged in terms of musicological criteria concerning texture, metre, rhythm, riff, chord progression, sound-recording, form; or in terms of the social functions of funk as a subcategory of late twentieth-century popular music, funk audience expectations and practices, funk musicians' intentions, the relationship of various funk groups to the music industry, and so on. At best, both these approaches – that focusing on 'notes' and that focusing on 'contexts' – are merged. For examples of such merging see Brackett (1995), Ford (1991), McClary (1987), (1991), Middleton (1990) and Walser (1993), amongst others.

Both approaches inevitably confront some problems in making claims to be the route to evaluating music. For example, within the classical style, the 'greatness' of various pieces has been analysed by critics and musicologists over the years, aiding their sedimentation into a musical canon which has been more taken for granted than explicitly questioned. But today the canon no longer remains closed to dispute both within traditional musicology, and by virtue of challenges arising from, for example, feminist musicology, popular music studies, ethnomusicology, the sociology of music and other areas. Likewise, with reference to folk, jazz, popular music and many other styles, there have been varying approaches to scholarship which remain fraught with disagreement as to which pieces, if any, are superior.

Limited or universal criteria

The second evaluative axis I wish to consider relates to the development of criteria. On the one hand, when evaluating music it is possible to employ various different sets of criteria, each set of which is limited, and specifically pertinent to the piece of music under consideration. Today a number of theorists are still wedded to an out-and-out cultural and aesthetic relativism which suggests that any piece of music should be judged only within its own terms, and cannot legitimately be said to be better or worse than any other piece. This position not only suffers from its relativism *per se*, but also from a tendency to keep a very dark secret of exactly *what* the music's 'own terms' consist of. More realistically, it is possible to judge individual pieces of music in relation to criteria that are specifically pertinent to the music's genre within a broader musical style – by comparison with other pieces that go together to make up that genre within that style.

On the other hand, we can apply a single, unified or universalising set of criteria by virtue of which we attempt to evaluate all and any kind of music. In practice, this approach often involves an implicit and unexamined assumption of the superiority of certain styles, or one particular style, of music; but it can alternatively reflect a conscious distillation of certain fundamental musical parameters that are empirically distinguishable across a diversity of cultures. Either way, the implication of such an approach is that universal criteria exist which are pertinent to all music.

Individual pieces or whole styles

The approaches outlined above seek to evaluate individual pieces, or individual musical events. But musical evaluation might equally well be addressed, not to individual pieces but to whole musical styles by comparison with each other. Surely, it is admissible to enquire, for example, not only how good a Beethoven and a James Brown piece are as individual pieces of music, but whether the *style itself* employed by Beethoven and that employed by Brown are equally valuable?

Problems and differences of opinion concerning the value of musical styles can arise when the 'notes' approach is used to attack the 'context' approach, or vice versa, and when the question of whether the evaluative criteria are drawn from either a limited or a universal paradigm, is not addressed. For example, Frith's recent book *Performing Rites* (1996), which takes a contextual approach to evaluating popular music, was criticised from a 'notes' point of view, by Roger Scruton in a newspaper review. Scruton writes:

> It is surely not difficult to establish the superiority of Cole Porter over R.E.M.; one only has to look at the incompetent voice-leading in *Losing My Religion*, the misunderstanding of chord relations, and the inability to develop a melodic line in which the phrases lead into one another with a genuine musical need.
>
> But, once you look at modern popular music in that way, you will come to see how gross, tasteless and sentimental it mostly is, and how far it is from our tradition of meditative polyphony. You will begin to see why it is that musicology still concentrates on the classical repertoire and continues to ignore the daily diet of modern youth.
>
> (Scruton 1996)

The problem is two-fold, or in other words, it arises both within and between Frith's and Scruton's respective positions. Although the subtitle of Frith's book is 'On the value of popular music', his concentration on contexts, including various ways in which different groups of listeners and musicians construct musical value, is to the exclusion of any comment from either himself or his subjects, on the notes or how they fit together at all. By contrast, Scruton's concentration on the notes, derives from approaches that are pertinent to classical musical stylistic norms (not even necessarily to Cole Porter's style!), and brings to bear criteria that are wholly impertinent to the style of the popular music in question.

The point of dissension between these two writers provides an example of the sort of problems that are encountered when trying to evaluate music without making explicit reference to the terms and 'language' of evaluation, such as those suggested by the three axes around which I have organised my discussion. That is, it would be helpful to clarify whether the evaluation is taking place in terms of the 'notes' *or* the 'contexts' of the music; whether it is taking place with limited reference to other stylistically similar pieces *or* with broad reference to universalising criteria; and whether it is the individual piece *or* the style which is being evaluated. In some cases it will be pertinent to examine both sides – for example, both notes and contexts in themselves and in relation to each other. Again, being explicit about such an approach is helpful.

Musical evaluation and music education

Musical evaluation, whether of 'notes' or 'contexts', whether with reference to limited or universal criteria, or whether of individual pieces or of styles, is of course by no means only a scholarly activity, but an informal part of people's everyday assumptions and unconscious judgements about music. Furthermore, it is something which is implicitly engrained into the very interstices of the school music curriculum. Teachers cannot avoid making judgements about musical value; but more than that, they are in positions which make it imperative, not only that they *evaluate* pre-existing music, but also that they *assess* the level of skill and knowledge which pupils exhibit in their engagement with different music and musical practices. Here I want to split the discussion in two, and address evaluation on one hand, and assessment on the other even though in school, as well as university and other music classrooms, the two are inextricably linked. I will focus my discussion on the school, although I hope it will have relevance to other areas of music education as well.

The evaluation of pre-existing music

The development of the National Curriculum was marked by high controversy over what music was considered valuable enough to be included, and what music was considered, not merely inferior, but harmful or pernicious enough to be excluded: see Gammon (1993), Shepherd and Vulliamy (1994), Swanwick (1992). As it now stands, the document indicates the inclusion of a variety of music. Below is the wording of the Key Stage 3 (generally for pupils aged 11–14) programme of study on repertoire. This adds to, rather than alters, that of the earlier Key Stages:

> The repertoire chosen for performing and listening should extend pupils' musical experience and knowledge, and develop their appreciation of the richness of our diverse cultural heritage. It should include music in a variety of styles:
>
> (a) from the European 'classical' tradition, from its earliest roots to the present day;
> (b) from folk and popular music;
> (c) from the countries and regions of the British Isles;
> (d) from cultures across the world;
> (e) by well-known composers and performers, past and present.
>
> (DFE 1995: 6)

This is not the place to examine the cultural assumptions of the document in its entirety, but it is worth discussing a few oddities in relation to the above passage. Given that classical, folk and popular music are all mentioned, it seems rather strange that jazz is not (particularly as jazz has for some years enjoyed a far more established position in Higher Education than have folk and popular music). It is also strange that the European 'classical' tradition is to be studied 'from its earliest roots to the present day', whereas folk and popular music are to be studied without any reference to their historical periodicity. The implication is that these musical styles have no history. The pin-pointing of 'countries and regions of the British Isles' under (c) also seems peculiar, since presumably those countries and regions would be already represented under (d), 'cultures across the world'. There seems to be an intention to prioritise the British Isles, without a willingness to admit doing so. What, in any case, the difference is between 'countries and regions' (with reference to the British Isles) and 'cultures' (across the world), one cannot help wondering.

Teachers appeared to be much more firmly committed to musical pluralism than were the Schools Council Assessment Authority and the government during the development of the National Curriculum. Although little recent national research is available on this, it is reasonable to suggest that the majority of schools now do include a wide variety of music in their curricula, probably wider than that implied in the terms of the programme of study cited above.[1] In choosing the music to be used, teachers can focus, among other things, on notes or contexts, they can apply limited or universal evaluative criteria, and they can consider individual pieces or whole styles. No systematic rationale for doing any of these has ever been produced, and yet many of these modes of evaluation go on all the time informally and unconsciously. For teachers, as for everyone else, musical evaluation will be greatly influenced by their own formal and informal musical and professional training, their acceptance or rejection of the 'received opinion' of various social groups, their taste, age, gender, ethnicity, class and so on.

For this reason it is important to be explicit about which kind of evaluative criteria are being brought into play when making decisions about what music to include in the curriculum. This would avoid unsupported statements such as the following, by Nicholas Tate, (chief curriculum adviser to the government), who made a speech quoted in *The Times* (8 February, 1996) containing the following sentiments:

> Schools must introduce their pupils to high culture and help them to escape the growing creed that sees no difference between Schubert and Blur. . . . A fundamental purpose of the school curriculum is to transmit an appreciation of and commitment to the best of the culture we have inherited. We need a more active sense of education as preserving and transmitting, but in a way that is forward looking, the best of what we have inherited from the past . . . we should aim to develop in young

people a sense that some works of art, music, literature or architecture are more valuable than others.

(Charter 1996)

I would very much like to hear Nicholas Tate explain exactly what his grounds were for implying that Schubert is better than Blur; and in making this request I am not suggesting that I think Schubert is, or that I think he isn't. What I am arguing should be made public, amongst other things, is whether Tate is referring to 'notes', to 'contexts' or to some other parameters characterising the music in question; whether the unstated criteria for his evaluation are different for Schubert than for Blur, or whether he has used a unified set of criteria that he considers equally pertinent to both Schubert and to Blur; and whether he thinks Schubert is better because he was a better composer within the classical style of the early nineteenth century than are Blur within the Brit-pop style of the late twentieth century; or whether he thinks it is the classical style itself which is better. In this chapter there is clearly no space to go any further into these questions with specific reference to particular pieces of music; but what I am suggesting is that such questions are helpful, and that all of us, including curriculum advisers, can benefit from thinking carefully about precisely why they make evaluative judgements and what governs particular choices concerning music in the curriculum.

The assessment of pupils' musical ability

These problems shift when, instead of *evaluating* the professionally or adult-produced music that we use for listening, history, analysis, performance, or as models for composition, teachers start to *assess* pupils' work. Here, the same issues articulated in the three axes suggested above – that of distinguishing between 'notes' and 'contexts', that of using different, limited sets of criteria or one, universal set of criteria, and that of evaluating pieces with reference to given stylistic norms or evaluating styles themselves – are transplanted onto pupils' performances and compositions. But they bring with them the added complexity; that we have to assess pupils according to what it is reasonable to expect of them as individuals and cohorts in connection with their age and previous musical experience.

An increasing amount of work has been done on children's musical development during the last few decades, some of which has suggested that children develop musically in stages not unlike Piagetian developmental stages. One of the most influential pieces of research (Swanwick and Tillman 1986) suggests that musical developmental stages are not so much age-related as logically sequenced. Thus any learner in music, it is argued, is likely to pass through the earlier stages before proceeding to the later ones. The research was conducted through analysing 745 compositions by 45 children, mainly aged 3 to 11. The compositions suggested that at the earliest stage, referred to by Swanwick and Tillman as 'materials', children are interested in the quality of musical sound, which they explore at a sensory, then a manipulative level. The next stage, 'expression' arises when some development of musical gesture, phrase, or some quality of mood or drama becomes apparent, at first rather spontaneously and sporadically, then in more organised forms bearing similarities to music that the children will have heard or performed. The next stage, 'form', occurs when experimentation, expressive characterisation, then idiomatic, stylistic references are made showing technical, expressive and structural control. The fourth level, 'value' (which might be reached by a 15- or 16-year-old, or not at all) involves musical communication, originality, the development of ideas, personal commitment and the systematic expansion of musical discourse.

This formulation has subsequently led to the development of assessment criteria not only for composing, but also for performing and listening, linked to each stage: see Hentschke (1993), Stavrides (1995) and Swanwick (1988: 1994). Indeed, using these criteria has enabled music teachers to reach a high level of consensus in assessing how far along the developmental sequence a pupil has gone. These assessment criteria purport to be relatively 'style-free', or in other words, they represent that single set of unified criteria mentioned as the second axis within this chapter, which are considered to be equally suitable for any music. Thus, although the criteria can help to measure how far along the developmental sequence a pupil has gone, what the criteria cannot tell us, is how far along the yardstick of musical value the piece of music being composed, performed or listened to has gone. Nor can they help us to judge whether different *styles* of music require less skill and knowledge, or are less valuable, than others.

I will now explore these conundrums with reference to music assessment through some concrete examples. In doing so, it is necessary to distinguish between the assessment of performance, and that of composition. In the assessment of performance, we are not supposed to be evaluating the music, but assessing the pupils' level of musical skill and/or knowledge, quite regardless of the value of the music being performed. In composition, we are both evaluating the music, *and* assessing the pupils' level of musical skill and/or knowledge as displayed in the compositional evidence. The ramifications of this difference are extensive and in the context of this book quite unlike some of the debates around evaluation in other subjects, where a distinction between performance and composition is either irrelevant or carries a different meaning. First of all, I will examine some of these issues with regards to performance.

Evaluating performance

Let us say we are assessing two performances. One pupil plays Beethoven's first piano sonata, and another pupil plays the trombone part in an arrangement of James Brown's 'Say it loud: I'm black and I'm proud'. We are to assess each pupil with reference to criteria provided by the examining body or by our own scheme of work, or whatever. The assessment is to be under-taken either within the limited terms of the accepted performance practices of each particular piece's genre and style, or within the terms of universal, style-independent criteria. In either case, one problem for the teacher is this: supposing the performance of each of these pieces is considered to be pretty good, say each performance is awarded a mark of 8 out of 10. But suppose the genre and/or style of each piece does not *afford* an equivalent exhibition, or does not *require* a commensurate level of skill? Is it then fair to give each pupil the same mark?

Traditionally, since the end of the nineteenth century the assessment of (generally defined) classical performance ability has been conducted through a system of graded exams that has existed in tandem with, but independently of, schooling.[2] The graded system means that, regardless of age, a candidate sits an exam in which the level of technical and interpretative difficulty of the pieces, has been pre-decided and is considered by the exam board to be approximately the same for all the pieces, and at a commensurate level of difficulty, appropriate to the grade being sat. The performance is then assessed against criteria governing agreed aspects of classical performance practice that musicians and teachers have developed over the years. These criteria vary to some extent depending on the instrument played and on the particular genre and style of the music. They involve a fine line between aspects of technique and aspects of interpretation. They refer, for example, to the candidate's tone quality, line, touch, accuracy, breath control, sensitiv-ity, phrasing, dynamics, control of tempi, or whichever of these is pertinent in the circumstances, and so on. This system has been very successful in promoting the instrumental and vocal education of hundreds of thousands of children in many countries of the world. It has sustained some criticism, for example, that it is inflexible, that it encourages teachers and pupils to work too narrowly towards the exam repertoire, and so on, but it remains a very strong presence in performance-related music education. Many of the music GCSE and A-level syllabi accept a specified grade of this exam system in place of or as an alternative to their 'own' exams, and many Higher Education courses specify particular requisite grades for applicants.

Problems with this system of assessment have arisen recently with the increasing desire of children and young people, as well as opportunities for them, to play or sing popular music and other non-classical styles. Tradition-ally one of the definitive marks of popular music, as well as jazz and other styles, has been that they are not taught in schools, or by professionally qualified private teachers. Given the intrinsically vernacular character of popular music, and the depth-embeddedness of existing informal mechanisms for passing it on, this situation will always prevail to some extent. But the recent entrance of popular music in some guise or other into the curricula of so many schools has brought a large portion of popular music firmly within the sphere of formal music education; jazz has been making in-roads into formal education at the conservatoire level for a few years and is also begin-ning to be incorporated in some schools; and the same goes for other musical styles from around the world, especially music associated with the ethnicities of various groups forming the catchment area of a school. This has in turn, led to a demand for the inclusion of particularly popular music and jazz within the existing graded system of performance exams described above. However, problems arise because the criteria that have evolved over many years for assessing classical musical performance are not necessarily pertin-ent to other kinds of music. The appropriate tone and touch for a folk guitarist would certainly fail a candidate on a classical guitar; the vocal tech-niques of soul or blues singers would be completely unacceptable in *bel canto*, and the required manner of interpreting notation, where applicable, in jazz would be almost sacrilegious in classical music. These problems have not been resolved, but music educationalists are working to develop new exam-ination repertoires and new criteria that are pertinent for different styles. For example, two current initiatives in developing graded systems, one in rock and the other in jazz, have recently received accreditation.[3]

In contrast to assessment within the school system, graded exams work regardless of the age of the candidates. You take the exam whenever you or your teacher thinks you are ready. Of course, this feature of music education has traditionally gone hand-in-hand with the fact that candidates for graded exams have tended to be either taught privately, or taught in small groups or individually by peripatetic teachers within schools. It is a system that emphasises individual ability and not the norms associated with a cohort. The graded system is not suitable for assessing pupils grouped together by virtue of a classroom context or year-group such as in the National Curriculum or the GCSE. Here, as opposed to everyone being at the same level regardless of their age, the opposite occurs: everyone is the same age regardless of their level.

One response to this dilemma has been the helpful procedure of using what are often referred to as 'difficulty multipliers'. Formally, within com-pulsory education, this procedure has only been used in the GCSE exam, but there is nothing to stop teachers using it autonomously alongside the National Curriculum assessment guidelines. The process involves making an evaluation of the level of performance-difficulty of a piece of music. This evaluation will of course be based on the sorts of criteria that are used, as described above, to select pieces at certain levels for the grades. Supposing we have three candidates all taking a GCSE performance test on the piano. One candidate plays 'Twinkle Twinkle Little Star' in an arrangement that is con-sidered easy, involving just one note in each hand, all the notes being either one beat or two beats long, the piece being played fairly slowly. The pupil plays the piece quite well, according to criteria similar to those used in the graded exams, and is awarded 8 out of 10. Because the piece is easy, we multiply 8 by an 'easy' difficulty multiplier of 1, making a total mark of 8. The next candidate plays a Scarlatti sonata which, by the same criteria, is considered to be of moderate difficulty. The pupil plays quite well and also scores 8 out of 10, but we apply a 'moderate' difficulty multiplier of 2, to get a mark of 16. The third candidate plays a Brahms sonata, again gets a mark of 8, and has it increased by a 'difficult' difficulty multiplier of 3 to gain an overall 24. Because the difficulty multipliers in this example range from 1 to 3, and because the performance is marked out of 10 before being multiplied, this means that the final mark is out of 30. Thus the 'Twinkle Twinkle' candidate gets 8 out of 30, the Scarlatti candidate gets 16 out of 30 and the Beethoven candidate gets 24 out of 30. In practice, difficulty multipliers are often used in fractions, to give a more sensitive final yield. Some exam boards use a different method of calculation to that described here, but with the same overall effect.

This system works well for assessing the performance of particular pieces of music, so long as there is sensitivity to certain factors, of which I would like to mention three. The first is that the ability of an individual to handle complex music can only reliably be assessed after accumulating evidence from a number of assessment points. The second is that the difficulty multiplier can only ever act as a gauge for the purposes of controlling validity and reliability: we are never assessing how well a pupil can play or sing 'difficult' music, but rather, how well a pupil can play or sing music *with musicality*, according to our pre-established criteria. Ultimately, 'musicality' will always elude precise linguistic definition, and can only ever be 'translated', using approximate equivalencies, such as 'sensitivity', 'expressivity', 'individuality' and such terms. Third, the criteria which are used to judge how easy or difficult pieces are, and to judge how 'musically' they are being performed, must be systematic and pertinent to the style of the piece in question.

However, problems arise as soon as new styles are introduced which seem to require new, and different criteria. Because of the history of music and of music education, there are very few people alive who are in a position to make really cogent judgements about exactly how difficult it is, for example, to sing in the accepted style for a nineteenth-century German Lied, compared to how difficult it is to sing in the accepted style for twentieth-century soul. Because Lieder singing has for a long time been taught within formal educational establishments, excellence in this pursuit has gained a reputation (deservedly so of course) for being very difficult to achieve. The almost complete absence of any formal educational mechanisms for singing soul, conversely, gives the appearance that excellence in this feat requires no education, and must be very easy to achieve. Scruton again exemplifies this dilemma: 'The assumption has been that we teach classical music because it requires disciplined study. Expertise in pop, on the other hand, can be acquired by osmosis' (1996). Typically, he has no grounds for this latter claim. Very little systematic musicologically-based research has been done on exactly how popular musicians go about learning their skills, although Bennett (1980) Cohen (1991) and Finnegan (1989) provide excellent anthropologically-based accounts of popular musicians learning and teaching. The best insight into the learning process is probably to try learning the skills oneself – and I would like to hear Scruton do this!

These arguments about how much 'discipline' and skill are required for the performance of different styles of music arise, then, not *necessarily* from any inherent qualities of the performance demands of the music or any contingencies of the musical styles in question; but from their social contexts such as, in this case, whether they are included in formal educational mechanisms or not. Although very little systematic examination of performance difficulty or performance quality in popular music has as yet formally fed into any school-based educational syllabi, current-day scholarly attention to a wider range of music than hitherto is beginning to suggest ways in which new definitions of value in performance might begin to impact on this area, and this changing agenda will undoubtedly inform assessment criteria within the music education of the future: see for example Brackett (1995), Middleton (1990), Moore (1993), Walser (1993).

My final argument about assessing performance is that the type of assessment of musical skill involved in the exams described above, tends to be focused on the 'notes' side of things. A small amount of credit is sometimes allocated to 'presentation', (a fairly ill-defined area implying dress, comportment and such like) but other than that there is no real consideration of the music's context: and this means, among other things, that the role of the audience within the musical style is left out of consideration. For some styles of music, such as classical chamber music, this is not a particular problem; but for others, such as some types of funk, it is problematic. The relationship of musicians to a noisy and responsive audience is part and parcel of their performance technique, and this would come across poorly, as larger than life in a room containing just one examiner or a small panel, as in the rather rarefied traditional performance exam conditions of the school, the graded system or the conservatoire. Only at undergraduate level in some universities, and beyond at post-graduate level, has a more realistic concert situation sometimes been possible, although even then, everyone knows that the examiners are sitting in the audience, making the event more like a competitive music festival than a real concert. Nevertheless, this kind of scenario does take place more frequently than one might imagine at school level in classroom performances, or at Higher Education level in the form of 'master classes'. An extension of such practices, involving the pupil or student-audience in peer-assessment and structured listening, might well be a positive strategy although it does require more complex classroom organisation.

Evaluating composition

Moving from performance to composition, I want to clarify that I use this word in the way it is generally used within school-level educational circles: to include individual and group composition as well as improvisation, notated in any form, or un-notated. Unlike musical performance, composition has been closely guarded by the academy, and until the 1960s was hardly ever practised at all until undergraduate level, and not really practised seriously until postgraduate level. The absence of composition from British schools changed gradually from the late 1960s, and composition is now a major part of the National Curriculum for Music and the Music GCSE exam.[4] In clear contrast with the history of performance exams, there has never been any system of graded exams in composition, nor do the exam boards or the National Curriculum Assessment Guidelines employ a difficulty multiplier.

The question I want to pose here is: if it is possible to assess the performance of a piece according to criteria which are sensitive to the level of difficulty considered to be involved in the performance, then why not assess the composition of a piece according to the level of difficulty considered to be involved in its composition? This question brings me back again to the three axes around which I've organised this chapter: first, that of whether we focus on 'notes' or 'contexts'; second, whether we develop a range of limited evaluative criteria or one unified set of criteria; and third, whether we attempt to evaluate individual pieces or to evaluate styles.

In attempting to establish a graded system or a difficulty multiplier for composition, one of the most intractable problems for classically educated music teachers, is that traditionally it has seemed as if there is a connection *between* difficulty and 'good' composition. Complexity and intellectual rigour are often valued within the musical canon and seen as justification for quality in and of themselves. This is not the case with performance. As we have seen, in the process of assessment, it is possible for a musician to give a performance capable of being considered 'good' (or even superlative), even if the piece of music being performed is considered very 'easy' (or for that matter, very 'bad'). A graded system or a difficulty multiplier responds at least in part to any unfairness or unreliability in the test, and a performance-candidate will of course always be advised to choose pieces that balance his or her ability with the grade or difficulty multiplier to maximum effect. But the distinction between what is 'good' or 'bad' and what is 'easy' or 'difficult' in composition is more elusive, at least as far as assessment mechanisms are concerned.

Defining 'difficulty' in the assessment of composition cannot just take into account 'technical complexity'. It would be possible for someone to compose a piece that was technically extremely complex, for example highly polyphonic, or totally serialised music, but which from an aesthetic point of view would be deemed lifeless and unattractive. The key issue here is that the kind of difficulty that is pertinent, the difficulty that contributes to musical value in composition, is not technical prowess, but the interaction of technique with those many factors which are impossible to describe accurately in words: factors, depending on the style and era of the music, such as expression in relation to the social and historical origins of the music, originality, or the relationship of the particular piece of music with the general style to which it alludes. Whereas in the assessment of performance, linguistically elusive factors such as 'expressivity' can be separated from the technical difficulty of the piece being performed, in the assessment of composition, they cannot so readily.[5] Here we come again to the conundrum of trying to find a language to describe what is (in music's case as well as other art forms) beyond language.

Another, related problem in the establishment of criteria for assessing composition is that any criteria must be sensitive to what musical possibilities are afforded by the *style* of the piece in question. The piece would then have to be considered in terms of how well or how poorly it represented that style. But so often in the history of music – whether classical, popular, or any other – what has been considered most valuable, is precisely that certain composers do *not* simply represent the style: they go beyond it.

The GCSE exam boards' criteria for the assessment of composition can be difficult to use. This is partly because while the boards mostly allow compositions to be submitted in any style whatsoever, they do not recognise anything akin to a difficulty multiplier with reference to composition, and they do not provide assessment criteria for composition that are tailored to suit particular styles of music. Instead, they provide that unified set of criteria alluded to in the second of my three axes: universal criteria, which go across styles, and are supposedly pertinent to any style. But what if one style is much more difficult, or requires much more originality, or affords more compositional virtuosity, than another style? I would like to examine this question with reference to four contrasting examples.

Pupil A composes a piece in sonata-form in the style of Mozart; pupil B composes a jazz piece in the style of early Ellington; pupil C composes a rap involving voice, pre-set drum rhythm and a bass line; and pupil D composes a John Cage-style aleatoric piece by throwing dice. All four pieces are to be assessed in terms of a set of unified criteria concerning generalised musical qualities such as balance, form, variety and so on. These criteria give no guidance about differences between musical styles, but in practice, teachers are bound to relate the given 'universal' criteria to the demands of the style of the piece of music in question: see Green (1990). Thus, let us say, all four of these pupils receive a mark of 8 out of 10. But the two pupils who composed the sonata and the jazz pastiche have demonstrated far greater understanding of far more musical *technical* parameters than the ones who composed the rap and the aleatoric piece. Is it valid, then, that they should all end up with equal marks? Clearly not, the reason being that the styles in which they are composing do not allow for equivalent possibilities in terms of technical manipulation. This problem is compounded at school level by the fact that no distinction is made in the National Curriculum or the GCSE syllabus between pastiche and original composition. Whereas the Mozart and Ellington pastiches require a high level of technical proficiency, as pastiche, the exercise does not so much warrant *expressive originality* as faithfulness to a model. By contrast, the rap requires little technical skill, but allows, at least potentially, for a high level of expressivity: it need not be pastiche and could well be original. The aleatoric composition, pastiche again, affords very little of either technical proficiency or expressivity.

The only thing to do then, in the present-day situation where in schools and universities we are often assessing pupils' and students' compositions in a large variety of musical styles, is to establish different criteria for evaluating different styles of music against each other, including a type of 'difficulty multiplier' to distinguish between different styles. Any attempt to do such a thing would be highly contentious and would undoubtedly lead to some heated debate between defenders on one hand, and critics on the other, of the styles involved. But, because educational assessment has to have a degree of not only validity and reliability, but also plain fairness, we *must* surely proceed along lines somewhat akin to awarding different value, in terms of the availability of marks, to different musical styles and compositional exercises.

The kinds of criteria that I would suggest in the present context, derive from the three axes around which this chapter is organised, and would be structured as follows:

Notes or contexts

Evaluation would be linked to both 'notes' and 'contexts'. Notes would be assessed in terms of pitches, rhythms, and the other similar kinds of parameters listed earlier on in this chapter; contexts would be assessed in terms of the music's meaning and value within its usual terms of production and reception. The views of pupils and students would be relevant here.

Limited or universal criteria

Evaluation would employ different, limited sets of criteria for individual pieces of music, according to the music's style. But at the same time, whatever specific evaluative criteria are used, all criteria must share certain overarching consistencies. Thus the relationship between whether we have a variety of limited criteria or one set of universal criteria is not a relationship of two equal and mutually exclusive alternatives; but a relationship of hierarchy. Limited, style-specific criteria and difficulty multipliers would make reference to particular stylistic norms and possibilities in terms of all manner of details. Overarching, universalising criteria would make reference to factors such as, for example, the tension between form and expression, unity and diversity, tradition and innovation, function and use. Even then, not all of these 'overarching' criteria would always be pertinent, as for example, in the case of evaluating the tension between unity and diversity in a piece of process music. To double check such contingencies, we could again include pupils' and students' own voices to some extent, not only in the assessment procedure, but in the evaluation of music as well.

Individual pieces or whole styles

We must recognise that when we *evaluate* an individual piece of music we are always also making an implicit evaluation of its style. Then when we *assess* pupils or students, we must be willing to acknowledge that some styles of music do afford different levels of technical skill, expressivity, originality or other factors, at different historical periods and in the terms of different exercises within and between performance and composition, than others.

Many musical qualities will always escape any system of either evaluation or assessment: as the history of music demonstrates, technical proficiency has often been unrecognised, expression has been taken for tastelessness or ousted as unwanted political comment, and originality has been judged as incompetence or insanity. This is not something to bemoan – rather the opposite, we can celebrate music's capacity to afford an experience that escapes language, that defies reason, that opens new realms, that communicates in ways we can barely understand. There will always be a level at which we simply cannot be sure that we are cogently evaluating music, or adequately assessing musical skills and knowledge. But at the very least, awareness of the nature and extent of some of the difficulties involved can help us to bring the stylistic musical diversity which so enriches our contemporary lives, into some sort of representative and fair educational context.

Acknowledgements

I would like to thank Charlie Ford and Keith Swanwick for responding to a draft of this essay, Simon Frith and Dai Griffiths for sending me copies of the Scruton review, Melinda Carr for giving me a copy of the article about Tate's speech, and Steve Ridley and Norton York for providing me with information about Rock School.

Notes

1 See, for example, the descriptions of professional reaction to the development of the National Curriculum in Gammon (1993), Shepherd and Vulliamy (1994), Swanwick (1992); or peruse the academic journal, *British Journal of Music Education*, or professional journals such as *Music Teacher, Music in the Curriculum* and *Primary Music Now*, for evidence of the extent of the commitment. At the time of writing I am in the early stages of some research which is indicating that popular music and world music now hold first position alongside classical music in the curriculum.

2 These are mainly run by the Associated Board of the Royal Schools of Music (ABRSM), Trinity College of Music and the London College of Music. They take place throughout the UK, the Commonwealth, and in several other countries. The standard is from beginner (Grade I) to advanced (Grade VIII), and then diploma level.

3 Rock School currently run a graded system similar to that described above, offering grades III–VIII on electric guitar, bass guitar and kit, covering a variety of

popular music styles including Latin, funk, rock, country and others. The ABRSM have developed a new syllabus for examining jazz, which was published in the spring of 1998.
4 For early teaching methods, ideas and materials with reference to classroom com-position see Dennis (1970), Paynter and Aston (1970), Schafer (1967), Self (1967). For further discussion see HMI (1985), Paynter (1982), Swanwick (1979). A large selection of teaching materials related to composing in the classroom is now available.
5 Green (1997) provides ethnographic evidence to suggest that teachers do in fact devalue pupils' compositions when they consider them to be 'merely' technically proficient; and that they place most value on those compositions which they deem to be 'imaginative', 'creative', or 'exploratory', even when technical proficiency is considered to be lacking. It will come as no surprise to many people, that in the research, it was overwhelmingly girls who were seen to produce the former type of composition, and boys the latter.

References

Brackett, D. (1995) *Interpreting Popular Music*, Cambridge: Cambridge University Press.

Bennett, H. Stith (1980) *On Becoming a Rock Musician*, Amherst: University of Massachusetts Press.

Charter, D. (1996) 'Schools must not blur culture boundary, says syllabus chief (Teachers told to put Schubert before pop to save heritage)', *The Times*, 8 February.

Cohen, S. (1991) *Rock Culture in Liverpool*, Oxford: Oxford University Press.

Dennis, B. (1970) *Experimental Music in Schools*, Oxford: Oxford University Press.

Department For Education (DFE) (1995) *Music in the National Curriculum (England)*, London: HMSO.

Finnegan, R. (1989) *The Hidden Musicians: Music-making in an English Town*, Cambridge: Cambridge University Press.

Ford, C. (1991) *Cosi? Sexual Politics in Mozart's Operas*, Manchester and New York: Manchester University Press.

Frith, S. (1996) *Performing Rites: On the Value of Popular Music*, Oxford: Oxford University Press.

Gammon, V. (1993) 'The new right and the making of the music National Curric-ulum', unpublished conference paper, The Place of Music Conference, University College London, September.

Green, L. (1988) *Music On Deaf Ears: Musical Meaning, Ideology and Education*, Manchester and New York: Manchester University Press.

Green, L. (1990) 'The assessment of composition: style and experience', *British Journal of Music Education*, vol. 7, no. 3, pp. 191–6.

Green, L. (1997) *Music, Gender, Education*, Cambridge: Cambridge University Press.

Hentschke, L. (1993) 'Musical development: testing a model in the audience-listening setting', Unpublished PhD thesis, University of London Institute of Education.

Her Majesty's Inspectorate (HMI) (1985) *Music 5–15*, London: HMSO.

McClary, S. (1987) 'The blasphemy of talking politics during Bach Year' in Leppert, R. and McClary, S. (eds) *Music and Society*, Cambridge: Cambridge University Press.

McClary, S. (1991) *Feminine Endings: Music, Gender and Sexuality*, Minnesota, Oxford: University of Minnesota Press.

Middleton, R. (1990) *Studying Popular Music*, Milton Keynes: Open University Press.

Moore, A. (1993) *Rock: The Primary Text*, Buckingham: Open University Press.

Paynter, J. (1982) *Music in the Secondary School Curriculum*, Cambridge: Cambridge University Press.

Paynter, J. and Aston, P. (1970) *Sound and Silence: Classroom Projects in Creative Music*, Cambridge: Cambridge University Press.

Schafer, M. (1967) *Ear Cleaning: Notes for an Experimental Music Course*, New York: Associated Music Publishers Incorporated.

Scruton, R. (1996) 'Review of Simon Frith, *Performing Rites: On the Value of Popular Music*', *The Times*, October.

Self, G. (1967) *New Sounds in Class*, London: Universal Edition.

Shepherd, J. and Vulliamy, G. (1994) 'The struggle for culture: a sociological case study of the development of a national music curriculum', *British Journal of the Sociology of Education*, vol. 15, no. 1, pp. 27–40.

Stavrides, M. (1995) 'The interaction of audience-listening and composing: a study in Cyprus schools', London University Institute of Education, unpublished Ph.D. thesis.

Swanwick, K. (1979) *A Basis for Music Education*, London: NFER Publishing Company.

Swanwick, K. (1988) *Music, Mind and Education*, London: Routledge.

Swanwick, K. (1992) *Music Education and the National Curriculum*, The London File: Papers from the Institute of Education, London: The Tufnell Press.

Swanwick, K. (1994) *Musical Knowledge: Intuition, Analysis and Music Education*, London: Routledge.

Swanwick, K. and Tillman, J. (1986) 'The sequence of musical development', *British Journal of Music Education*, vol. 3, no. 3, pp. 305–39.

Vulliamy, G. (1976) 'Definitions of serious debate' in Vulliamy, G. and Lee, E. (eds) *Pop Music in School*, Cambridge: Cambridge University Press.

Vulliamy, G. (1977a) 'Music and the mass culture debate' in Shepherd, J., Virden, P., Wishart, T. and Vulliamy, G. (1977), *Whose Music: A Sociology of Musical Language*, London: Latimer New Dimensions.

Vulliamy, G. (1977b) 'Music as a case study in the "new sociology of education"' in Shepherd, J., Virden, P., Wishart, T. and Vulliamy, G. (1977), *Whose Music: A Sociology of Musical Language*, London: Latimer New Dimensions.

Vulliamy, G. and Lee, E. (eds) (1976) *Pop Music in School*, Cambridge: Cambridge University Press.

Walser, R. (1993) *'Running with the Devil': Power, Gender and Madness in Heavy Metal Music*, Hanover, New Hampshire: Weslyan University Press.

6 Measuring the shadow or knowing the bird

Evaluation and assessment of drama in education

John Somers

A teacher needs to know whether, and to what extent, his [*sic*] students are understanding and learning, and to achieve such knowledge is assessment. To fail to assess is to fail to teach. What form that assessment should take is, of course, another matter.

(Best 1992: 75)

Introduction

This chapter focuses on the school subject of Drama as it exists within the English education system, although I hope that it will have resonances in the work of other countries. It considers approaches to evaluating the dramatic artefact, that which might be supposed to result at the end of a creative process within the drama lesson. At one level that would appear to be an easy matter. We can all make judgements about the levels and effectiveness of skills employed within a piece of drama, and especially given that Drama in the UK has been externally examined since the 1960s, one would imagine we must surely have got it sorted out by now. But we have not and in spite of recent arguments such as Ross and Kamba (1997: 35) that there is increased student confidence and clarity about drama, and despite the fact that the past twenty-five years have clearly been significant for the development of the subject, I would suggest that we are still floundering in the areas of evaluation and assessment.

I feel the problem primarily stems from our inability to define what kind of learning is taking place in the drama lesson; and only when we are clear about that issue can we begin to consider how to go about evaluating it. Of course precisely *how* we evaluate learning in drama is, in itself, no simple process and can give rise to a number of methodological debates. The issue is more complex than simply making external judgements about the quality of dramatic product – that is those dramas or performances at whatever level of sophistication or theatrical panache made by students – because making judgements about learning is qualitatively different from making judgements about aesthetics and the arts in general; although there are points of overlap. For example, before students' dramatic output may be judged to be of interest to anyone outside the process of making, there is a need to assess its levels of interest and suitability for the participants. That is, the material chosen has to be capable of making good drama, but also must be meaningful and of interest for the participants. In this context I see the drama (that is both performance skills and its structure or dramaturgy) as *form*, and those matters that are dramatised within the medium through the use of the form as the *material*. These two facets of the drama constitute its content and are central to my discussion of what makes up 'drama learning'.

In other words our attitudes to evaluation and assessment will be greatly affected by our views of what Drama in Education is. So, before we can address the issue of evaluating the quality of students' work (and, most importantly, the worth of the process from which that product emerges), we need to look more closely at the issue of what drama is for. Historically, drama education has been bitterly divided on this point. On the one hand, there is the notion that drama is a means to personal development, and this is frequently confused with vague ideas about conceptual understanding:

> Although it is quite proper that Drama should be child centred, a growing body of theorists and teachers . . . consider that the focus should be on the child's *Learning* rather than his [sic] maturation.
>
> (original emphasis, Cook 1992: 42)

But what kind of learning are these authors suggesting? Is it true to say that the subject finally shed its need to justify drama chiefly in terms of 'personal development'? And, if this is the case what is left? Does the value of the subject come down to a matter of judging the students' competence in mastering the skills of the medium? Or, as Hornbrook provocatively asks, is there another function to assessment and evaluation, that is to do with the student's *relationship* with the dramatised material and the process that leads to the publication of product?

> If drama is a learning medium in which students are expected to learn through the drama, shouldn't the proper focus of the assessment be what they learn rather than the drama itself?
>
> (Hornbrook 1991: 125)

The duality of drama's intent and the matter of assessment and evaluation

I would argue that drama developed a set of dual intentions, either to develop good people or good drama, as a consequence of post World War Two developments in education, chiefly in the UK. In the first major work to describe and attempt definitions of Drama in Education, *Child Drama*, Peter Slade describes the educative aims of what he called 'Child Drama':

Cleanliness, tidiness, gracefulness, politeness, cheerfulness, confidence, ability to mix, thoughtfulness for others, discrimination, moral discernment, honesty and loyalty, ability to lead companions, reliability, and a readiness to remain steadfast under difficulties, appear to be the result of correct and prolonged Drama training.

(Slade 1954: 125)

This notion, that drama could affect the development of the 'whole person' sprang from a romantic, Rousseau-esque view of educational philosophy in which the child was conceptualised as a gentle seedling that needed careful nurturing in an educational environment in order to protect it from the ravages of everyday life. It is not surprising that this was a dominant approach between the wars in Britain. Conditions for many young people were extremely poor – both materially and spiritually – and the purpose of post-Victorian education was mainly still utilitarian. There was a tremendous waste of young people's talent and the life-opportunities on offer were still chiefly determined by social class. The 'Hadow' Report of 1931 recognised schools' shortcomings:

Is their curriculum humane and realistic, unencumbered by the dead wood of formal tradition, quickened by enquiry and experiment, and inspired not by an attachment to conventional orthodoxies, but by a vivid appreciation of the needs and possibilities of the children themselves? Are the . . . lines on which their education is planned, of a kind best calculated to encourage individual work and persistent practical activity among pupils, initiative and originality among teachers, and to foster in both the spirit which leaves the beaten path and strikes fearlessly into new fields, which is the soul of education?

(Report of the Consultative Committee on the Primary School 1931)

The need to change the rigid orthodoxies of pre-1940s education gave rise to a flowering of educational experiments in Britain, experiments that firmly placed the child at the centre of the educational experience leading to the establishment of 'child-centred' education, subsequently vilified by the post-1979 Thatcher governments.

These notions of the arts as a means to develop personal qualities gave rise to 'new' arts genres that were seen as exclusively educational – Child Art, Child Music and Child Drama, (see, for example, Viola 1942). Their developmental aims, informed by an awareness of the uniqueness of the individual, ensured that the teaching approaches employed in such classes were a far cry from those still to be seen in many schools at the time – such as serried rows of children chanting choral lines or copying images from the blackboard. This child-centred approach infused the development of post Second World War drama in schools which was often defined as much by what it was not – theatre – as what it was. Indeed, this divide between the study or practice of theatre and the practice of developmental drama has been maintained well into the 1990s and, as this chapter suggests, is still forming an important backdrop to so many discussions about drama.

In the 1970s, Learning Through Drama preserved the duality. It maintained that the drama teacher's role was twofold:

> To encourage the child to deepen and challenge his [sic] perceptions of himself and his world so that he gradually begins to make sense of the complexities and subtleties of his experience; acknowledges, accommodates and reassesses his world view in the light of new experience.
>
> To do this through enabling the child to use and express himself through the symbolic process of the arts.
>
> (McGregor *et al.* 1977: 23)

Of course, this emphasis on personal development (and an implicit rejection of the academic study of theatre) was naturally opposed to any practice of taking measures and making judgements – if only because the object of drama had become the individual students. However, this attitude almost left the subject untenable within the school system and it began to change. In its 1974 enquiry into examinations in Drama, The Schools Council detected a changing attitude, stating that 'the belief that dramatic activity is too sensitive and personal to be examined is still held by many, but it is being challenged' (Schools Council 1974: 5). The Council was well aware of the dominant orthodoxy of the time and how it came into conflict with the examination system:

> To examine or assess drama would imply the imposition of a structure which is not necessarily obvious or desirable. An examination syllabus moves towards an end product, whereas drama is not concerned with such a result . . . Drama lacks an accepted or easily identifiable body of knowledge which is the mainstay of examination syllabuses in most subjects . . . Much of the value of any creative or artistic activity lies in the satisfaction of the individual's need – to play and to create – which may be unrelated to any objective or external standards of attainment.
>
> (Schools Council 1974: 12–13)

Indeed this document recognised, as this chapter also acknowledges, that the root of the problem was that no consensus existed about the subject: 'The peculiar difficulties of examining drama arise just as much from divergent and imprecise definition of the areas of drama to be examined' (Schools Council 1974: 11).

After years of debate about the educative purposes of drama (see, for example, Clegg 1973), David Hornbrook, controversially at first, articulated a coherent case for students to be judged solely on their ability to use the dramatic medium. He scorned drama teachers' attempts to teach social or moral issues:

> Some drama teachers came to believe that a principal aim of drama was to expose forms of social and historical oppression, such as racism and sexism, while generally there was a preoccupation with the exploration of topical issues of all kinds.
>
> (Hornbrook 1991: 7)

Having rejected drama as a means of personal development, Hornbrook focused on the more academic traditions associated with the study of the theatre as a way of defining the basic elements which constitute dramatic art. It is proficiency in these which define how we measure progression in drama (see Hornbrook 1989: 132). Indeed, Hornbrook identified the root of the drama teacher's problems as being the desire to see drama as nothing else other than an expressive art form:

> Another major weakness, of the expressive, developmental and peda-gogic models which dominated practice for so long was that they had no conceptual means of addressing fundamental questions of quality and assessment.
>
> (Hornbrook 1991: 70)

But in spite of the profound influence Hornbrook's critique has exerted over the field and the apparent security that flows from many years of operating various assessment and grading system, we are still troubled by the dilemma of whether we try to assess the quality of dramatic *experience* in terms of its effect on students or just by judging the *product* they make – or both. And whatever we assess, how do we do it?

Notions of evaluation and assessment

Assessment in education is popularly used in the sense of 'fixing the amount of'. As such, it usually employs normative criteria to make sum-mative judgements and comparisons between students – although used sensitively it can also have a formative effect. For a variety of reasons it is usually conducted by the teacher, although students can have a hand in it. It is expected to be as objective as possible, although as I demonstrate later, such objectivity is hard to achieve. Evaluation is usually used in the sense of 'determining the value of' and is often used in the context of attempts to discern the value to the individual concerned. It involves the unpacking of an experience to better understand it and to make decisions about where to go next and how to best get there. Although it is usually based on the reflective processes of the individual, insights gained will usually be harnessed for the good of the group. Because of its perceived subjectivity and the possible absence of verifiable criteria, it is often frowned upon as a method of calibrating experience and output although it may be of great use to individuals who engage in it. It is best served by qualitative methods that do not have as their aim the comparison of the individual with others.

For the reasons outlined above, formal assessment in drama was firmly resisted until the 1960s. When it did arrive, the argument centred on the notion that, if drama's main purpose was to develop people, how were assessment criteria to be devised? A system of examining 'Speech and Drama' work – the rather rigid exercises of the voice and body associated with the theatre schools and private education – had existed for some time but was of little help. The first examination to affect drama assessment in the UK was the Certificate in Secondary Education (CSE) which was introduced in 1965. This examination was designed to embrace the large percentage of British children who were considered not able enough to be entered for the 'Ordinary Level' General Certificate of Education (which attracted entries from only the top 12 per cent of the school population). There were widespread misgivings about the notion of drama being examined but drama teachers, reluctantly in my own and many other cases, came to accept that the subject should fall within the CSE system.

Our decision sprang from a degree of political pragmatism as to whether or not we could continue to argue for the inclusion within the overcrowded curriculum of a subject that refused to submit its content to examination. There was also a feeling that students who chose to do drama post-14 should receive external recognition for their efforts. The Schools Council recognised the political strategy involved:

> Whatever the difficulties of constructing either valid or reliable examination procedures, if the effect of having an examination is to ensure that more drama is done during the five years before the examination, and that teachers and pupil feel more secure about their engagement in the subject, these gains may be felt to be sufficient justification.
>
> (Schools Council 1974: 11)

The Mode 1 Southern Region Examinations Board CSE examination that I taught in 1977 included in its criteria for assessment such notions as 'absorption and concentration', 'involvement and relationships', 'flexibility' and 'grace'. There were seventeen criteria in all and each should have received a numerical assessment at the end of each of the five terms of the course. The difficulty of interpreting and applying these criteria meant that in practice the teacher placed individuals in rank order, decided who should get a grade one, who a grade two and so on, and then filled in the individual marks to produce the right total to support that grade (see Hornbrook 1989, ch. 2). Subsequently, the CSE/GCE examinations were replaced by the General

Certificate of Secondary Education and teachers have now become accustomed to carrying out assessments through their familiarity with these examination systems.

During the 1980s, UK teachers generally came to accept the necessity of the examination system although there were those who fought rearguard actions. In 1986, for example, Malcolm Ross wrote:

> So no assessment . . . at the heart of any form of evaluation in this sacred domain . . . will be self-evaluation. We must learn to know, and hence to judge, ourselves. . . . There can be no conventional examining in this reserved part of the curriculum: no grading; no norm or criterion referencing; no national criteria. This is a world in which 'the good' is pursued for its own sake; here, the child's work gives rise to pleasure and appreciation rather than a set of marks; it is the child who will deliver the final verdict on his or her achievement.
>
> (Ross 1986: 92–3)

Ross continued to advance passionate argument to support this point of view, maintaining that:

> For many children, assessment means enduring a form of mental and emotional derangement, the morbid exchange of a warm, living experience for a cold, dead reckoning. Accountability has to be rescued from the accountants – mere reckoning must make way for the lively exchange of human insight and intuition.
>
> (Ross *et al.* 1993: 168)

Here, more general educational debates about the Arts and assessment in education were pertinent to the debate within the subject drama between child-centred progressivism and advocates of the study of theatre. In the early 1990s it seemed that a consensus would soon exist bringing an end to the child development/form divide. The tide of antagonism seemed to be turning. But even in research published in 1997, Ross still detected the old ambivalence: 'Teachers of the arts . . . espouse an "arts for all" policy and make the "personal development" of the individual student their top curriculum priority' (Ross and Kamba 1997: 66).

However, even if such values underpin arts education in many schools there are a number of practical reasons why the formative systems of evaluation, associated with such values, are not more widespread. One is the lack of time in the modern school to conduct in-depth evaluations of the work of individuals. A UK drama teacher might teach around 450 students in a week, making sophisticated, in-depth monitoring impossible. This very factor led to most evaluation being based on some form of summative assessment giving prominence to normative criteria and introducing notions of comparison and competition (see Ross *et al.* 1993).

In addition, there was also concern about the effect of making judgements on the students themselves – especially when awarding low marks. Many drama teachers, among others, had traditionally operated in the belief that there was a need to encourage all. Ross, again best sums up this approach:

> teachers instinctively wish to reward their pupils with public praise and acknowledgement, indeed many arts teachers see this kind of personal endorsement as perhaps the only contribution they can make to their pupils' development. Praise is indeed the principal duty of the teacher as first-perceiver of the pupil's work.
>
> (Ross *et al*. 1993)

The ranking and division of students' efforts was also alien to the culture that had developed – not least because many drama teachers believed that, in the absence of clear criteria that proved otherwise, they were making judgements about the personal worth of individual students. Indeed, the problem with the philosophical critique of formal assessment, advanced by Ross, amongst others, is that in practice, it ignores the equally unpalatable fact that evaluation had become yet another means for teachers to make moral judgements about the individual worth of their students, as people. Although such attitudes had been criticised by the Schools Council in 1974 they had become deeply embedded in the professional practices that characterised generations of drama teachers.[1]

One important solution to this problem of teachers making judgements about students was to involve the students themselves within the evaluation process. Indeed, this method was considered all the more desirable in that it explicitly valued the capacity of students to become self-critical which, it has been argued, is a central part of arts education (see Ross *et al*. 1993). 'Appraising' is another term sometimes used in this context to describe the role of the student as a reflective practitioner. In the 1993 Consultation Report issued by the Northern Ireland Curriculum Council, for example, appraising is said to involve the student in:

> applying the skills of reflection, analysis and evaluation to the process of making in order to enhance understanding and to consider how meaning may be expressed through using dramatic skills. Appraising involves evaluating the work within a context of known forms and conventions so that its effectiveness can be judged, and moving forward the drama based on this evaluation. Appraising should occur continuously during and after the drama, both in and out of role. At some stage in every lesson, therefore, pupils should have opportunities to:
>
> • assess what they are doing and why they are doing it;
> • deepen their understanding of characters and situation;
> • make judgements about their own and others' progress and work;

- reflect on, analyse and evaluate the stage of development of the drama so that they can continue to learn from the process.

Pupils should also have regular opportunities to make choices about the kind of appraisal they wish to apply.

(Northern Ireland Curriculum Council 1993: 19)

I shall return later in this chapter to this model of evaluation – although I am not suggesting that, in itself it is a system that circumvents some of the problems I have just outlined. Nevertheless, the attention to the role of the student within the evaluation process is an important corrective to the model of hierarchical assessment promulgated by recent governments.

Some modes of evaluation and assessment

By contrast, and in common with curriculum developments in all subjects, the dominant strategies for evaluation and assessment in drama are, of course, teacher-centred. I give the following examples only as indications of current practice and thinking and they do not form an exhaustive list.

GCSE syllabi

The most systematic procedures for assessing drama in the UK have been developed in relation to formal examinations. Entries to GCSE Drama examinations have shown the fastest growth of any subject taught in UK schools (National Drama 1997). The Southern Examining Group (SEG) GCSE Drama and Theatre Arts (3390), 1999 syllabus has three main aims. Although the priorities quoted from McGregor *et al.* (1977) on p. 110 are reversed, numbers two and three here, continue to reflect the 'personal development' intent of the work:

To encourage candidates to develop, through the process of drama and theatre arts:

1   an interest in, and understanding of, a range of drama and theatre experiences;
2   an increased group and self awareness;
3   imaginative, creative, cognitive, communication and social skills.

However, in a concession to the 'anti-assessment' philosophies discussed in the preceding section, the document recognises the difficulty of assessing aspects of these aims in practice, stating that 'some of the above aims are reflected in the assessment objectives; others are not, as they cannot readily be translated into objectives that can be assessed' (SEG 1997: 5).

The assessment objectives assess candidates' ability to:

1   demonstrate knowledge and understanding of practical skills and tech-
    niques in drama and theatre arts;
2   respond to material for dramatic presentation, demonstrating that they
    can: organise the response in the appropriate form for communication;
    work with sensitivity to the needs of group relationships and inter-
    action; analyse and evaluate the effectiveness of their own ideas and
    those of others.

All of the judgements relating to assessment are made by the teacher. An
external moderator, usually a teacher of drama, visits and certain of the
course performances and improvisation sessions are presented. These are
marked by both teacher and moderator who negotiate a mark. In 1995, the
Schools Assessment and Examinations Council (SEAC) decreed that no
examination should be conducted by coursework alone and all examining
groups introduced written examinations. The Midland Examination Group
(MEG) allowed examination by coursework and a choice of two forms of
written examination: one based on a set text with questions relating to performing, design, direction and stage management; and the other based on
stimulus material and its potential for drama making. This Board also offered
an alternative (which satisfied SEAC's decrees) by introducing a requirement
that students work in groups for sixteen hours devising a dramatic piece
(termed a 'realisation test' by the Group), arising from one of three stimuli
provided by the Board in a sealed examination package. A moderator visits
the students at some point in the sixteen hour period and tracks students
identified by the teacher as being the most and least able, and of average
ability. The moderator also asks for those and other students to execute
certain tasks and exercises in order that he/she may verify the intended
assessment levels. Ninety per cent of the assessment is based on practical
work and 10 per cent on a written folder of drama 'evidence' relating to
the practical work undertaken during the hours of the realisation text. The
'marking criteria' are:

- To select and employ Drama genres/styles/conventions and shape the
  drama.
- To reflect upon their work at all stages.
- To negotiate in and out of role.
- To make appropriate use of available sources (for example people,
  materials, facilities).
- To communicate deliberate meaning(s)/atmosphere(s) by using chosen
  structures.

(MEG 1997: 13)

In this syllabus, claims for the developmental role of drama are greatly
diminished in favour of an attention to dramatic skills and the understanding of dramaturgical concepts. However, the rather tortuous examination

procedure, designed to get round oppressive regulations, does at least give students an opportunity to demonstrate proficiency in drama through the process of making.

Teacher assessment

Assessment of this GCSE course and most other systems of assessment and evaluation of student's drama work currently in place put great emphasis on the ability of teachers with a variety of levels of experience to make judgements about the quality of students' drama work. However, research studies suggest that such faith may be misplaced. For example, drama has been part of the Dutch National Curriculum of basic education (11–15 years) since 1994. Working at The Dutch National Institute for Educational Measurement (CITO), Jose Noijons has developed tests of Drama to be administered at the end of basic education (Noijons 1997). Students are assessed on their ability to 'play', 'give shape to a role and scene' and 'reflect on drama'. Noijons looked at how closely those who are asked to 'rate' the (videotaped) drama performance agree on where it fits within accepted, normative criteria. He sought ways in which observers, or 'raters' as Noijons terms them, can reach greater agreement in their judgements. To eliminate the variable of dissimilar dramas, students are given a common assignment with clear instructions setting out the parameters of the drama exercise. The resulting performance is rated, as is a worksheet in which participants are asked to identify a number of dramaturgical features such as the beginning, middle and end of the piece; the characteristics of the scene in terms of its action and how it is represented; the central motif; the situation of the scene; and the time at which it takes place. Students are also asked to identify the characteristics of their role – the mood and type of person.

The observers rate the participants on a three-point scale. The outcomes showed that 'raters' generally get the students into the right rank order and that their overall scores show good levels of agreement. Echoing my own aberrant practice at assessing individual aspects of my CSE students in the 1970s, however, there is much less correlation between the scores against individual criteria. They also found difficulty in distinguishing the work of an individual from the work of the group – a good student may be pulled down by lack-lustre companions, whilst a poor student may be pulled along by others, for example. There are problems, therefore, even using such simple and restricted assessment criteria.

The unreliability of teacher judgement is echoed in other studies. Virginia McGowan enquired how consistently dance teachers assessed the same solo dance pieces using common criteria. She found great disparity in the outcomes both in terms of the percentage marks given by the individual examiners to each solo, but also in the weighting that examiners would attach to the six criteria used (McGowan 1982). Susan Philpott's research showed that merely providing assessors with criteria to use in the assessment, does not alone produce more accurate assessment in terms of a significant agreement about the ranking within a group (Philpott 1986: 173). Nor can this be attributed to lack of experience in the field for she found that even teachers with extensive experience of dance teaching and assessment did not share a consensus view of the relative merits of a group of dancers.

Reflective conversation

If teachers' judgements are unreliable, to whom do we turn for more accurate evaluation and assessment? As I have already suggested, many maintain that students' own evaluation of their work should be paramount in any system of formative evaluation and, possibly, summative assessment. Malcolm Ross conducted a research programme that investigated reflective conversation as a means of evaluating artistic experience. The work was founded on the belief, articulated in an earlier book by Ross, that students should be directly involved in an appraisal of their work and the process that gives rise to it. Ross argued that only the student can know what he or she has experienced and that it is unreasonable and unreliable to depend on the teacher as interpreter and mediator of child art.

> Assessment in the arts ceases therefore to begin and end with the teacher's perceptions, judgements and statements and turns right around to restore the work to its maker, the pupil. And so a new role emerges for the teacher: to equip the students with the reflective skills to monitor and assess their own work.
>
> (Ross *et al*. 1993: 159)

From this perspective Ross proposed four aspects of student understanding in the arts:

Conventionalisation – an awareness and ability to use the conventions of the art form.

Appropriation – embracing, for personal use, the available expressive forms.

Transformation – in which the student searches for knowledge and meaning through the expression of 'feeling impulses'.

Publication – the placing of the result in the public domain.

However, it is not entirely left to the student to ascertain their own understanding of these processes. The teacher conducts an interview aimed to encourage reflection. This, of course, only serves to highlight how much the *principles* of evaluation are determined by pragmatic reasons, given that the systems of evaluation and assessment that are currently practised in schools owe a lot to the need for speed and ease of operation and bureaucratic tidiness. Perhaps rather idealistically Ross recommends that the reflective interview should be conducted after the completion of each work of art and, that the work itself should be the focus for discussion.

> Pupils must first know what they have done before they are in any position to judge how they have done. This principle underlies the assessment conversation; the pupil and teacher as assessors must first recover and discover the imaginative object (image) as a real presence before attempting to assess competence, skills and understanding.
>
> (Ross *et al*. 1993: 165–6)

How this can be achieved in drama is problematic as drama is an ephemeral happening and video-taped records usually do not capture the work satisfactorily. Nevertheless, Ross is adamant that reflective conversations have great potential for uncovering important information about the creative process. His argument is worth quoting at length as it sums up the need to pay attention to students' contribution to the evaluation process:

> pupils are capable of rich and sophisticated responses to and understandings of their own work and seem well able to develop these responses and understandings in collaboration with their conversation partner. This phase of creative and expressive production in the arts is, we believe, considerably underrepresented in schools' practice and yields a field of opportunity for aesthetic knowing as well as appraisal of enormous potential; but, we must hasten to add, only when conducted in the reflective mode, which means that many teachers will have to discard present practices based almost entirely upon the principle of technical rationality. It could be argued that arts teachers need to behave more like real artists and less like bureaucrats.
>
> (Ross *et al*. 1993: 161–2).

This approach has many resonances with several other chapters in this volume, notably on Art, Media and forms of gallery education.

The reflective journal

In an attempt to preserve something of this notion of the student as reflective practitioner, there is much use of the students' journals and production notes as a means of capturing important aspects of the creative process. Research conducted by Sally Mackey and Kathleen Dacre attempts to show the value of this approach. They argue that the journal should contain 'personal accounts of observations, feelings, reactions, interpretations, reflections, hunches, hypotheses and explanations' and maintain that 'practice and reflection on practice can constitute a body of knowledge in itself' (Dacre and Mackey 1999).

There is a distinguished history in the arts of using such journals but their purpose is often confused. In the initial phase of writing this method lacks the interactive component of Ross's model of reflective conversations, although the journal can form the focus for productive discussion. It is not clear what 'added value' accrues from such student discussions as opposed to solely writing the journal. However, students who are more comfortable writers will, of course, express themselves more fluently in the journals and this can disadvantage those students who may be able in drama but unconfident writers.

Profiling

Profiling attempts to make use of a range of judgements concerning a student's ability, presenting them in a manner that allows them to be 'read' in ways which help the student to be more aware of their comparative strengths and weaknesses. In an example of this, Frank McKone (1997) outlines a simple matrix to produce an assessment profile. His imperative was to construct a scale that would produce a numerical grade. He justifies this procedure, in use for four years, through the need for students to 'count their drama course in the university entrance package'. He expects teachers and students to take part in the profiling process so that the results are open to scrutiny. His matrix tabulates five 'types of drama knowledge' with three levels of 'quality of participation' by students. When the points on the matrix have been plotted, a 'line of best fit' is drawn between the points marked to produce a grade that represents the student's 'overall quality of participation' in that teaching unit.

McKone has subsequently re-examined the criteria he used in arriving at the assessment of student involvement as a result of research by Christine Warner (1997) which reveals that students may be deeply involved with the process of making drama whilst appearing not to be contributing. Warner shows that members of a group may engage with the making process in different ways and that the 'listeners' and 'outsiders' constitute necessary parts of the drama group dynamic. She argues for teachers to provide a variety of ways in which students can contribute, ways that augment and support the more obvious physical and verbal contributions of some group members and which are, none the less, vitally important to the group's efforts and the development of the individuals so involved.

Once again, teachers' appraisals are seen to be unreliable. Like Ross, Warner believes that students' judgements should be central to any evaluation of what is happening in the drama as they are 'very aware of their own elaborate engagement patterns'. They are also very conscious of how they personally learn best and what kind of methods work to enhance their learning' (Warner 1997: 41). On this basis other, more sophisticated profiling approaches have been developed in schools, often with an intention to facilitate formative evaluation.

Taking account of 'giftedness'

A considerable amount of effort has gone into the identification of 'able and gifted' children in UK schools. It is part of the system of identifying the special needs of students and it is driven by the requirement to show that comprehensive schools have mechanisms to develop effective learning for all. Teachers of drama may well be asked, therefore, to identify those students who have special drama abilities. Cheryl Starr (1997) tackles the issue of what constitutes giftedness in drama, and whether a curriculum can be developed that caters for the 'gifted'. She maintains that she, and other teachers have little difficulty in identifying 'dramatically gifted students' but in a real plea for help with the development of accepted criteria she says:

> how do we define what it is we are seeing? How do we break it down into manageable pieces that can have numerical value attached to it? What do we tell parents when, intuitively, we know their child isn't ready for the advanced drama classes but they are so sure their child is gifted in this area?

> (Starr 1997)

This is another example of how teachers believe they can identify successful drama practice but cannot produce reliable criteria to back up their judgements.

What kinds of learning?

As I stated earlier, the key to assessment and evaluation lies in what sense we make of the nature of students' learning. I will now try to situate this problem in the context of a recent teaching experience where I worked with some 12 year-olds in an Exeter Middle school. In this example, which I would suggest is a relatively common drama experience for students of this age, I identified five kinds of knowledge and abilities which synthesised some of the different traditions within the subject. These were our explicit objectives during discrete phases of the project. In particular, I was keen to reconcile the value of using drama as a means to learn about other subjects and ways of living, with an attention to understanding its communicative structure and form. I was also keen for students to find the experience personally meaningful and to use the activity to reflect on their progress as students of the subject discipline. The five dimensions or phases were:

1 A knowledge of the facts and issues that underpin the story being created
2 A knowledge of which aspects of what has been discovered in (1) have most relevance to them as individuals.

3   An ability to discern which aspects have most relevance for the dramatic creation
4   An ability to capture material effectively within the medium and to communicate it to others.
5   An ability to reflect on process and product and to build knowledge gained into future work.

Having outlined the intention to devise a presentation about the Black Death in fourteenth-century Exeter, the class conducted a great deal of research into the disease: how it was contracted, its symptoms and effects, who caught it, what avoidance was tried and what the outcomes were (phase 1). We then explored selected aspects of this information through the drama, discovering their interest for the students (phase 2) and their potential to make good drama (phase 3). Finally we crafted our explorations into a polished piece, with music and narration, for performance to other students and parents (phase 4). It is, of course, difficult to separate these operations as, often, they happen in parallel with each other. Infusing all operations, for example, were the students' powers of discrimination based on their sense of what is most interesting and relevant to them as individuals – how the story connects with their own emerging story (phase 2). Subsequently, the class teacher encouraged the students to reflect on the project so that they might engage more successfully in their next drama unit (phase 5). My discussion of this project is structured around the learning objectives.

Knowledge of the facts and issues that underpin the story being created

At first glance the research and learning carried out in this phase was of a kind not unique to drama. It seems it could just as well have been a precursor to work in other curriculum areas. This may have been true for some of the time, but I believe in this phase the students were already researching with a particular regard for phases 2 and 3. It is also likely that I had shaped the kinds of research they were undertaking to ensure that they encountered material that had the best potential for drama making. It would be possible, however, to discover what factual knowledge the students had absorbed from this phase through accepted forms of testing.

Knowledge of which aspects of what has been discovered have most relevance to them as an individual

There is evidence that we come to know new things only in relation to knowledge we already possess (e.g., Bruner 1966). It is part of the teacher's duty to provide research resources that contain material that has this potential and choosing aspects of a topic that connects with individuals is a skill. I also believe that that material which has the most relevance to an individual also has the most potential to change students' attitudes and, as I have argued elsewhere, attitudes can and do change as a result of the drama experience (Somers 1996). Perhaps the only way of judging the quality of the material studied is to assess the student's identification with it. While I would not advocate the use of the extensive methods used in my research, I would argue that teachers need to take into account changes in student attitudes to the topic being taught.

Developing attainment targets and realistic assessment procedures for this area is difficult. And yet drama teachers do harbour a belief that by attempt- ing to raise and experience certain 'life areas' in drama, we are doing good – that students are gaining more humane attitudes, that they can demonstrate an informed understanding of the issues. Recent research I conducted with experienced UK secondary school drama teachers illustrates that to believe otherwise would be naive (Somers 1999). On the one hand, teachers main- tain that their chief criterion for choosing material to work on in lessons is its suitability for making good drama. Additionally, they state that they do not aim to achieve attitude changes and that, even if they did, such changes would be impossible to assess. On the other hand, when asked if they would be happy if a more negative attitude was being taken by students to, say, old age following a series of lessons on this topic, they were adamant that they believed there was a positive effect. This suggests that the tradition, discussed above, that drama changes students 'for the better' as a result of their contact with issues embedded in particular lesson material runs deep in the subject teachers' philosophies.

There can be little doubt that learning in drama is linked to the pupil's existing store of knowledge, understanding and experience. In a booklet entitled *Seeing Ourselves As Others See Us: Drama and Assessment*, Phil Chris- topher (1993: 15) makes explicit claims that drama experience may modify future behaviour and advocates direct contemplation of possible links between the educational activity and real-life actions through the addressing of questions such as:

- Has something like this happened to you?
- Did you feel the same (as the character you played)?
- How did you cope?
- What did you do?
- What was outside your control?

The finished drama product is an obvious use of the form and various kinds of performance (including theatre) traditions, but it also constitutes a 'means of understanding'. Bolton (1986: 220) suggests that when we are looking for progress we must look, above all else, for the quality of meanings the participants sought and found in the material.

An ability to discern which aspects have most relevance for the dramatic creation

In this phase students are predicting which material has most dramatic potential. They discriminate using criteria distilled from previous practice and explore the material by trying it out in the drama. It may be possible to assess the students' ability to do this although it would be fraught with difficulties given the idiosyncrasies of a creative process which sometimes allows us to make excellent drama from the, apparently, most unpromising material – and vice versa.

An ability to capture material effectively within the medium and to communicate it to others

The making of the drama and the acquisition of performance skills that allow it to be 'published' constitute the most easily assessed area because we are looking for communicative fluency. I am not suggesting that teachers will not have different evaluations of students' abilities here, but that because the 'communicability' of a piece is explicit, we do not have to investigate understandings which may be hidden away in our students' heads. In polishing and ordering the knowledge that distilled from the first part of this phase, the students were clearly engaging in processes special to drama. They were demonstrating their understanding of how drama works. They added music, simple lighting properties and costume and narration to bind the piece together and to make it an effective vehicle for publishing the results of their research.

An ability to reflect on process and product and to build knowledge gained into future work

Future work will be informed by effective reflection on that which has been created and how that creation was achieved. These qualities can only be evaluated by the quality of student reflection through conversations or written forms; and the tracking of student progression. In this respect making final judgements here is always going to foreclose the full potential of the experience. As for the social learning so valued by the early pioneers, a degree of this is inevitably taking place, but drama cannot claim uniquely to do this, although it may do it better as a result of the kinds of structures that operate in drama activity and the nature of the student/student and staff/student relationship in these lessons (see Verriour 1994).

Conclusion

I have attempted to show that a number of forms of learning are taking place in drama sessions. The most easily observed by all concerned is the acquisition of the skills necessary to give students a command of the dramatic form, but this cannot exist in isolation from the other elements of the experience. All of these operations should be evaluated by the students so that they become aware of the phases involved in making and reflecting on drama. There should be no mystery about drama making. The more that students understand how they and it work, the more autonomous and empowered they will be. The teacher should also consider the learning phases in assessing work, taking due note of the effects and demands of group work for, as Warner (1997) and others have shown, the interpersonal dynamics involved in drama-making exist in many forms.

For example, I recently watched a group of twelve year-olds making a spy story. One of the girls, (A), appeared not to be contributing to the group discussion and decision making. For some of the time she lay on her back apparently disassociating herself from the group effort whilst another girl (B) talked animatedly about the possible story line. Girl (C) listened intently but said very little whilst B consolidated the story. When it came to working in the drama, however, A was brilliant at portraying the spy and C became an animated director figure to bring B's story alive. If we are to acknowledge the complexity and subtlety of the efforts needed to make drama, we have to use realistic and appropriate criteria.

This chapter fails to come up with definitive models and leaves a range of unanswered questions regarding forms of assessment and evaluation. This is clearly an area in which we need renewed effort and increased research activity to produce a more useful and practical approach to both assessment and evaluation. Hornbrook makes a powerful case to make assessment in drama subject specific (1991: 131); and he outlines a possible series of Attainment Targets (Making, Performing and Responding) and associated Statements of Attainment in Drama (1991: 141–61). But when we encourage students to make decisions about how a piece of drama can be improved, do we refer *only* to the medium? In a scene, for example about the First World War trenches, while our aim is to make better drama, 'making it better' cannot be divorced from making it more sensitive, more subtle, more redolent of the actual human condition and predicament of the characters being portrayed. In other words, focusing on the *technical* aspects of making and performing do not describe the complete aims of the subject.

In drama then, we cannot separate form and material. We can concentrate on one or the other in the preparation phases, but they are inseparable in the exciting fusion of doing drama. Drama is only successful if the participants have developing mastery of the form *and* are engaged by the material being explored or expressed. So how such material is chosen should also be of interest to the Drama in Education community. Here teachers need to be clear if, or when they are working with a model of child development. If, as my research has suggested, drama teachers believe the subject has the capacity to change attitudes, what implications does this principle have for our choice of material within the drama? Above all, we will need to decide whether it is sufficient solely to concentrate on the quality of the form (which is unique to drama) in the expectation that, when the drama is effective, all of the four additional areas of learning outlined above will follow. As Ross *et al.* found out, teachers are much exercised by these matters:

> Looking back at our early interviews with teachers, we can now redefine their problems with assessment as stemming from a fundamental difficulty as to how to reconcile the so-called 'teachable' elements of the arts curriculum with what is essentially 'untaught': conventional forms and expressive materials transformed by subjective feelings.
>
> (Ross *et al.* 1993: 166)

And, of course, there is a danger of only testing the testable and ignoring that which cannot be easily categorised and measured; of elevating, for pragmatic reasons, the role of summative assessment over that of formative evaluation. In drama we cannot use the product alone as a means of assessing the value of the experience for the individuals concerned: it ignores essential aspects of individuals' learning. The evidence is not all in the product.

I want to end by suggesting that research has a major function in helping to bring clarity to these issues. Research can deal with those esoteric areas that, due to the huge amounts of time and effort required to conduct subtle enquiry, are not open to regular evaluation and assessment. It is beholden to researchers (and in this I see teacher-researchers as the major force) to clarify what is happening in the creative and expressive processes so that the more manageable and practically realisable methods of evaluating and assessing drama work can proceed within a more confident knowledge of what is the whole drama effect.

Rudolph Arnheim states that all we can ever do in understanding art is to go after the bird's shadow in flight which, 'when cast upon the ground, is reachable, measurable, two dimensional' and to 'glance mindfully and gratefully at that high apparition to which we owe it all' (quoted in Winner 1982: v). Productive study and understanding of the bird itself, however, will be the yardstick of our success.

Notes

1 In discussing criteria for assessment in drama, the Schools Council argued:

> frequently [the criteria] are sociological and psychological (for example, group dynamics, personal background, degree of co-operation, in class or group etc.). When these criteria are not applied, teachers often resort to theatrical judgements in their assessments which can be equally misleading.
>
> (Schools Council 1974: 12)

References

Best, B. (1992) *The Rationality of Feeling*, London: Falmer Press.

Bolton, G. (1986) 'Assessment of Practical Drama' in David, D. and Lawrence, C., *Selected Writings* [on drama in education], London: Longman.

Bruner, J. (1966) *Towards a Theory of Instruction*, Cambridge, Mass.: Harvard University Press.

Christopher, P. (1993) *Seeing Ourselves as Others See Us: Drama and Assessment*, London: Edge Hill College.

Clegg, D. (1973) 'The dilemma of drama-in-education', *Theatre Quarterly*, vol. 3, no. 9, pp. 31–41.

Cook, P. (1992) 'Evaluating Drama', *2D* vol. 2, no. 1, pp. 37–45.

Dacre, K. and Mackey, S. (1999) 'Self-interpreting animals: action research and the reflective drama journal', *Research in Drama Education*, vol. 4, no. 1, p. 68.

Hornbrook. D. (1989) *Education and Dramatic Art*, Oxford: Blackwell.

Hornbrook D. (1991) *Education in Drama*, London: The Falmer Press.

Report of the Consultative Committee on the Primary School, (The Hadow Report) (1931) London: HMSO.

McGregor, L., Tate, M. and Robinson, K. (1977) *Learning Through Drama*, London: Heinemann Educational Books.

McGowan, V. (1982) 'Assessing Practical Mode 111 CSE Dance', *2D*, vol. 1, no 2, pp. 31–6.

McKone, F. (1997) 'Engagement and assessment in Drama', *Research in Drama Education*, vol. 2, no. 2, pp. 215–16.

MEG *Drama (Syllabus code 1825 [1999])* (1997) Cambridge: Midland Examinations Group.

National Drama (1997) 'Examination in Drama; statistical report', London: National Drama

Noijons, J. (1997) 'A study of rater agreement in tests of Drama', paper presented at conference, Researching Drama and Theatre in Education, University of Exeter.

Northern Ireland Curriculum Council (1993) 'A Report on the Statutory Consultation for a Programme of Study and Attainment Targets for Drama', Belfast, NICC.

Philpott, S. (1986) 'Assessment in Dance' in Ross, M. (ed.), *Assessment in Arts Education*, London: Pergamon Press.

Ross, M. (1986) *Assessment in Arts Education*, London: Pergamon Press.

Ross, M., Radnor, H., Mitchell, S. and Bierton, C. (1993) *Assessing Achievement in the Arts*, Buckingham: Open University Press.

Ross, M. and Kamba, M. (1997) *The State of the Arts*, Exeter: University of Exeter Press.

Schools Council English Committee (1974) 'Examinations in Drama', London: The Schools Council.

SEG (1997) *GCSE Syllabuses 1999 (1997)*, *Drama and Theatre Arts (3390)* Guildford: Southern Examinations Group.

Slade, P. (1954) *Child Drama*, London: University of London Press.

Somers, J. (1996) 'The nature of learning in drama in education', in Somers, J. (ed.) *Drama and Theatre in Education: Contemporary Research*, North York, Canada: Captus Press.

Somers, J. (1999) 'How teachers choose what to do in drama lessons', in Miller, C. and

Saxton, J. (eds) *Drama and Theatre in Education: International conversations*, Victoria, Canada: AERA & IDIERI.

Starr, C. (1997) 'What is giftedness in drama? Developing a model for gifted education' paper presented at conference, Researching Drama and Theatre in Education, University of Exeter.

Verriour, P. (1994) *In Role: Teaching and Learning Dramatically*, Markham, Ontario: Pippin Publishing.

Viola, W. (1942) *Child Art*, London: University of London Press.

Warner, C. (1997) 'The edging in of engagement: exploring the nature of engagement in drama' in *Research in Drama Education*, vol. 2, no. 1, pp. 21–42.

Winner, E. (1982) *Invented Worlds: The Psychology of the Arts*, Cambridge, Mass.: Harvard University Press.

7 Making the grade

Evaluating student production in Media Studies

David Buckingham, Pete Fraser and Julian Sefton-Green

The act of evaluation inevitably brings into focus many of the most problematic dimensions of teaching and learning. Far from being a neutral or straightforward process, evaluation is often beset by considerable uncertainties and contradictions. While they may have several causes, these difficulties often point to unresolved questions about the aims of our teaching, about what counts as valid knowledge, and about how we identify evidence of what students have learnt. This may be particularly the case with relatively 'new' subjects, or those which have had to struggle to establish their educational legitimacy. In this respect, Media Studies is an interesting case in point.[1]

In fact, there is a long history of teaching about the 'mass' media in schools and it is possible to identify several traditions or versions of media education which continue to co-exist – and, to some degree, to conflict (see Alvarado and Boyd-Barrett 1992; Alvarado, Gutch and Wollen 1987). Traces of these different traditions can still be detected in the 'official' version of media education, which is enshrined in the GCSE and A-level Media Studies syllabuses that are increasingly being taken up in schools and colleges. The conflicts between them are particularly apparent when it comes to practical media production – an area which, despite government restrictions on coursework, continues to constitute between one third and one half of most Media Studies courses.

Alongside the discursive writing that constitutes the bulk of their assessed work for examinations, most students who take Media Studies are therefore required to produce artefacts in several media – primarily video, photography, print and audio. These typically range from small-scale exercises or plans (storyboards, treatments or mock-ups) to more finished productions. Many – perhaps the majority – take the form of simulations of professional practice, which are explicitly designed to generate questions about the established forms and conventions of mainstream media (for examples, see Buckingham, Grahame and Sefton-Green 1995; Grahame 1994).

In general, students are highly motivated by this kind of work: it is the promise of 'making videos' that many identify as their primary reason for opting to take the subject in the first place. Yet for many teachers, production is an area of the course that they often approach with considerable trepidation. Of course, there are some good reasons for this. The majority of Media Studies teachers were initially trained as English teachers, and very few have substantial expertise in media production. Media technologies are currently evolving at a frightening rate; yet the challenge of enabling twenty-five students to make videos with a couple of camcorders and a makeshift editing set-up should not be underestimated.

However, the anxieties teachers often experience here are not merely to do with the difficulties of managing technology. On the contrary, they reflect some of the most significant tensions and uncertainties that continue to characterise the field. Addressing the question of how teachers and students *evaluate* production work, as we intend to do in this chapter, raises fundamental questions about the aims and purposes of media education, and about what students learn from it.

'Theory' and 'practice'

It is important to emphasise here that Media Studies is not primarily a 'creative' subject like the majority of others considered in this book. Indeed, in some respects it has more in common with Science than it does with Drama or Art – subjects with which it is often grouped in the secondary school curriculum. While it certainly contains 'creative' elements, Media Studies is perhaps more accurately seen as a contemporary social science or humanities subject. Its aims are defined in primarily *conceptual* terms – that is, in terms of a series of abstract understandings about the social and cultural dimensions of the media (e.g., Bazalgette 1992). While there is some variation between them, most Media Studies syllabuses are organised in terms of a set of 'key concepts' or 'aspects of knowledge and understanding' that typically include *media language*, *representation*, *institutions* and *audiences*. Although some syllabuses have elements of a more process-based approach – which rewards students for their skills in group work or research, for example – they nevertheless stipulate that student productions should be assessed primarily in terms of their demonstration of these conceptual understandings.

This emphasis on conceptual learning inevitably raises some significant questions about the aims and purposes of student production work – and in particular, about the relationship between practical production and the critical analysis of the media. Is production something that has value in its own right, or is it primarily a means to another end? Is it a way of *illustrating* pre-existing conceptual understandings of the media – or is it an activity that can *generate* new understandings? In either case, how can we identify *evidence* of those understandings in students' productions? What, ultimately, are students expected to *learn* from making their own media products, and how can we tell that they have learnt it?

This relationship between 'theory' (or conceptual understanding) and 'practice' (or media production) has been a focus of considerable debate throughout the history of Media Studies (see Sefton-Green 1995). The gradual establishment of Media Studies as a legitimate academic subject in schools has involved a troubled, almost schizophrenic, stance towards student production. On the one hand, the inclusion of such practical activities has been seen to define Media Studies as an essentially vocational or creative subject. In the traditional academic hierarchies that continue to prevail, in which the 'mental' is privileged above the 'manual', this has effectively marked it out as a low status subject for low status kids. On the other hand, for many students across the whole range of 'ability', it is the promise of getting their hands on cameras or of doing creative work with computers that often motivates them to choose the subject in the first place.

Nevertheless, advocates of Media Studies as a specialist subject have traditionally adopted a sceptical, even hostile, attitude to practical production. The most influential writers in the field in the 1970s and early 1980s tended to condemn the majority of such work as politically suspect and as educationally worthless. Len Masterman's book *Teaching About Television*, published in 1980, was the most influential book for a whole generation of teachers. Yet its chapter on practical work was very much the shortest in the book, and much of it was extraordinarily negative. What happens, Masterman asks, when you give students video cameras?

> In my experience an endless wilderness of dreary third-rate imitative 'pop'-shows, embarrassing video dramas, and derivative documentaries courageously condemning war or poverty, much of it condoned by teachers to whom technique is all and the medium the only message.
> (Masterman 1980: 140)

What is striking about this quote now, twenty years later, is its reliance on precisely the kind of Leavisite critical criteria that the rest of the book sought to challenge (see Leavis and Thompson 1933). Students' work is condemned as 'derivative' and 'third-rate', in exactly the same terms that one might find Leavis condemning a novel that had failed to gain entry to the Great Tradition. Yet this tone can also be found in other writings of the period. Bob Ferguson, writing in *Screen Education* in 1981, condemned practical video work in similar terms:

> Many groups ended up just clowning around with the equipment . . . the camera was often 'squirted' at its subject and the dizzy, boring and incoherent results thus obtained could be justified as experimentation. When plots were attempted they were puerile and in further education often incorporated obligatory punch-ups in pubs and discotheques.
> (Ferguson 1981: 44–5)

Significantly, Ferguson's main criticism was directed against the notion of 'creativity' which he saw as deriving from Art and English teaching, and which he condemned as mystical and individualistic. This approach, he argued, reflected a dangerous 'romanticisation of the working class': it led to work that was 'intellectually undemanding' and that merely institutionalised low expectations of students.

Likewise, Masterman's *Teaching the Media*, published in 1985, gives over little more than a page to practical production, in what claims to be a comprehensive introduction to the field – and in this respect, it is similar to other handbooks for teachers published at that time, many of which simply neglect student production altogether (Masterman 1985: 26–7; and see also Alvarado, Gutch and Wollen 1987; Clarke 1987). Again, most of what Masterman says is negative. The new concern here, however, is with what he calls 'the technicist trap'. In the wake of the 'new vocationalism', it seemed to be vital to challenge any attempt to reduce media education to a form of technical training. This kind of training, Masterman argued, represents 'a form of cultural reproduction in which dominant practices become naturalised'; it is a kind of ideological 'enslavement' which produces 'deference and conformity'. The alternative, it would appear, is to encourage students to produce 'oppositional' texts which directly challenge and subvert the norms of professional media practice.

As these quotations imply, these criticisms were partly motivated by a fear of *imitation*, which in turn derived from a wider suspicion of the deceptive pleasures of popular culture. Imitation was seen to be an inherently *unthinking* process, through which the 'dominant ideologies' of media products were simply taken on and reproduced. An emphasis on production was therefore seen to be at odds with the radical political mission of Media Studies, and its struggle against the ideological hegemony of capitalism. Media Studies was essentially – and, for some, exclusively – a matter of ideological critique.

For Masterman and other authors writing at this time, the only form of production work that was seen as acceptable was in the form of 'deconstruction exercises'. While this approach had precedents in the 'film grammar' approach of earlier decades (Sefton-Green 1995), it was essentially derived from the application of semiotic theories of 'visual language' which were popular during the 1970s. According to Masterman (1980: 142), deconstruction exercises involve the practical analysis of the dominant 'codes' of television: '[deconstruction] allows individual conventions (of framing, camera positioning, editing, etc.) to be isolated, experimented with and broken while variations in their meaning are explored'. Thus, students might undertake exercises on the conventions of TV interviews or news presentation; or they might be required to produce 'exercises in style' designed to demonstrate their understanding of a particular genre such as film noir or horror. This approach explicitly seeks to oppose and subvert dominant forms of professional practice; and in the process, the 'expressive' or 'creative' potential of production is rigorously subordinated to the demonstration of critical or conceptual understanding.

Along with many other aspects of Media Studies, this perspective on student production has been significantly challenged and revised over the past decade. These changes have arisen partly as a result of the increasing status of the subject, and its institutionalisation both in public examinations and in higher education. The attempt to distance Media Studies from any association with the 'manual labour' of production is no longer such a powerful imperative. These changes are also a consequence of technological developments, and of the increasing accessibility of production equipment. Media production has increasingly come within the reach of the domestic consumer, and managing production work with scarce resources is no longer quite the daunting prospect it used to be.

Furthermore, there has also been a more wide-ranging reconsideration of the fundamental aims and methods of media teaching in recent years (see, for example, Buckingham 1990; Buckingham 1998; Buckingham, Grahame and Sefton-Green 1995; Buckingham and Sefton-Green 1994). By addressing hitherto neglected questions about children's existing knowledge of the media, and about how they learn, contemporary teachers are now beginning to question many of the grandiose political claims about media education made by its pioneers. The notion that media teaching would 'liberate' students from the chains of the dominant ideology has given way to a more realistic – and, we would argue, more effective – approach. Broadly speaking, the sense of burning political mission that characterised media education in the 1970s and early 1980s has given way to a more neutral emphasis on developing students' critical understanding of – *and participation in* – the media cultures that surround them.

Setting limits

On one level then, student production is no longer so comprehensively marginalised or suspected as it was in earlier decades. Nevertheless, its status within Media Studies remains problematic. In our experience of examining A-level Media Studies, for example, the tensions between 'theory' and 'practice' have frequently loomed large. Some syllabuses have relegated practical work to the status of a bolt-on extra, which is probably included as a 'sop' to schools and colleges needing to attract student numbers, rather than from any more principled commitment to student production. Several refer to 'production exercises', implying that the fundamental aim of the practice is to 'prove' the theory; while some examiners' reports have been taken to imply that the written essays that are required to accompany productions will be more highly valued than the productions themselves.

For example, the first version of the Cambridge A-level syllabus – which is generally more committed to student production than some others – required students to devise productions within four broad categories. The range of work was very diverse, but in our experience there were some clear patterns that emerged. For the *Images in Context* category, still images were the most commonly used: students frequently explored photography and representation using different images of themselves, following approaches developed during the 1970s and 1980s at the Cockpit in London (Dewdney and Lister 1988). Found images tended to be heavily used here, often in order to create 'alternative' representations. For the *Exercise in Style* category, work varied from a broad-based genre exercise, such as the creation of a story-board for the opening of a film noir, to much more narrowly focused def-initions of style, such as 'in the style of a Heineken advert, create a new Heineken advert' (a genuine example!). *Non-fiction* work often took the form of newspaper front pages (tabloid and broadsheet versions of the same story were a frequent example); although it also led to a heavy emphasis on some-what worthy 'issue-based' productions, such as documentaries about the homeless. The *Free Choice* category was very varied and often included work which seemed to bear little resemblance to mainstream media forms. Yet even here, the fact that the syllabus emphasised 'small scale' activities was often taken very literally: the majority of print-based work, for example, consisted of single-page products, often using basic cut-and-paste and drawing techniques.

As this implies, most of the work – even at this advanced level – is fairly limited; although this is at least as much to do with the constraints of the assignments set by teachers as it is to do with the imagination of the students. In this respect, the anxieties of earlier media educators continue to be appar-ent in a good deal of contemporary classroom practice. Production is still implicitly defined as an adjunct of 'theory', or as an opportunity to demon-strate pre-determined theoretical principles. This is particularly reflected in two dominant tendencies in current practice: the use of simulations and the approach which might be termed the 'impossible text'.

Of course, most media production work in classrooms is simulated, in the sense that it rarely approximates to the conditions of 'professional' practice. Yet the explicit use of simulations, in which students are invited to take on the roles of 'real' media producers, has become the dominant model for production in most contemporary media classrooms (for good examples of such activities, see Grahame 1994). Students are typically provided with a 'brief' which requires them to work within specific – albeit imaginary – institutional or economic constraints, and/or to target a particular audience.

In some respects, simulation could be seen as a kind of compromise between the theoretically over-determined approach of 'deconstruction exercises' and a more open-ended, 'creative' approach. Nevertheless, it remains a comparatively *conceptual* technique, in the sense that creative self-expression (whatever one might conceive that to mean) is ultimately sub-ordinated to the consideration of abstract theoretical issues. The key moment in such simulations is the 'debriefing', in which students are required to make explicit the reasons for their choices, and to analyse their potential consequences, for example in terms of audience responses (see Buckingham, Grahame and Sefton-Green 1995: ch. 8). The use of simulation thus invites a direct analytical comparison with 'dominant' or professional practice – not so much in terms of the technical quality of the finished product (or the lack of it), but in terms of the formal, generic and representational aspects of the text. In practice, the difficulties and limitations of 'debriefing' – whether in written or spoken form – can prove particularly problematic. Yet the central aims of such activities – and the terms by which they are largely assessed – are essentially defined in terms of theoretical or conceptual understanding.

In many instances, however, the requirements of media simulations are in themselves highly contradictory. Anxieties about 'political correctness' – or about the dangers of what used to be called 'ideological reproduction' – often seem to lead to a recipe for the 'impossible text'. This is the text which is simultaneously 'dominant' *and* 'oppositional'. Thus, students can be required to encode 'oppositional' content within a 'dominant' form; or (less frequently) 'dominant' content within an 'oppositional' form. Thus, media teachers will routinely ask older students to produce 'alternative' soap operas or 'non-sexist' teenage magazines or even 'anti-realist texts', when they have rarely had a chance to explore the possibilities of the technology, or indeed to gain much experience with the dominant forms they are supposedly expected to be moving beyond. If not 'impossible', such assignments are at least unrealistic, not only in terms of what can be achieved with the technology but also in terms of the internal contradictions of the tasks themselves.

As this implies, there is a continuing suspicion and anxiety about student production among Media Studies teachers. Some of this might be traced to a fear of technology, or a more general sense of uncertainty about the subject – neither of which are surprising given the fact that few teachers have had the benefit of specialist training in the field. Yet the forms of practice that have been inherited and are now (to a greater or lesser extent) enshrined in the syllabuses still reflect the political and pedagogic anxieties of an earlier era. The privilege accorded to 'theory' means that practical production may be reduced to the point where it serves merely as a means of demonstrating or illustrating pre-determined theoretical positions.

Assessment and evaluation: problems in practice

These tensions and anxieties are particularly apparent when it comes to *assessment* – that is, to the ways in which teachers grade students' work.[2] To some extent, the problems here are the same as those most frequently encountered in arts education, and described by other contributors in this book. Inevitably, published criteria for assessment are largely comparative, although precisely what is being compared often remains unclear. Grades are expected to be allocated on the basis of whether the candidate displays more or less of a given quality, yet the criteria for identifying this quality are only rarely specified. Words like 'capable', 'effective', 'confident', 'coherent', 'perceptive', 'appropriate', and so on, frequently recur in this context (e.g., Worsnop 1996).

As this implies, assessment is a *discursive* practice that takes place within specific institutional settings. Over time, examiners come to share a terminology and a set of meanings that obviate the need for precise specification: they agree, in other words, that they are talking about the same things, without necessarily having to identify precisely what they are. What might from the outside be condemned as mere subjective intuition becomes institutionalised: we might say that it becomes sedimented in discourse.

With subject areas that are comparatively new, this process is obviously more open to debate and contestation. Our experience of examining in Media Studies suggests that there is often considerable uncertainty – and no little controversy – when it comes to the business of allocating grades, particularly for student production work. We have participated in moderation and INSET meetings where the same piece of work has been awarded marks at opposite ends of the scale. In practice, the published criteria for assessment – however rigorously they may appear to be specified – often seem to provide little basis for agreement. As we shall indicate below, teachers and examiners frequently use a whole range of criteria, some of which may be quite irrelevant to the aims of the teaching, and which may prove internally contradictory. 'Intuition' still appears to play a very significant role. It is perhaps no surprise that teachers so often complain that there are 'hidden criteria' in operation here.

As we have noted, examinations in Media Studies typically require students to produce a written essay to accompany their production work. At GCSE level, this piece of writing is sometimes termed (with shades of *Star Trek*) the 'production log'; while at A-level, it is expected to be a more discursive, analytical account. In both cases, however, the written account is intended to present a rationale for the production and an evaluation of the outcomes in the light of the student's broader understanding of media theory. At least in principle, then, it is through the systematic process of written reflection that connections between 'theory' and 'practice' will be developed and made explicit.

In our previous work, we have sought to develop a theory of learning in media education that draws critically on Vygotsky's analysis of concept formation (e.g., Buckingham and Sefton-Green 1994: ch. 8; Vygotsky 1962). One of the key points here is the emphasis on the importance of reflection and self-evaluation. The aim of media education, we have argued, is not merely to enable students to 'read' – or make sense of – media texts, or to enable them to 'write' their own. It must also enable them to reflect systematically on the processes of reading and writing, to understand and to analyse how they themselves make meaning as readers and as writers. In the case of practical production, this means asking students to reflect back on the process in the light of their own and others' readings of what they have produced. Did they communicate what they set out to communicate? Why did they make particular choices, and what effects did they have? How might an audience interpret what they have produced, and what can they learn from this?

In this context, writing would appear to have a particular value, which derives at least partly from the specific characteristics of written communication, as compared with talk or other methods. Elsewhere, we have studied the development of two students' writing in GCSE Media Studies, and have argued that much of the value of writing in this context derives precisely from its individual, private nature (Buckingham and Sefton-Green 1994: ch. 8). This is not, however, to suggest that it is somehow asocial: on the contrary, it functions as a form of dialogue with an imagined other – or what one of the students, Michael, aptly calls a 'conversation with yourself'. Michael argues that, while he finds writing difficult, it does serve as a prompt for reflection – that it helps him to discover things that he didn't know he thought.

A further argument for the value of writing in this context can be drawn from work on the development of 'Knowledge About Language'. In his theoretical overview of the area, John Richmond (1990) argues that self-conscious reflection upon the characteristics of language can be developed through the 'translation' between language modes. Writing about talk, or talk about reading, for example, can make the specific qualities of these different modes much more explicit, and thus contribute to the development of a systematic understanding of how languages work. A similar argument could be made about the relationship between media production and writing, which effectively involves a similar form of 'translation' between one language mode and another. In the process, it could be argued, students are inevitably forced to make their implicit knowledge explicit, to make it systematic and thence to question it.

However, it is important to emphasise that these pieces of writing are produced primarily for the purposes of *assessment*. Indeed, it is the written account or commentary that, in practice, represents the major form of evidence for the examiner of the conceptual understandings that were entailed or developed in the production process – and hence exerts a crucial influence on the allocation of grades.

In fact, most media teachers would probably agree that this is a practice that is rarely done well. Reading logs at GCSE or even written accounts supporting production work at A-level can often be a dispiriting experience. Most teachers will have read logs that make *The Secret Diary of Adrian Mole* look like Proust. Examiners' reports frequently note that – particularly at GCSE – the written account is the assessment category in which the lowest marks are registered, and that candidates tend to engage in lengthy description rather than 'genuine analysis'.

As an assessment practice, this reliance on a written account rests on all sorts of assumptions. It implies, for example, that the thinking that counts is the thinking that can be made self-conscious – whereas of course one would not assume that a visual artist or a musician was necessarily the best person to explain or analyse their own work, particularly in written form. It implies that what took place in a collective process can (and should) be individualised; and that the writing will be somehow *honest* – that it will serve as a true reflection of what really went on in the student's mind, rather than as an exercise in self-justification designed to maximise marks in the examination.

One might go on from here to develop a strong critique of this approach. Thus, it could be argued that the written account is simply imposed by the institutional practices of examining – by a system that seeks to individualise and thereby to discriminate between students, that values writing above other forms of expression, and that sees learning as a matter of students regurgitating what they have been fed. As Jenny Grahame (1990) has argued, a great deal of what is most valuable about practical work may be lost in the transition to writing. Many of the students who contribute most to practical production, for example in terms of their technical or 'artistic' skills, or their role in group work, tend to lose out when it comes to writing. One could well argue that, like other forms of assessment, the primary aim of insisting on writing is to discriminate in favour of students who have skills in particular forms of communication, and against those who have other abilities; and that this serves merely to perpetuate existing social inequalities.

In our experience, this kind of written self-evaluation is often seen by students as an artificial, abstract requirement on the part of teachers or examiners. Rather than being integral to the process, it is seen as something extraneous to it, that is merely tacked on at the end. It has no *motivation* other than to please the examiner. In this context, writing can easily become an exercise in self-presentation rather than self-evaluation. As 'process-oriented' styles of pedagogy have become increasingly popular in recent years (most notably in the context of vocational courses), it has become apparent that students can develop a facility in using the *discourse* of self-evaluation which may in fact say little or nothing about their learning (see Bates *et al.* 1984). The most successful students may be simply those who are best at presenting themselves; and in the process, educational evaluation may become little more than a form of public relations.

As this implies, the use of writing in this context tends to conflate – and even to confuse – *assessment* and *self-evaluation*. It is at once a demonstration of learning and a form of self-justification, and its status is therefore quite problematic. Yet, as we have implied, some examiners appear to grant a considerable degree of credence to this written account: they effectively use it as a guide in interpreting the productions themselves. Yet how far should we trust what students say about their own work? To what extent can student productions be assessed 'on their own merits' – even assuming that we can agree upon what those merits might be? And what is the status of either as a means of identifying what students know and understand?

Assessment in practice

Research undertaken by one of the authors of this chapter (Pete Fraser) clearly illustrates some of the tensions and uncertainties that arise in this situation – both for teachers and for their students. This research involved asking groups of students and teachers to undertake 'trial marking' of some short pieces of student video and their accompanying commentaries, according to the published examination criteria. Using transcripts of the discussions, the aim was then to identify the discourses that both groups used in attempting to justify their grading decisions. In comparing the different readings of student productions generated by students and by teachers – as well as those of 'insiders' who were involved in the productions and 'outsiders' who were not – it is possible to detect some diverse (and frequently contradictory) sets of criteria in play. These point in turn to some quite contrasting views of the relationships between 'theory' and 'practice', some of which seem quite at odds with those contained within the syllabus.

Of course, the act of assessment – particularly in a trial marking situation – is a social act, which can serve a range of social functions. Teachers (and in this instance, students also) are being invited to construct 'evaluative identities' that must be negotiated and sustained alongside those of others.[3] Most obviously, they can choose to define themselves as more or less rigorous or stringent in their expectations; but in the process, they also inevitably situate themselves in relation to the various definitions of the aims of media education, as discussed above. In addition, as we shall indicate, all sorts of 'hidden' criteria that are quite extraneous to those identified by the syllabus may come into play. Like any other kind of discourse, the discourse of assessment situates its users in relations of social power and ideology. To pretend that assessment is an objective performance is perhaps a necessary fiction, but it is a fiction none the less.

Thus, in our experience of trial marking at examiners' meetings and INSET events, there is often a great deal at stake in not being seen to be 'too soft'. Participants are often reluctant to award A grades – although they might be rather less so in relation to their own students' work. (Despite public criticisms of Media Studies as a 'soft option', the proportion of students gaining A grades at A-level is in fact significantly lower than in most other subjects.) In addition, there can be a sense in which individuals self-consciously present themselves as 'representatives' of particular positions, some of which relate to the hierarchy of the education system itself. Thus, there is often a distinct difference between the way teachers from higher education (who are still involved in examining at this level) will present themselves compared to those from schools or further education. These 'academics' are often perceived to have idealised expectations of student work, and to pay obsessive attention to irrelevant details – expressing outrage at a student's 'poor grammar' or the fact that Roland Barthes' name has been wrongly spelt.

More broadly, of course, participants will bring different experiences and expectations of the media themselves. Student work within some genres – pop video, for example, or horror – may be valued rather less highly than work in other genres – news or documentary – simply because the latter are closer to the tastes and preferences of the majority of teachers. In the case of student production, these expectations become governed not just by the forms and conventions of media texts but by assumptions about what student work itself should be. Here again, the 'serious' (documentary) may be valued above the apparently 'frivolous' (pop video), particularly if the latter is seen to reflect a kind of subversive resistance to 'official' student identities. These judgements may be further complicated when we come to read students' writing about their productions, where attempts at academic self-justification may appear to contradict our initial experience of the work.

Finally, the diverse criteria which will be brought to bear in judgements about student production may also reflect differing and competing definitions of Media Studies itself. Teachers initially trained in different subject disciplines, or with different experiences of media production themselves, are likely to make very different judgements. What one teacher perceives as creative innovation may be seen by another as self-indulgence or incoherence; what one perceives as technically polished may be seen by another as suspiciously 'flashy'. Still others may operate according to strictly political criteria, forcefully condemning productions that are seen to 'reproduce dominant ideologies' – or even simply to fail to challenge them sufficiently explicitly.

Teachers' perspectives

One of the productions used in this research was a video made by a group of A-level students to accompany a song, 'Tales of Love' by an unsigned band 'The Geography of Love'. The video took a narrative form, in which a teenage boy dreams about a woman in red preventing him from leaving a room by taking the key and hiding it in her cleavage. We see them separately waking up in the morning and see her appear in his bathroom mirror, then disappear. We see her leaving home, apparently for work. Each chorus is accompanied by shots of Valentine's Day paraphernalia in shops, 'found' footage from romantic films (including *Some Like it Hot*) and repeated shots of a cupboard door having a torch shone on it to reveal the song's title jumbled into different anagrams. The narrative continues with the boy apparently seeing the woman at a bus stop, in the library and in the park, only for her to disappear each time. It ends with him arriving at the dentist's surgery, where she is revealed as his surgeon, unmasking herself as he has momentary flashbacks to earlier scenes.

In our previous experience of trial marking sessions, teachers had been particularly critical of this video on the grounds that it was 'not challenging' and 'full of padding'. One teacher immediately responded to the cleavage shot by saying 'I bet this was made by boys' – thus implying a form of ideological disapproval that is very familiar in Media Studies.

We asked a group of teachers to grade this video and one of the accompanying commentaries according to the syllabus criteria. While they gradually arrived at a consensus about the grade they would award, they were less sure about how to actually interpret the video in the first place:

MARY: C/D . . . I suppose the first thing I'd say is that without having read the explanation I wouldn't have known that's what they were up to. My reading of it was not what they've written here. I didn't understand all the business of the woman all the way through being his dentist and being part of his imagination.

CHARLES: Wasn't the dentist deliberately meant to be a twist in the tale? That's how I read it, the intrigue was his fascination with the woman.

MARY: No, well I didn't even understand that well, because I thought in fact that the two of them, I didn't realise that she was actually being so resistant to him. I know she kept disappearing but what we were supposed to understand was that quite deliberately she was running away from him whereas I felt that for some reason or other they never quite get together, he couldn't quite get to her in time.

LOUISE: The male was equally interested.

CHARLES: It didn't quite tie up with this ending because I read it as she was this elusive female but couldn't quite figure out why and yet she was in some kind of power relationship to him.

JIM: The thing about the power relationship was that he didn't quite have the knowledge as to why she was there. There was that one chase scene where she was moving away from him which suggested that he didn't have the knowledge, who was she?

LOUISE: Then there was the bit where she undressed him.

The condensed and (we would argue) deliberately ambiguous nature of the video clearly creates problems, particularly at a first reading. The teachers here attempt to interpret the tape in terms of conventional forms of narrative – in which things have to 'tie up' at the end – and conventional styles of editing – with 'intrigue' and 'chase scenes'. In fact, the video can be understood in these terms, although the overall air of uncertainty is clearly intentional. An additional problem here is that the students are using a form with which the majority of teachers are comparatively unfamiliar. Without resorting to a kind of generational essentialism, one could suggest that the students are likely to be much more at ease with the fragmented montage editing style, the comparatively rapid pace, and the general air of ambiguity of this kind of text, since it is the kind of thing they watch on MTV all the time.

In fact, the teachers did draw attention to some of these 'technical' or aesthetic devices:

JIM: I thought a lot of the media techniques, the technical stuff, like the editing, was excellent, like the one with the mirror, [that] was a very clever idea.

LOUISE: And the door with the jumbled up sentences. The pace was good – fast pace.

JIM: The bit where she walks through the door and they cut to the other side, that was well constructed, which I think was good.

In this instance, however, the attention to technical detail seems to provide a way out of having to deal with the difficulties of interpretation. The text comes to be seen as a compilation of 'good bits' and 'clever ideas'. Nevertheless, its apparent failure to render itself instantly understandable creates a space for negative criticism. As if to resolve their own confusion, the teachers now look to the students' written commentary:

LOUISE: There was a paragraph on what makes their video unconventional from which you can deduce that that's what they were told to do. I didn't think it was particularly unconventional, the only thing that's unconventional is that they haven't got the band in it.

MARY: I think what's brought up here for me is an interesting point about how to grade it. I mean if I was just looking at the video I'd be maybe wanting to grade it one way because it was maybe technically it has interesting things in it but then when I read this alongside it, it kind of changes my view.

LOUISE: They're better in the evaluation on signs and connotations than they are on analysis of the narrative. They're wrong in their analysis of the narrative. They haven't done what they think they've done. They haven't stood back and been self-critical enough about it but they are good in other ways. I wanted them to say more about the audience for this video because they are a bit vague about that and I thought they could have been trying to capture a female audience because the girl in the video just having her in the video means a sense of identification but they don't really mention that. And they don't really mention the age group they're aiming at, which I think with music videos you have to be quite clear about, because there's a different genre for the 12–16 age group than there is for a 16–25 audience.

The criteria for judgement shift again here, to ground on which the teachers appear more confident. As we have noted, 'audience' is one of the key areas of the Media Studies syllabus. Yet there are some questionable assumptions here about media-audience relations. Louise confidently asserts that having a girl in the video means that girls would identify with her, and that the audience for music videos is clearly segmented in terms of age. Yet the evidence for these assertions is somewhat questionable: they seem to derive from simplistic assumptions about 'identification' and from a mechanical form of demographics that most researchers in this field would find highly dubious. Likewise, Louise asserts that the students are simply 'wrong' about their own narrative, although the basis on which she makes this claim is unclear – particularly in the light of the teachers' overall uncertainty and disagreement about this.

Louise's comments also suggest that she is seeking a very high degree of control and self-reflexivity here. The students are expected, not only to 'do what they think they've done' (in this case, to produce an 'unconventional' example of a given genre), but also to analyse its 'signs and connotations' and its 'narrative' (using semiotic or structuralist methods), and to define its audience in very precise terms, for example of age and gender. There is a striking contrast between these expectations and those that might come into play in production work in Art or Music, for example – or indeed within the media industries themselves. Would we expect professional video makers, for example, to be able to conceptualise their own work in this way? Yet students, it seems, are expected to display *both* a high degree of facility as producers *and* an ability to stand outside this process and analyse it object-ively – despite the fact that they are likely to have had very little experience of media production, and are subject to considerable technical constraints. Louise's confident rejection of what the students themselves say about their work represents a further escalation of these expectations: the students are not to be trusted, and the teacher alone seems to be able to discern their 'true' intentions.

Louise's initial comments above do reflect an obvious technical constraint, however. One of the problems raised for students making a pop video is that in the real world of pop promos, the main aim of the video is to showcase the band. There are relatively few pop videos which do not consist largely of shots of the artists themselves. Unless they pretend to be the band, students' videos are likely to use forms and conventions largely alien to the form. In this case, however, this seems to provide some grounds for condemning the students for departing from the teacher's brief:

MARY: The other thing that they seemed quite happy to report is this thing about the video being more like a short film than a pop video. What they don't then say is how they might have – in a sense if their brief is to produce a pop video then maybe there they need to comment on how in a sense they might have done it better to have made it a pop video.

LOUISE: That seems to be the implication. They've left that comment as if therefore it's a good thing isn't it . . . because they then go on to say in fact we were advised that it shouldn't have such a complicated narrative.

Of course, Mary and Louise are attempting to reconstruct the teacher's original motivations on the basis of the students' comments about 'what they were told to do'. Nevertheless, it would seem that honesty is not the best policy here. Admitting that you were unable – or simply failed – to follow the teacher's 'advice' is effectively admitting to failure. There is a sense here in which simple either/or choices have to be made: either it is a pop video or it is a short film – and, according to Mary, it is simply 'better' to do what teacher wants. Rather than judging what the students have produced on its own terms, it is judged in terms of what it is not – a kind of idealised text which the teacher has imagined.

In this group, the teachers hedged their bets for some time before arriving at a grade. As in most such discussions, they were unwilling to step out of a consensual line. Mary's initial C/D is gradually pushed upwards, but there is a distinct reluctance to go much higher:

CHARLES: So what are we looking at?

MARY: How do we mark it? [sighs: long silence]

CHARLES: I think in terms of a lowish B . . .

LOUISE: I thought another weakness in the report was not saying much about audience. I thought they were quite good on forms and conventions . . . I'll go for a B – based on guesswork!

MARY: I think I'm being much harsher than all of you lot 'cause I just think in many respects, mostly because of their commentary, they ended up doing themselves a disservice because I watched again in much the same way as they said here. I thought, 'this is looking like a little film, it's not looking like a pop video' . . . but because I was kind of confused by the story I stopped being entertained, because I just wanted to know what the hell was going on. And then their commentary tries to – I mean, I can see that they ought to be rewarded for the fact that they had good intentions and they knew what they were aiming at, but I'm not sure how successful they were.

LOUISE: I think that would prevent it from being an A in that it's not very clear and it doesn't link up and it doesn't have quite enough impact, but I still think technically it's good enough to be rewarded. I might give a C for the report though. I don't think the report even on its own terms in comparison with the video isn't as good. I could imagine a better report than this.

MARY: But then I wonder if that's because we're used to reading English, you know what I mean, it seems to me there's lots more they could have come out with . . . B with C inclinations.

The way in which these teachers privilege the written commentary is, in our experience, typical of the assessment of students' media production work. The commentary becomes the lens through which the video is viewed: ultimately, it alone provides the evidence of whether the students are sufficiently analytical and clear in their intentions. Aside from the 'technical' aspects, the only learning that counts is the learning that is *demonstrated* in the form of discursive writing. The video itself only counts as a measure of the students' failure to do what they claim to have done – at least in the eyes of the examiner.

Mary's final comment is particularly revealing in this respect. As we have noted, the majority of Media Studies teachers are initially trained as teachers of English; and the criteria that are invoked here are drawn from the model of the 'literary critical' essay. There is a great deal that might be said about the textual fixation of this practice, and the implicit belief that meaning – and indeed cultural value – are somehow inherent in the text, awaiting recovery by the truly sensitive critic. The key question here, however, is whether this is appropriate in the case of students' writing about media production – where they are effectively required to apply the analytical skills they have been taught in relation to other texts to their *own* creations. There are assumptions here about how 'theoretical' understandings might *transfer* to 'practical' activities which are in need of much more sustained investigation.

Finally, there is a striking contrast here between the confidence with which the students' work is judged and the seemingly 'intuitive' teacherly tone in which the grades are ultimately identified. The teachers have few reservations about privileging their own readings of the production in preference to those of the students themselves; and they persistently compare it to an 'idealised' or pre-given model of what the text *should* be. There is a degree of power here which they can collectively agree to share. Yet it is in the actual awarding of the grade (a lowish B? a B with C inclinations?) that the consensus – established early in this discussion – is in danger of being disturbed.

To sum up, then, there are several discourses and sets of assumptions that are brought into play here. On the one hand, there are *aesthetic* judgements, for example in the comments about the 'clever ideas' or the 'well constructed' editing. These overlap to some extent with 'technical' considerations, which are partly about 'technique' and partly about how effectively the available equipment has been used. Finally, there are the broadly *theoretical* and indeed *political* concerns of Media Studies, which are most apparent in the teachers' use of the commentary and their references to notions of audience, narrative and genre.

In this case, the former considerations are clearly subordinated to the latter; although in our experience they can often conflict much more directly. Thus, we have encountered teachers and examiners who are suspicious of what they perceive as more aesthetically pleasing and technically accomplished work, tending to mark it down because of an apparent lack of theoretical rigour. In a different group discussion, one teacher awarded a C to this video on the grounds that it did not 'challenge the mainstream' – although quite what the 'mainstream' might be in this context is (in our view) increasingly difficult to identify. Pop video seems particularly problematic for examiners in this respect. In this case, the students are criticised for breaking the conventions of pop video by not featuring a band; yet we have also seen examiners' reports which attack pop video work which features the students acting as the band on the grounds that it is merely 'self-indulgent'.

Students' perspectives

In an attempt to discover whether similar criteria were in play for students, the video was shown to several members of the A-level group, including one of the pair of students who made it (Alison). Like the teachers, they were then asked to discuss how they would grade the production, using the assessment criteria provided in the syllabus.

Similar questions about the technical constraints and the relationship with 'real' music videos were quickly raised:

PAUL: Well I was just saying that Alison's one, I don't think [it] would be an A because it's not a pop video.

ALISON: Well they're not judging it for that though.

PAUL: Well they should.

ANNA: Yeah but she wrote in her thing how they deliberately tried to avoid the conventions of pop video.

ALISON: I mean it says if you look at number two here [from the Syllabus criteria], it's got all the formal aspects of film production and awareness of mise-en-scene and whatever.

PAUL: Yeah that was good. I mean it's a good film but –

ALISON: I mean you could say it was going against the conventions of pop videos because that's what we did say.

PAUL: Yeah, but the point is you just *don't* go against them.

ANNA: But how do you define a pop video? It's pop music with a video so it must be a pop video.

ALISON: I mean it's not actually obligatory that you have to have the group in the video.

PAUL: No, that's okay.

ALISON: And that's what we didn't do.

CHRIS: But when you put it alongside other ones it's very different.

ALISON: Yeah, but I was saying though . . . that if you actually take it apart the only thing you can find is that it just hasn't got the group in the video but instead it's got a very strong narrative.

Paul's assertion that the production should be judged on how well it conforms to the conventions of the genre provokes an interesting exchange about the criteria for assessment. The implicit assumption, discussed above, that student production should challenge 'mainstream' or 'dominant' forms – and therefore their 'ideology' – rather than merely imitating them, is thrown into question here. Alison attempts to rationalise the technical limitations of her situation (the lack of a real band) by arguing that her failure to observe the conventions was in itself a challenge to those conventions; although she also justifies her work as a 'film' in terms drawn from the syllabus criteria. As the discussion proceeds, it becomes more difficult to define precisely what is the 'dominant'

generic form to which the students should (or should not) be adhering.
Similar problems arose in attempting to define the ideological content or
'message' of the video:

ANNA: Did yours have a deep hidden message in? Or was it just supposed to
be sort of fun?

ALISON: No. Ours had a deep hidden message in . . . it was about the changing role of women and men sort of thing and doing it from a female
point of view.

ANNA: So yours did have a deep hidden message?

ALISON: Yeah, no longer having a male protagonist and all this phallocentrism and stuff.

ANNA: What about all those shots of Laura's bust though?

ALISON: Yeah I know that's where the key goes down, that's because he was
completely absorbed, yeah? Like he thinks this woman is a sex goddess
and he keeps seeing her appear all over the place and you think well 'how
come he hasn't got her in his life?' sort of thing. Then you realise it was a
dentist and all that time it was his imagination. I mean that whole thing is
a drama with the key, 'cause he wakes up or whatever. I mean, it's just
like the way he perceives her and he's completely scared of her 'cause he
thinks – how am I going to get out of this room? I've got to get the key
from down her bust – oh no! oh no! sort of thing. That's why.

ANNA: So men are afraid to be in touch with their sexual feeling.

ALISON: [laughs] It was just reversing roles, 'cause in most videos all you get
is just the female sort of prancing around and she lands up sort of
snogging the lead singer at the end you know.

There is a considerable degree of irony here, which serves several purposes.
On one level, the girls are disclaiming the 'serious student' identity that is
potentially available here: their mocking references to 'deep hidden messages' at the start of this extract, or the laughter that surrounds Anna's
assertion that 'men are afraid to be in touch with their sexual feeling',
suggest that they are unwilling to represent the production as a serious
statement about gender roles. Yet at the same time, Alison clearly does want
to claim that the video is more than just a promo: she presents it as an
authored text with a serious feminist purpose, and goes to considerable
lengths to refute the suggestion that the 'shots of Laura's bust' can be seen to
undermine this.

Alison's comment about 'all this phallocentrism and stuff' is particularly
interesting in this respect. The term 'phallocentrism' (unlike, say, 'reversing
roles') clearly derives from a particular academic discourse – in this case,
probably from the work of Laura Mulvey and other feminist film theorists
whose work had been introduced to the students earlier in the year. Yet the
offhand addition 'and stuff' reflects a kind of embarrassment at deploying
this academic discourse – and the 'serious student' role that accompanies it –

in this more informal context (in discussion with peers). Yet, on the other hand, presenting one's work as a critique of 'phallocentrism' clearly represents a legitimate, academically respectable justification for what one might otherwise describe as just a lot better than watching females 'prancing around' and 'snogging the lead singer'.

Either way, however, such a possibility was largely missed by the teachers who examined this video, for whom the presence of 'Laura's bust' was enough to condemn the tape to ideological disgrace. In our experience, even this limited degree of subtlety or ambiguity often seems to be ignored by teachers. Despite the heavy premium on questioning images of gender in Media Studies, it seems that such questioning has to be extremely literal if it is to be rewarded. Thus, a typical assignment in which students are required to produce contrasting 'positive' and 'negative' images of women is frequently valued more highly, because it appears to spell out an explicit political position of which the teacher can approve. When, as in this case, students claim to be questioning gender roles in the context of a text without such an explicit purpose, it is almost as if it is too subtle – or at least insufficiently *demonstrated* – for the teacher to see.

At the same time, however, the students recognise that such representations are *bound* to be ambiguous, and can be read in diverse ways:

PAUL: You get the hard-to-get [woman] as well, that's another stereotype.
ALISON: Yeah, oh yeah.
ANNA: I didn't feel it was a stereotype.
PAUL: I thought she might be a figment of imagination.
ALISON: Well, that is what she is for most of it, and then it turns out that he's just been dreaming about this woman who's actually his dentist.
CHRIS: Well I thought the dentist was part of the dream as well.
ALISON: Ahhh! Well it's obviously open to loads of interpretations. So MTV would actually play it so many times that the viewers would finally grasp what it was about – except they wouldn't!

As Alison recognises, a crucial feature of pop videos is that they are designed to be seen more than once. On one level, this potentially offers rewards for the viewer who misses 'deep hidden meanings' first time around; although, on another level, videos could be seen to require a level of ambiguity if repeat viewing is to be at all tolerable. As academic analyses of the form have shown, the use of pastiche and parody in pop videos makes them almost impossible to pin down ideologically: they defy many of the objectivist analytical strategies of film theory, from ideas about realism and narrative to notions of 'the look' (e.g. Goodwin 1992; Kaplan 1987). Similar problems are bound to apply to assessing pop videos produced by students:

ANNA: Do I detect a lack of distance in judging these media products? I still haven't read these criteria.

ALISON: Well, basically they just have the same criteria except they put better as they go up the scale . . . a better understanding . . . an even better
understanding.

ANNA: I think what you really want is these five things . . . formal aspects,
representation . . .

ALISON: I mean 'cause part of the idea of having very good skills is understanding the form of something is by changing it and challenging it. You
know, you actually get marks for challenging the genre or something.

ANNA: So you should put you're challenging genre in it. 'We challenged the
idea that men always have to lip synch in their videos thus attacking the
dominant ideology' [laughter].

On one level, the students here are simply sending up the discursive 'rules of
the game', both those which relate to the activity of 'trial marking' and those
of Media Studies more broadly. They are able to identify the vagueness of
the mark scheme, and to detect its 'hidden agenda' – 'marks for challenging' –
and to identify ways in which they might use the written commentary for the
purposes of a kind of ideological impression management. There is an
explicit acknowledgement here that 'theory' is just another discourse that
can be manipulated to your own advantage.

In attempting to assess their own and each other's productions, these students therefore use a range of potentially contradictory discourses or sets of
criteria. On the most immediate level, there is an *aesthetic* discourse – a
discourse of personal taste – which includes comments on the quality of the
acting as well as the look of the finished video ('it was a good film'). Beyond
this, there is a *theoretical* discourse, in which they use specialist academic
terminology to support their assertions, however inappropriately ('all this
phallocentrism and stuff'). This is in turn related to an *ideological* discourse,
in which notions of being challenging, innovative and 'politically correct' are
prominent ('it was just reversing roles'). There is a *self-evaluative* discourse, in
which students attempt to reconstruct their own motives and assess them in
the light of audience responses ('it's obviously open to loads of interpretations'), as well as technical constraints. Finally, there is a potential conflict
between *professional* and *pedagogic* discourses, in which the text is compared
with pre-existing models – and which in this case leads to the debate about
whether the production is or is not a pop video.

As this example shows, these discourses can come into conflict, or be
combined, sometimes in unpredictable ways. Thus, for example, some of
these discourses place a premium on *originality* – whether on aesthetic or
political grounds – while others seem to emphasise the need for *conformity* to
pre-existing aesthetic or professional models or standards. Perhaps most dis-
turbingly for some media teachers, these students show a highly self-
conscious awareness of the educational *and* political games they are being
asked to play.

This discussion took place several months after the event of the production itself, and indeed of the formal assessment of the work. This may in itself account for its fairly relaxed, and occasionally ironic, tone. Nevertheless, and for all the game-playing and jockeying for position that goes on, we would argue that this kind of self-evaluation should be seen as a crucial dimension of learning in media education. While there is certainly a value in doing this in written form, there is a qualitative difference when it comes to engaging in a dialogue of this kind with one's peers. In this instance, Alison is effectively forced to articulate her aims and to argue with others' interpretations of the results. Presenting one's work to a real audience and having to reflect upon the interpretations of that audience will not necessarily make the work 'better', but it might help students to think more clearly and critically about the relationships between intentions and outcomes.

Some conclusions

We suspect that much of what we have identified here will be very familiar for experienced Media Studies teachers. Yet it will probably seem quite strange for most other readers – particularly those whose backgrounds are in creative arts subjects. The reasons for this largely derive from the distinctive aims and status of student production in Media Studies. Of course, media production could be seen to have a whole range of potential aims – from the relatively instrumental ones of developing technical or communication skills through to the more grandiose cultural aims of some arts educators. Yet as we have shown, the central aim of production in the context of Media Studies is defined in terms of its contribution to developing students' *conceptual* understandings – and it is predominantly in these terms that it is assessed.

Yet even if we accept this primary aim – and it is, in some respects, a peculiarly limited one – there remains a continuing problem in identifying *evidence* of students' understanding. The production itself is obviously one major form of evidence, although (as we have implied) it is not always easy to read in its own right. It is often difficult to 'read past' the inevitable technical limitations of student productions, or to infer their authorial intentions. We must inevitably make all sorts of assumptions about the students' experiences and understandings of the genres and formal conventions they appear to be using; about their perceptions of the nature of the audience; and about their interpretations of the assignment itself. As we have suggested, these assumptions can often be mistaken; and our expectations of the *kind* of learning that students might reasonably achieve are often quite unrealistic.

So what are the implications of our arguments in terms of future practice in Media Studies teaching? We would like to put forward some fairly blunt and polemical conclusions here, in three main areas. First, we would argue that there is a need to rethink the kinds of production assignments that teachers set. Student production in Media Studies should be *more* than just a 'critical' act, or a means of displaying pre-determined theoretical positions.

We do not believe that the best way of developing students' conceptual understanding of the media lies in requiring them to produce 'radical' or 'oppositional' texts – even assuming that we could agree about what those might be. They will learn a great deal more from reworking forms with which they have greater familiarity and a personal engagement already. They also need a *regular* and *frequent* engagement with production throughout the course, in addition to the limited number of 'one-off' assessed productions that are required by most Media Studies syllabuses. Students need to be given opportunities to experiment with the technology in less constrained ways, to revise and 'redraft' their work, and to learn from their own mistakes, without the requirement for such work to be assessed. This in turn suggests that we need to pay closer attention to teaching and refining skills connected with the use of the technology, rather than regarding these as marginal.

Second, we need to be much more explicit about the criteria we are using in assessment, and ensure that these are fully understood by students themselves. Elaborate checklists of the kind developed by Chris Worsnop (1996) could be seen as unduly bureaucratic and mechanical, but they have the significant virtue of openness and clarity. While it was intended primarily as a form of research, the kind of 'trial marking' conducted by the students here might prove to be of more general value in this respect, insofar as it makes the criteria much more explicit. Beyond this, however, we need to find more active and positive ways of engaging with what students actually produce and how they then account for their work, rather than assessing them in terms of what we might prefer them to produce. Above all, we need to avoid reducing assessment to simply a matter of detecting evidence of theoretical understanding. In this respect, the more process-based mark schemes that are used by some examination boards (such as those recently developed by Cambridge) do begin to provide ways of valuing a much broader range of learning outcomes. Such forms of assessment give teachers and students the responsibility for providing evidence in support of their grades, rather than relying on external moderators' assessments of the finished products.

Third, we need to develop more innovative approaches to self-evaluation, that go beyond the limitations of the discursive written essay. In particular, we need to find ways of *motivating* self-evaluation – that is, giving it a function and a purpose beyond that of simply writing for the examiner. Jenny Grahame (1991: 103) provides some interesting possibilities here, for example using forms of oral and visual presentation, role-playing, group presentations, and so on. One of the most significant problems here is that the large majority of student production never finds an audience beyond the immediate peer group and the teacher/examiner. Presenting work to a real audience, and taking account of the responses of that audience, may encourage more spontaneous and self-critical form of reflection, that can in turn feed into the formal self-evaluation that is presented for the purposes of assessment.

Notes

1 In this chapter, our primary emphasis is on Media *Studies* – that is, the specialist subject courses that are provided in the upper years of secondary schooling (and in further education) in the UK. We use the more general term 'media *education*' to refer to teaching about the media wherever it occurs in the curriculum. There are of course many forms of media production that take place outside specialist Media Studies courses – for example, in vocational training courses and in other curriculum areas such as English and Art; although these are beyond the scope of this chapter. (A brief overview of these approaches can be found in Buckingham 1992; and an historical account in Sefton-Green 1995.)

2 Like other contributors, we are making a distinction in this chapter between evaluation and assessment. We take *assessment* to refer to the process whereby teachers make comparative judgements about students' achievements in relation to external norms or criteria. It almost invariably involves the allocation of grades or marks. By contrast, *evaluation* focuses more broadly on the relationship between intentions and outcomes. Both for teachers and for students, this is likely to involve an element of *self*-evaluation – a process which we would regard as a crucial means of forging connections between 'theory' and 'practice' in media education. While evaluation often accompanies assessment, it should not be reduced to it. Indeed, as we imply, the two processes may in some respects prove incompatible.

3 The approach we are using here is drawn from methods of discourse analysis developed within social psychology. See, for example, Potter and Wetherell (1987).

References

Alvarado, M. and Boyd-Barrett, O. (eds) (1992) *Media Education: An Introduction*, London: British Film Institute and The Open University.

Alvarado, M., Gutch, R. and Wollen, T. (1987) *Learning the Media: An Introduction to Media Teaching*, London: Macmillan.

Bates, I., Clarke, C., Cohen, P., Finn, D., Moore, R. and Willis, P. (1984) *Schooling for the Dole: The New Vocationalism*, London: Macmillan.

Bazalgette, C. (1992) 'The politics of media education' in Alvarado, M. and Boyd-Barrett, O. (eds) (1992) *Media Education: An Introduction*, London: British Film Institute and The Open University.

Buckingham, D. (ed.) (1990) *Watching Media Learning: Making Sense of Media Education*, London: Falmer Press.

Buckingham, D. (1992) 'Practical work' in Alvarado, M. and Boyd-Barrett, O. (eds) *Media Education: An Introduction*, London: British Film Institute and The Open University.

Buckingham, D. (ed.) (1998) *Teaching Popular Culture: Beyond Radical Pedagogy*, London: UCL Press.

Buckingham, D. and Sefton-Green, J. (1994) *Cultural Studies goes to School: Reading and Teaching Popular Media*, London: Taylor and Francis.

Buckingham, D., Grahame, J. and Sefton-Green, J. (1995) *Making Media: Practical Production in Media Education*, London: The English and Media Centre.

Clarke, M. (1987) *Teaching Popular Television*, London: Heinemann Educational Books.

Dewdney, A. and Lister, M. (1988) *Youth, Culture and Photography*, London: Macmillan.

Ferguson, R. (1981) 'Practical work and pedagogy', *Screen Education* 38, pp. 42–55.

Goodwin, A. (1992) *Dancing in the Distraction Factory*, London: Routledge.

Grahame, J. (1990) 'Playtime; learning about media institutions through practical work' in Buckingham, D. (ed.) *Watching Media Learning: Making Sense of Media Education*, London: Falmer Press.

Grahame, J. (1991) 'The production process' in Lusted, D. (ed.) *The Media Studies Book: A Guide for Teachers*, London: Routledge.

Grahame, J. (1994) *Production Practices*, London: English and Media Centre.

Kaplan, E. (1987) *Rocking Around the Clock: Music Television, Postmodernism and Consumer Culture*, London: Methuen.

Masterman, L. (1980) *Teaching About Television*, London: Macmillan.

Masterman, L. (1985) *Teaching the Media*, London: Comedia.

Leavis, F. and Thompson, D. (1933) *Culture and Environment*, London: Chatto and Windus.

Potter, J. and Wetherell, M. (1987) *Discourse and Social Psychology: Beyond Attitudes and Behaviour*, London: Sage.

Richmond, J. (1990) 'What do we mean by knowledge about language?' in Carter, R. (ed.) *Knowledge about Language and the Curriculum: The LINC Reader*, London: Hodder and Stoughton.

Sefton-Green, J. (1995) 'Neither "reading" nor "writing": the history of practical work in media education', *Changing English* vol. 2, no. 2, pp. 77–96.

Vygotsky, L. (1962) *Thought and Language* (trans. Hanfmann, E. and Vakar, G.), Cambridge: MIT Press.

Worsnop, C. (1996) *Assessing Media Work: Authentic Assessment in Media Education*, Mississauga Ontario: Wright Communications.

8   Whose art is it anyway?

Art education outside the classroom

A discussion between Roz Hall,
Steve Herne and Alistair Raphael,
chaired and edited by Rebecca Sinker

For this chapter I invited a small group of artists and educators to discuss their different experiences in formal, gallery and community arts education and artists' residencies, because as I shall outline below, these sectors challenge a number of conventions about the purpose of young people's creative production. As a debate, the discussion highlights differences in approach and expectation between these cultural sectors and schools, throwing up points of controversy; but it also identifies areas of shared practice. The conversational format reflects the dialogic and occasionally argumentative nature of the processes of making and evaluation, of making judgements and expressing opinions, and raises questions about these processes as they occur in different contexts. I have edited the participants' contributions and included some of their retrospective comments on the transcripts.

Education in the arts has existed in a number of forms outside the formal system, from the extra curricular activities of the drama club and junior orchestras, to the cultural initiatives of arts and community centres, or to the education programmes of museums and galleries. Young people might experience creative production in any of these sectors as well as privately at home. Unlike other areas of the curriculum, the arts (particularly visual and performing) are distinctive in the way that professional practitioners in these disciplines are regularly invited to work within schools, and this is generally recognised as an important part of pupils' understanding of the subject. Though not unknown, the incidence of doctors or chemists working in residence in the science department, or archaeologists in history is almost certainly less prevalent. One reason for this may be the work commitments of these professionals who are more likely to have full-time careers, whereas artists or musicians tend to have more flexible working arrangements. Another is that artists will often become involved in education work as a way of financially supporting their practice, which is not to say that they don't feel challenged by and committed to this kind of work, but that other professions might have less of an economic motive. But perhaps a more significant reason, is that the pedagogy of non-arts subjects does not tend to view experience of professional practices as central to a full understanding of the subject. Geography education does not stipulate that students work with a meteorologist in order to understand weather systems, although they may have the opportunity to visit a weather station or even watch storm-tracking satellites on the internet. While the National Curriculum document for Art does not state that young people *must* be given the opportunity to work with artists, several art educators, for instance Binch and Kennedy (1994b: 25), have noted that Attainment Target 2 has impelled teachers to extend pupils' experiences of art into contexts beyond the school. These contexts are described separately below but in many cases they are directly related, having emerged out of a common history.

The artist in residence

The artist who visits, or is resident in a school, is there *as an artist* and not as a supply teacher. His or her role is to stimulate interest in, and provide insights into, the particular areas of work in which he or she is expert.

(Gulbenkian 1982: 121)

Most artist's workshops or residencies are collaborations between the school, the artist and a funding body or art organisation. All the publications which advocate artists working in schools (see Binch and Clive 1994; Binch and Kennedy 1994; Binch and Robertson 1994; Dahl 1990; Gulbenkian 1982; Sharp and Dust 1997) stress that these relationships should be negotiated partnerships. Most young people will only know of artists through their work, from books or videos or perhaps gallery visits. The aim of the residency is to provide the opportunity to meet and work with professional artists, thus giving direct contact with their work, affording an insight into their working practices and possibly enabling the young people to produce new work in a collaborative project. The teacher can contribute pedagogic skills and an understanding of the curriculum, as well as detailed knowledge of the individual students. In this relationship the teacher is to some extent the 'broker', preparing the students for the visit as well as helping the artist to work in the school environment. But it is an important professional development opportunity and the artist may well be involved in some form of INSET in addition to working with the pupils and pursuing their own practice.

The gallery

If you look at a work of art in a gallery or a studio you can begin to look for clues, look for evidence that justifies the very act of making that we are asking our students to do.

(Kennedy in Binch and Kennedy 1994: 11)

The gallery is a space designated for the exhibition and often collection of art work – a secular shrine to the visual. A modern invention which largely grew out of the social and political ideas of the nineteenth century coupled with the rise of the middle class, the social role of galleries was as a place of learning: visitors came to see and value the objects on display, to 'appreciate' the art. But this notion of art appreciation is easily used as a disguise for taste, marking out those who don't share approved aesthetic values from those who are ignorant of 'quality' culture. With the rise of popular culture and the leisure industries, going to galleries has became an increasingly marginal activity and pressure has increased on these publicly funded organisations to become more accessible to a broader audience and to represent more culturally diverse perspectives. One result of these changes has been the development of education programmes in galleries. Another is the diversification of arts opportunities to cater for minority groups and the emergence in special interest, community initiatives such as Black Arts, Disability Arts and Youth Arts. In gallery education, the chosen term to promote the public understanding of art became 'interpretation', which implied more flexibility in the construction of meaning, suggesting a dialogue between the maker and viewer. Interpretation aims to encourage debate not only into the meaning of an individual piece of art but also the context of that work's production and exhibition.

Community arts

> If community arts is anything, it is the manifestation of an ideology . . . all community artists shared a dislike of cultural hierarchies, believed in co-authorship of work and in the creative potential of all sections of societies . . . For many the aim was to produce cultural change, to change society's attitude to art and to artists.
>
> (Morgan in Dickson 1995: 18)

The term community arts has its roots in the cultural and political movements of the late 1960s and early 1970s, which sought to challenge the view of art as an elite pursuit and to promote its social relevance as an agent of communication, cohesion, expression and education, as well as dissent or change. Very often run as co-operatives, community arts organisations had a high number of volunteer staff and usually involved their key constituency in the decision-making processes. The notion of arts in the community was built on left-wing ideals of social inclusion, local provision, access for all and multiculturalism, and was, at least in part, a response and an alternative to an art establishment which was largely white, adult, male and middle class. Community arts were also seen as a challenge to an education system, which was judged to replicate or even instigate social and cultural hierarchies, disenfranchising sections of the community and closing off their opportunities for creative production. Among other things, community arts centres set up initiatives aimed at giving young people the opportunity to express themselves through creative arts practice, particularly in urban areas of poverty and deprivation:

> When it comes to (arts) centres' educational roles some are actually achieving what education is not able to accomplish, particularly in the aesthetic, cultural and social spheres, for those alienated by formal structures and for others to whom these are not agreeable.
>
> (McDonald 1987: 11)

Unlike formal education which has a 'captive' audience, creative work in community arts settings is often piecemeal because it is dependent on periodic or one-off funding and is usually undertaken on a project-by-project basis. Similarly, gallery education has a transient audience and has traditionally been tied to education events, coinciding with the exhibition programme. In addition, organisations are more or less required to work with a changing constituency, for reasons of equal access and in the name of audience development. This makes long-term process-based work more difficult, unless of course such work can be defined as forms of 'training', in which case it becomes the subject of vocational criteria and can attract other sources of funding.

Defining the work of these organisations thus raises the spectre of evaluation, without which, none of these informal institutions have the possibility of developing coherent education programmes because they cannot describe themselves as meeting 'educational' criteria. But evaluating educational programmes merely serves to raise further questions. For example, who does the evaluation and for whom is often related to the question of funding; and dependence on educational funders can easily supersede the needs of a non-paying audience. Most galleries and arts organisations now have education officers: indeed almost all funding seems to be dependent on an 'educational' element and the cynical might suggest that some education programmes are only there to bring money into the institution. What is undoubtedly true is that most education officers are not as well paid as their curatorial colleagues and that education projects rarely get equal billing with the main programme, nor do they carry the kudos of working with well-known artists. Even while the most innovative work of an arts organisation may be initiated under the auspices of the education department, its perceived lower status is often related to issues of quality, specifically the way that the products of such work are judged in relation to professional work. Many people committed to working in this sector would argue that this is largely related to limited production funding. With the increasing use of digital arts technologies and particularly web-based projects, it is suggested that the lines between professional and amateur are blurring and the curatorial 'quality' control of the physical gallery space is being bypassed, enabling a new generation of artists to reach new audiences.

The participants

ALISTAIR RAPHAEL: I am a practising artist and educationalist. I studied Fine Art at Falmouth School of Art and later at Chelsea College of Art and Design, graduating with an MA in 1989. Since then I've consistently worked in the independent visual arts sector and within higher education, as an artist. I have contributed to the education programmes of some of the larger art galleries in London, including the Whitechapel, the Hayward and the Barbican and worked for about three years as the education officer at Photofusion Photography Centre in South London. I've taught part-time and as a visiting lecturer on various Fine Art courses including Winchester School of Art, Northampton Institute and London Guildhall. Currently, I contribute to the Education and Research programmes at The Institute of International Visual Art (inIVA) and I'm also an advisor to the Education Unit at the Visual Arts department of the Arts Council. Most of my recent art practice was made to commission for public art galleries – mainly photographic, sculptural and large-scale.

ROZ HALL: I have a background in photography, and as a practitioner I've used photography, digital imaging and multimedia. Since I graduated from the Polytechnic of Central London, a lot of the work I've been involved in, alongside my own practice, has been with young people and photography or digital imaging. That's been in a range of contexts outside formal education, starting off working informally from such places as Barton Hill Photography Project – a community darkroom project in Bristol – and then working with young people who were excluded, for whatever reasons, from mainstream education, within Stage 5 Centres, or residential schools for young people with emotional and behavioural problems. I spent four years at Watershed Media Centre, where I co-ordinated the part-time photography and digital imaging courses and programmed the community-based project work in photography and digital imaging. I'm now at Jubilee Arts in the West Midlands and the University of Central England, on a three-year research project into young people's creative uses of digital technology outside formal education. The main focus of this research is how young people's informal creative uses of this technology could inform the development of practice both within and outside formal education.

STEVE HERNE: I trained as a visual artist, as a painter and a print-maker, and then became a secondary school art teacher. Actually my first job was in charge of a light-and-sound room, where I dealt with early video and photography – it was black-and-white video in those days. So I've taught in secondary art departments for a long time, and part of that time I taught photography. More recently, I was a local authority adviser in

Tower Hamlets and I also act as an art inspector. I've also been a project co-ordinator and an education adviser for the London Arts Board, so I do assessment work there. I've been involved in one or two curriculum development projects connected with media arts. I wrote a chapter about assessment in my M.Phil. and I'm currently a lecturer in art and teacher education at Goldsmith's University. In addition I'm developing a website with the London Association of Art and Design Education (LAADE).

The discussion

Assessment and evaluation

Ideas of evaluation and assessment would appear to mean different things to different people in different contexts. Within the broad area of arts in education there are a range of entwined cultures: the cultures of art (incorporating visual arts, craft and design), education and schooling. Each have aims and agendas which may or may not match and so the criteria for assessment and the elements deemed 'of value' are likely to vary depending on who is evaluating what, why and for whom. In any case, it is vital to be transparent about these things to avoid confusion (see Binch and Robertson 1994: 110). Is it simply that we assess a piece of work and evaluate a practice or are there accents and nuances, through formative and summative approaches, which determine which term we use? People have warned against an assessment-led National Curriculum for Art (Hughes 1998, Steers 1994) which values a formula approach to making a finished product above an exploratory process through which work in a range of media might evolve. Such an approach might also be at odds with the way many artists explore ideas and impede an understanding of how they are making evaluative decisions in and through their work. But outside formal education there are similar pitfalls, where the demands of institutional accountability might overshadow the individual experiences of the participants involved in creative production. So how do we define these terms, how flexible should they be and what form do they take in practice?

STEVE: From an educational point of view, there's a very clear body of writing connected to the National Curriculum in relation to assessment. There's the TGAT Report [TGAT 1987] which came out just before the National Curriculum, setting up the whole system and defining different kinds of assessment for schools: terms like *formative* assessment, *summative* assessment, *evaluative* assessment. So, for any debate about assessment in formal education these definitions are the ones used. I'm not sure there have to be *fixed* criteria, and within education, formative assessment is a day-to-day interaction taking place in any situation, wherever teaching occurs. I would say it's largely intuitive and perhaps unconscious. I get the feeling from some of what's been said that 'assessment' is a dirty word, associated with formal education and the product as opposed to the process – but some elements of assessment are natural parts of interaction in teaching.

REBECCA: But you call this *assessment*, as opposed to evaluation?

STEVE: Yes. Within the educational community there are documents shared by everyone where *assessment* is very much the word used. I suppose to me, assessment is to do with making judgements about how children are doing. *Ipsitive* assessment, for example, is assessment in terms of the child's own previous level and where they are going, while *negotiated* assessment is based on the criteria which evolve between the teacher and the child through ongoing conversations. So the criteria needn't be external. To me, evaluation is much more qualitative, to do with values – whether something is good or not in a more general sense. Within the TGAT Report, there's a sense that you *start* with formative assessment and proceed to summative assessment, to sum up at the end of a unit of work, often related to giving grades or marks. To me, assessment is to do with individual children and making judgements, but it needn't be formal, or measured in terms of external criteria. And evaluation is more open and qualitative.

ROZ: For me, evaluating something is very much about identifying its value, which does imply a subjectivity process, because something might have value for one person and not another – value isn't necessarily fixed. That's why I think the idea and the term, evaluation, implies that it (the process) is part of something bigger: there is a reason for doing it in terms of building upon a certain experience and developing a practice. The criteria for such evaluation are determining factors in the effect or impact of such a process. If these criteria are constructed less through discussion with the producers of what's being evaluated and more aligned with values *imposed upon* those producers, then that's closer to what I think of as assessment. I identify assessment with something being perceived as *successful* or not, which is quite different from thinking in terms of value. Success necessitates certain clear criteria by which you measure something, perhaps criteria defined by the dominant cultural discourse. So for me, evaluation implies the possibility of using a variety of criteria, which could be negotiated between the different partners in any creative process.

ALISTAIR: When I began to look at evaluation and assessment in preparation for this discussion, I became aware that I'd never really *examined* them before, either specifically in terms of what I do, or in relation to formal ideas of education. For me, evaluation and assessment are both inherent parts of *making*. To have a set of criteria for evaluation, set up by another body, an external structure that encases your practice or sets up a dialogue with and about your practice, is quite a complex set of relationships. And because the meanings or readings of an artwork are fluid and changing, I find the notion of somebody 'making an assessment' of it problematic. Also, the value judgements a person holds may change as they go through primary and secondary school, and certainly beyond the life of the school. I feel it might be potentially detrimental to *fix* this at school, so that young people go off with a static set of value judgements about looking at things without any idea of how these can and do change.

Establishing criteria for evaluation

If a shared understanding of the criteria for evaluation is required, who decides that criteria? Is it dependent on a shared notion of 'quality' and a common set of values? Are these value systems those of a dominant culture and what happens when people feel excluded from that? Who is work made for – the maker, the teacher, the examiner, the artist in residence or a wider audience, and might this predetermine the kind of work produced?

STEVE: Alistair, you said that if judgements of our children are made externally, then they will take those judgements, those views with them when they leave school – and you're questioning the validity of the judgements made in that school context?

ALISTAIR: Not just their validity but their fixity – and their authority. You have these very different experiences of something that is so subjective, so particular and potentially so personal. In some ways this system seems almost contradictory to the nature of making.

STEVE: I'd argue that in a good art department, the kind of formative assessment that happens can be a good model. A lot of assumptions are made about formal assessment in schools and how it is based on external criteria.

ALISTAIR: I suppose my response is fuelled by exasperation, having worked in secondary schools, where value judgements are placed on what is made by young people and how it's made, without those young people having the chance to question those values or that process.

ROZ: My work is usually outside formal education but some of my experiences endorse what you're saying, Alistair, relating to young people's involvement with creative processes after they've left school, as well as outside of school, before they've left. More than once, I noticed these young people specifically directed their work to fulfil what they see as a pre-determined agenda, even though I haven't given them one. When I was working with a group in the Internet Café, one girl made her piece of work around issues of identity and communication of your own identity, because those were the types of issues that we were initially talking about (see Figure 8.1). It could be argued that the discussion had initiated a thought process which made her consider these issues. But I really felt that she was actually trying to fulfil an agenda which she saw me as having determined, even though I hadn't specified any agenda or brief for the work.

STEVE: But isn't that one approach to learning anyway? In a social situation where young people are learning, they're searching for a pattern or format to copy?

ROZ: It's an approach yes, but at the same time perhaps it undermined her ability to explore the potential of the media in any number of other ways. What is problematic for me about a formal assessment structure is that it often proves a barrier for new ideas and restricts opportunities for exploration of a creative process.

STEVE: In my experience formal assessment doesn't really happen until right at the end, when the students put up an exhibition.

Figure 8.1 Annabella Moore/Anita Kaushik. Café Surf Workshops

ROZ: Yes, but there's the anticipation of it.

ALISTAIR: I think Steve's point about that being one way of learning is a really good one. But one has to look at the different audiences inside and outside school and who the work is being made for. Kids make some work that may not be seen by anybody, or only by their peers. They also do things that will not only be seen within the public environment of school, but beyond that, by adults and by 'others' – that is by people of a different age group, and quite possibly another class, or race. So you will get a range of assumptions, expectations and aspirations there. This happens with adults as well. I spent the morning with a group of architects and I found myself presuming what *they might want* from this potential commission, instead of starting from my own practice. I think we all do that to some extent.

Making judgements

How do we arrive at judgements? Is this process something we want young people to achieve through conveying ideas about art and art practice? If so, can we teach this, without an established framework or criteria for making critical decisions? Is there room for shades of opinion or dissent? How do self-evaluation and reflective practice figure in processes of assessment?

ROZ: Probably the strongest basis for young people to become engaged in some form of critical dialogue with their work is through an active involvement with the evaluation process. This requires examining how the evaluation process is itself *integral* to the making of work – it has to be acknowledged as taking place during the creative process. I think it's crucial for young people to identify and acknowledge their own skills – which many of them don't get the opportunity to do – partly because it builds self-esteem and confidence. They might make something and it's assessed and graded, but this doesn't acknowledge what it is that those young people, individually, are skilled at or the ways in which they've personally developed. In order to be able to evaluate the work they're making, to acknowledge their own skills, the evaluation criteria must be partially based on their own cultural experience. I think this is pivotal because young people's own cultural experiences are markedly different from people who aren't young. I think we have to acknowledge that the cultural experiences young people bring when they look at their own work are just as valid as those the teachers and the arts workers bring.

ALISTAIR: But how does one endorse somebody else's experience, if one has no notion of that experience? If the evaluation is being facilitated by people with a very different experience – through age, gender, class, culture or whatever?

ROZ: That's why I'm saying that it needs to be based around an exchange of those experiences, rather than one dominant experience being used to measure the work.

STEVE: I agree. In my opinion the best work in the formal sector does draw on children's cultural and social experience and becomes very individual. Obviously, a programme of study has to include teaching of skills and group projects, but the best GCSE exhibitions do have this individual quality where students are really involved in exploring their own identity or particular issues which are important to them from their cultural perspective. I think there are quite a few schools doing this, where children are having the opportunity to operate as artists and make work which isn't just done to get the certificates, but actually has an impact on their own life and experience and the way they look at themselves.

ALISTAIR: Thinking about all the ways that I make things, I would agree that evaluation is an integral part of making for me. That process of taking a step back and looking – you could think about that as a contemplative or evaluative moment. But what you're looking at, the thing that is half-finished or half-assembled, also becomes part of the judging process. In a way you set the piece against itself, so it becomes embroiled in its own evolution. It's not that there are parallel processes of evaluation – one subjective and one objective. It's much more tangled than that, and tangled up with you, the maker, too.

STEVE: There's a constant feedback loop, isn't there, between you and what's happening in the world that you're shaping. Sometimes it's imperceptibly quick and at other times it's much more studied. 'Sit back and make a real judgement: let's pin that on the wall and have a look at it'. Good art and design teachers and presumably good media studies teachers too, would get children involved in a negotiated dialogue about the development of the work as it goes through this process. Also, when you're looking at a work of art, you're actually making it for yourself, aren't you? I mean, you're using your own experience to interpret what's there.

ROZ: There's no reason why you should take from the image the same thing that . . .

STEVE: . . . that was encoded into it, exactly. I was marking some students' work at Goldsmith's recently: the top marks were given to the work which really did look professional and I admit I wasn't totally clear about what this work meant to the student who made it, but everybody who encountered this particular work found it profound, memorable, moving, and we were probably all taking different things from it. It was deemed to be a very successful work of art. I didn't feel I had to actually fully understand it, its intentions. I interpreted it in my own way. I think in a good model of evaluation you go in with an open mind and allow the criteria to develop out of the situation, gradually moving towards making a kind of critical judgement based on your exploration and the ideas which develop in your engagement with that work. When I've seen teachers trying to develop reflective practice in art, it often starts out as a kind of formal sequence. The children are taken through stages in quite a formal way. They're expected to write a bit of evaluation in their sketchbook, which does risk becoming formulaic. But it should become more than just an exercise. It's part of an ongoing process of interaction between the teacher and the child, where both are learning about the work.

ROZ: Do you think that there is enough freedom within the time-tabled structure of formal education, to allow young people to develop their practice in that way? Or do you think that having periods of time allocated to specific tasks, often seen as separate learning experiences, is problematic?

STEVE: Well it is possible. . .but it's not necessarily very easy.

The difficulties of assessment and the challenge for art

Are there some practices which are more difficult to assess than others? If art education should progress to accommodate new modes of making and the evolving nature of contemporary practice, can assessment criteria and procedures keep pace or are we stuck in a modernist mould?

STEVE: I see no problem at all with the assessment process in the art GCSE, for instance, accommodating multimedia artwork. In my experience, that assessment process has been able to cope with almost every new development in media, including group work. In twenty years I've seen all sorts of 'cutting-edge' practice emerge and people would say 'Oh, we'll never be able to get that through', but, basically, you can. I suppose group work has sometimes provided a problem because examinations are set up as an individual test. But I've put it through GCSE. Obviously you show the group piece with accounts by you or the children themselves, of what parts they've played. In the past, video work was seen as something that couldn't be submitted but my partner, who's involved in GCSE moderation, has assessed videos, performance pieces and installations. You throw it at the system and I think it can accommodate it (see figures 8.2 and 8.3).

ALISTAIR: Or it absorbs it, and hybridises it, to make it function. For me, a

A study to look at the way Corbet created the glowing effect in his painting with the contrasts, it is like magic when you begin to see the colours next to each other in the above format you understand much more clearly how colours affect each other. If I was doing this with children I would do it with larger squares because it's quite difficult to fit them in. It's very interesting to see how many subtle shades you can create in the colour brown or red. I think it would be useful in the classroom because it concentrates on hue + tone without having to worry about form and realism it's a good way of building a language of colour.

Figure 8.2 Deborah Poland (BEd student), Goldsmiths College. Reflective journal entry 1

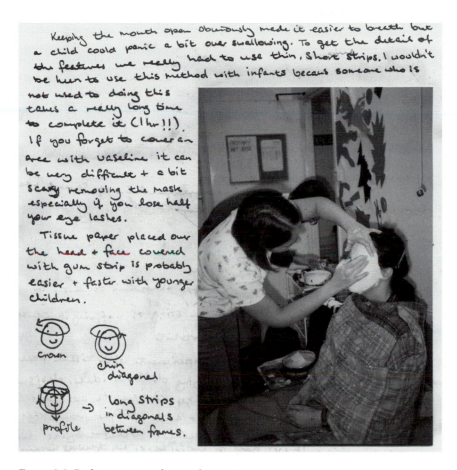

Figure 8.3 Reflective journal entry 2

key issue arises here. The classical model for formal education in this country – in terms of syllabi, subject divisions, assessments, with its categories and hierarchies – is so dated already. It's more appropriate for the last century than the end of this one. In a way art has been fitted into this model, because it's had to be in there somewhere, and it's sometimes had to borrow the language of other subjects to endorse it. What's interesting now, with the development of new technologies, is that this affords different ways of thinking about education, about knowledge, of thinking about information and accessing that information. The huge fundamental changes in education stress computers in every class and 'Grids for Learning' and all of this, but ironically *don't* seem to be able conceptualise the social changes that accompany them and the different needs children will have in twenty or thirty years time for communicating – exactly the sort of skills and language and ways of thinking that I think *art* can provide. You could say that art is the most vital model, and it's been waiting for education to become appropriate.

STEVE: Well, I would agree with that, but then I'm biased! Maybe it's also true of Drama or Media, perhaps the arts in general but certainly it's so in visual art. It's one space in the school where the child is seen as a human being with a personality, not a vessel that has to be filled up with this body of knowledge or that has to attain certain levels.

ALISTAIR: Also I would say art is one of the few subjects where it's possible not to produce anything but still to have valuable discussions about ideas or responses to things. Of course, ideas and responses are quite difficult to assess, to pin down and quantify, but they're obviously valuable processes. In fact, the skills involved in that sort of collaborative action and negotiation are possibly more appropriate than many of the factual things that we still learn in other models.

Domains of meaning – beyond the visual

With regard to talking about what you're making, what is the relationship between the languages of critique and of communication, the verbal and the visual? As well as enabling young people to articulate their feelings and critical responses in written and verbal language, should there be room within evaluation for *non*-verbal, *non*-written responses? What about the meanings embodied within a piece of work and equally the response to a piece of work which can't fully be articulated through words?

ROZ: Where language is impoverished, it isn't that it can't give us a way to discuss the visual, it's much more that, it can't always give us an appropriate means of articulating our emotional responses to work. But it's difficult to envisage how a purely visual response to something visual could be seen as a valid evaluative process within a formal education context, although I think it's a valid form of response myself and it might be accepted in higher education. There's a project I'm working on at the moment, where a group of young people have made a website (http://www.dmc-uce.co.uk/imagenit) which is mainly visual (see Figures 8.4 and 8.5). It's called 'Young, Queer and Safe' and we've started a guest book for written responses. But the real aim is for young lesbian, gay and bisexual people to be able to contribute to the website in a visual way, responding to images already up there, with their own. It explores this as a type of evaluation, but also as a communication process or dialogue. It's about those young people saying, 'Yes, but actually this too,' or 'No, actually this is how . . .'. But it's about how identifiable images – which might relate to specific experiences these young people have had – can be a springboard for creative work amongst others. So I suppose there

Figure 8.4 Mistress Jill/Danya Cleghorn. Young, Queer and Safe?

are three different elements: evaluation, communication and creative trigger.

ALISTAIR: I think that language has several relationships to making: to a finished product or a product in the process of being made, but also in relation to things that never get made and this is an important part of making. Many things don't ever get made, they exist as ideas or as conversations, which inform an ongoing process. There's another point I want to make in relation to language and art: it's about a shift in meaning. Historical and political shifts can affect the debate and change the language used in talking about art, while the artwork itself hasn't actually changed at all – it's finished, it just exists – but its meaning has moved on, and the critical dialogue around it is still as substantial as the artwork. Sometimes critical debate can become a weight around the artwork, making it difficult to re-visit . . . to shake off or reshape the debate around the work. But what can happen is that the talk, the critique, becomes more important than the work itself. This happens in education as well in the art world and I think it can be detrimental because it's like diluting the most potent form (the visual) that you've got.

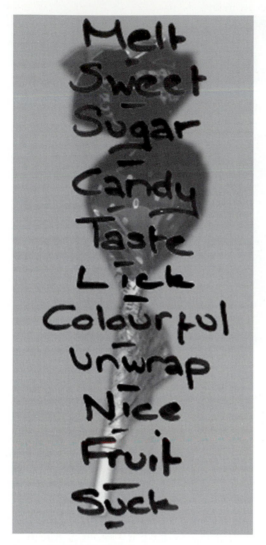

Figure 8.5 Marie Delany. Young, Queer and Safe?

ROZ: Yes. That's really interesting in relation to things I've been thinking about, such as how community arts practice employs the evaluative process. Within community arts, there is an emphasis on evaluating the *process* of production rather than the end product. Mark Webster claims in his book that 'There is always a trade off when you are working on group projects, as you balance the quality of the process and the quality of the product' (Webster 1997: 49). For me this presents an interesting parallel to what you were saying. If the process is what's assessed or evaluated why should the value of the product necessarily suffer? I think it's nonsense to see it as an inevitable result of this type of evaluation. Often it's just used as an excuse for low production values or to avoid the debate around lack of funding within community arts practice. Low production values tend to be associated with a working practice which emphasises the process when actually it's much more to do with there being not enough money to realise the project. So when an audience looks at work made within a community arts context, it carries all this baggage. They presume that community arts work is all about what people gain from the creative process and about its social and cultural impact on people's lives. These things aren't *negative* but I think they can negate the value of the actual work produced.

The institutional contexts

The place of production, the context of making and the time available all affect the outcomes and the relationship between process and product. How much time or opportunity is there for development and progression? Is a one-off opportunity better than nothing? How are the differing expectations and assumptions negotiated and where do young people find a voice in collaborative work? How does a critical vocabulary develop beyond 'I really enjoyed this project'?

STEVE: Gallery education work also often suffers from lack of funds. They're usually very short-term projects, and the people running the workshops know very little about the children involved. Comparing museum and gallery education arts-making with art in formal education: clearly one difference is that in formal education a teacher develops a coherent programme over a long period, which actually moves children along. That is very different to creative activities where groups of children come into an exciting space to do a certain activity. Some gallery education projects take place over a much longer time, with the possibility of a dialogue developing through the relationships made. But the quality of much gallery education art-making is low-level because it's this kind of creative workshop. It's a valuable activity, it's certainly a strong *learning* activity, but it doesn't go a long way.

ROZ: I agree with what you say about how problematic a short timescale can be. Very often there is scope for further development and it's frustrating if you're just building a relationship with young people when you have to go. But I question the issue of not knowing the young people – I usually find that less of a problem than the communication between school staff and the arts worker. I'll start working with a group of young people and we're building a relationship but then a member of staff involved in the project finds it necessary to give me some negative background information like, this person isn't able to write their name and address. I try very hard not to make a judgement based on this but the very fact that the teacher thinks it relevant is problematic and symptomatic of a particular kind of pre-judgement of ability.

ALISTAIR: Gallery education is distinct from community arts education in its aims. Also, there is a huge variation in how different galleries have worked with schools, short term and long term, but very often they're putting children and artists together for the first time. I go into schools sometimes and you just know the kids have never met anybody who makes a living from making art. They might never have considered that a woman or an Asian person can be artist, or even that an Asian can come and teach in their school. One thing I've been trying to do through the education programme at inIVA, working with a school in Camden over five years, is actually get artists to work everywhere in the school *apart* from the art department (see Figures 8.6 and 8.7). We're working on this idea that Art (the subject) isn't the only focus for looking at art, because the debates in visual culture permeate every aspect of our education or home life, especially within contemporary practice. But in schools the visual elements get removed from mathematics, from geography, from science and all the other non-art subjects. So, as well as making that direct contact, galleries can provide this link to contemporary issues and cultural issues, which I'd say are as valid in the process of teaching art, as passing on figurative skills.

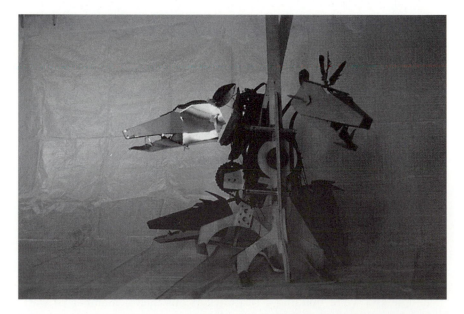

Figure 8.6 Four Nomadic Warriors. Coyote – Brother Heads On. 1997 (photo Fernando Palma)

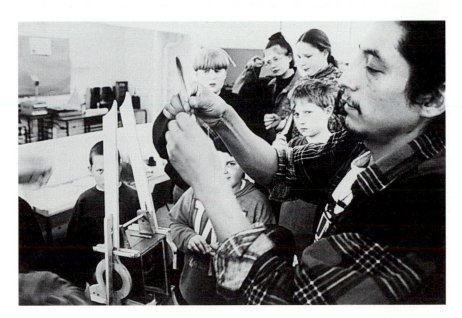

Figure 8.7 Artist Fernando Palma with Year 7 Technology Students. Alcland Burghley
School. (photo: Michael Williams/inIVA).

STEVE: I wouldn't argue with that. What you've described are very valuable
experiences, which we'd like more children to have. The point I was
making is this: if you're teaching art in school, you have to have a coherent programme of art education over a period of years. You see children
on a weekly basis, which is very different to the kind of opportunist
programmes run by gallery education departments. The school round
the corner from the Whitechapel Art Gallery might go there once a
month but there are other schools out in leafy suburbs or rural areas
who may never go. I'm not criticising gallery or museum education,
because it's one place where curriculum development happens. But if
the advocacy of artists' residencies and museum and gallery education is
accompanied by a blanket criticism of the formal art education system,
as somebody who evaluates the whole area, I'm just not willing to accept
that. My vision is of partnerships of respect between these different
players, not this dismissive 'formal education is a load of crap' attitude.
Some is bad – it's a national system – but I think the work happening in
good art departments knocks the socks off anything you see in museum
or gallery education, or artists' residencies, or even in some art colleges.

ROZ: For me, the only way of combining the various agendas of these
institutions, concerning how you might evaluate such a collaborative
project, would be to make the participants' self-evaluation the pivotal

element, so that they define what their own aims and goals are within the project.

STEVE: Would that always be possible, or does it depend on the kind of critical vocabulary and experience of talking and discussion the children have?

ROZ: I can't really imagine a lack of vocabulary undermining a young person's ability to engage in that type of process.

STEVE: Clearly, children do learn to engage in critical discussion and some might learn that through talking to people generally, but most of it happens in school. You can't cut the formal education system out of the development of young people's engagement with critical discourse. It varies, but in the art departments where there's a culture of talking about art, a level of articulacy is reached. But, I wouldn't be confident that all children were equally able to engage in critical discourse.

ROZ: That's not what I'm saying, and I'm not trying to imply that formal education or the collaborating arts organisation has no part in the evaluation process, or in developing young people's ability to engage in a critical discourse about their work. All I'm saying is that if the young people's own aims are central to the evaluation process, this should be the point at which collaborating organisations meet. Unless young people have a chance to define their own aims and goals, through an understanding of their own creative processes, it will become very difficult for them to engage with that process beyond this sort of collaborative education project.

ALISTAIR: Should the participants, the young people, necessarily be the ones defining the parameters of the evaluation? What about the actual quality of the work?

ROZ: But whose idea of quality are you talking about?

ALISTAIR: Well what about established notions of quality, historical notions of quality, artists' notions of quality? As you said, there's a danger everyone's so bent on recognising the value of the process, they're actually not looking at the art – then the whole thing becomes about a therapeutic exercise.

REBECCA: Doesn't that contradict what you said at the beginning, about the danger of accepting established values of quality and judgement?

ALISTAIR: Well, what is criticism? A group of kids running across a gallery floor and stopping in front of one painting to look at it for longer than they looked at another? Does that qualify as being a criticism of the work – is it a negotiated group criticism or an individual criticism, or a dialogue between the kids, the work, the artist, the environment? We haven't really spoken about how developing the critical skills of a group of young people to engage with art practice might benefit them in the long term, however they go on to use it. Not everybody who engages with visual art culture within a school art department is going to become an artist. In a class of thirty, the vast majority of those kids will later participate in visual art culture as viewers. I don't think formal education teaches us how to be audiences; it doesn't teach us how to participate without making. I think it's also the responsibility of formal education to introduce the idea of being a viewer, being somebody who talks about art, being somebody who commissions art, being somebody who teaches about art and all the various social, cultural and economic roles within art as an industry.

STEVE: Well I think this already happens. The National Curriculum does require children to talk about art and to use critical vocabulary. If you look at the Art GCSE, it has firmly established notions of the child as producer and the child as critic. We've moved away from the old, one-dimensional view of the 'child-artist'. Looking at some of the available models for art education, for instance, discipline-based art education in America, which has been very influential in this country. It's built around the idea of the artist, the art critic, the art historian and the aesthetician. There you've got four different roles in society represented by real people who you could bring into your art department. This particular model argues that an artist draws on each of those four discip-lines when they're making art. In fact you could go beyond that: I think that to these four you should add the curator, because in contemporary practice that role has become very important.

Challenging practice

Are there some kinds of work, or some ideas, which are inappropriate to explore in formal education? Many of the issues that contemporary art deals with are challenging and complex, as are many of the cultural experiences which young people deal with, and can touch on very personal or sensitive subjects, for instance in the areas of race or sexuality. Artists might be raising a social issue, while at the same time challenging such art conventions as siting work in a gallery. Or they might simply be delighting in being conten-tious and breaking taboos. How feasible is it to accommodate this work within the curriculum, let alone make value judgements about it?

STEVE: Well, looking at your project Roz, I would say work dealing with homosexuality and children's sexuality is very difficult to deal with at the moment in mainstream formal education because of Clause 28. It's not that teachers are afraid of these issues, although some might be, it's more what's happening in education now, where something can leap out of a school context and into the tabloids, in a very destructive fashion, as with OFSTED and schools put on special measures. That's what people are afraid of.

ROZ: I'd say with a project like this that it's as much to do with young people's perception of being within a safe space. These particular young people said during the evaluation process that they would not have been able or felt supported enough to make that work within school. In the context where the project took place they're surrounded by people who they feel comfortable with and relate to in many ways. And there was something about the personal nature of it – whether dealing with sexuality or other issues – they felt they could be much more open, contribute more of themselves within this project than they could within a school context (Maypole 1999).

STEVE: I'm sure that's true in this case. Some schools have dealt with very personal issues in children's art – I'm thinking of children making art about somebody very close to them dying, or children from refugee situations. For instance, George Orwell School's 'Safe in Another Country' and the related multimedia 'Portrait Project' (see Chapter nine).

ROZ: Yes it's specific to the particular school environment where those young people are.

ALISTAIR: Much of that issue-based art, or art that is time-based or site-specific, doesn't happen within formal art spaces, which is another argument for acknowledging the presence of art in all the different learning environments. But I do think it gets really complicated with so-called 'problematic' art because you are asking people that aren't necessarily specialists to talk about something that's highly specialist and requires a complex understanding. It's very difficult to be asking young people to engage critically with something when you don't feel confident about that critical engagement yourself.

STEVE: I think the limitations are the teachers and their experience. With a teacher who left art college when the trend was for a modernist approach, it's unlikely you'd be able to make issues-based, postmodern installations in their department, unless they have kept up with current work.

ALISTAIR: I think you're being generous suggesting that teachers who keep up with a current art practice could engage with this work in the classroom. I suspect it would be hard to find an art teacher who was comfortable talking about experimental video art in the late 1960s or Orlan's performance work, which relates to the female body and video art as well as traditional art-historical ideas about beauty.

STEVE: Well, in one school I visited all the sixth form went to the Turner Prize exhibition. They'd also been to 'Sensation' and in their sketchbooks and writing, they were picking up on the artists who'd interested them, by exploring their work further. They could have gone in any direction; they didn't have to stick with the artist or the practice as presented by the teacher. The teacher introduced them to a way of connecting with it.

Teacher education

How is teacher education addressing the changing nature of art practice? Are approaches to teacher training evolving to accommodate contemporary art and issues or are they impeded by time constraints and statutory directives? What other opportunities are there to broaden your professional development and your practice, once you're in post? While there is money for ICT skills training, it's not a simple question of a one-day INSET to acquire keyboard skills. And do teachers capitalise on the informal knowledge of popular culture which young people bring with them?

ALISTAIR: Can we get art teachers out of schools and say, 'Go and make some work' or 'Go and do some research' or 'Go to another country and get familiar with a different cultural tradition'? Because I think those are quite reasonable demands, really. Steve, I know you've got much more experience of talking to art teachers than I have, but I've met a phenomenal number who can't name three contemporary non-white European artists – and I find that absolutely depressing. In another industry, that would be a complete non-starter, totally unacceptable, people have to stay informed and keep up with contemporary trends.

STEVE: I'm sure they'd love to. Teachers who are up-to-date with contemporary culture and art practice have acquired this knowledge themselves, out of interest. There is no structure to keep the teaching force abreast. You can only get out of school in connection with target-setting these days. But as an art teacher, you have to be competent across a wide range of different practices and you end up teaching drawing, painting, print-making, art history, critical theory, with a group of thirty-three children. The best ones can do that, in London certainly, teachers have been working with and looking at multicultural approaches to art for several years. They do keep up, through teachers evenings at galleries or whatever, but whether it's realistic to expect the whole teaching force in formal education to be up-to-date with contemporary art, I don't know? And for some children, their only experience of art is in that art room over the six or seven years of secondary education. Many never get into community art contexts or visit an art gallery.

ROZ: That's important to acknowledge. Obviously a lot of young people don't engage with any type of contemporary or historical art outside formal education, informally or otherwise – but they *do* engage with popular culture on a day-to-day basis and one way I feel formal art education is impoverished, is by not building on the learning opportunities presented by young people's daily, often quite sophisticated, engagement with popular culture. In Karen Raney's book (1997) – she said something like, 'Does understanding a Silk Cut advert help us to understand an abstract painting?' I think this sentence is the wrong way round, because actually, day-to-day, it's more important for young people to understand a Silk Cut advert – where it's coming from and what it's trying to communicate – than to understand, say, an Orlan video.

New media

Since we seem to agree that there's a strong argument for enabling children and young people to work with media which has cultural significance for them, can we capitalise on the increasing use of digital technologies in school to investigate contemporary issues and popular culture? And do these media forms introduce new criteria into the process of making and evaluating?

ALISTAIR: Viewing new technology or multimedia as this 'great liberating force' that allows you to think about the curriculum and across the curriculum simultaneously brings its own set of problems though. This relatively unformed and unexamined medium is being introduced into a long, historical tradition of art and art-making. But digital technologies *appear* technologically very sophisticated. It's as if through these new technologies you can speak with the authority of science but the spectacle of art.

ROZ: I think the potential use of digital technologies within education as creative tools for production has highlighted the need for the area of evaluation to be questioned. But I feel quite strongly that talk about a 'lack of benchmarks' for evaluating is something of a red herring. The real reason why digital technology seems to problematise evaluation is more to do with the specific relationship young people have to this technology as perceived by most adults. In fact, I think this relationship is far more complex than it's portrayed, which is often full of assumptions based on the marketing strategies of soft- and hardware manufacturers. Still, it has highlighted the tension between the sort of popular culture that young people engage with on a regular basis, including digital applications, and a cultural hierarchy where a dominant culture sets expectations for young people's working processes. This isn't specific to digital technologies – there's a broader tension related to young people's experiences and what's expected of them, as well as those things they *anticipate* will be expected of them.

I encountered another problem thrown up by these assumptions, when I was working at a pupil referral unit recently. The work they made was received with some surprise by the staff, because it greatly exceeded their expectations. Given those young people's lack of experience with the technology it transcended my expectations too, but at the end of the project, the interview with the teacher was very revealing. He basically said, 'The kids valued the work they did with you; they looked forward to working with you. I suppose for them it was a non-academic way of passing some time.' The unit staff constantly referred to this work, using computers, as a form of playing. They also repeatedly talked of it as a 'high-status incentive'. They obviously thought these young people just wanted to get their hands on the hardware. I think such attitudes completely undermine the value of any work young people make using these media.

STEVE: I really feel that within Art as a school subject, new technology can be taken on as just another medium with its own qualities and the assessment/evaluation applied will be equal in quality to any other media used.

ROZ: There is the problem of being dazzled by the new, but there's also a danger of being dismissive by viewing this as 'merely playing'. There were several ways the experiences gained by those young people could have been used or built on within a range of subject areas. But the teachers never really acknowledged this. Perhaps this instance is extreme, being a referral unit, but it's based on power relationships – which you find in all mainstream education – and the perceived relationship between young people and digital technology. It's assumed that young people have a greater knowledge or experience of these media and that can threaten the power relationship between staff and pupils. In this instance it definitely did.

ALISTAIR: That idea about the shift of control in the relationship is interesting, even if it's based on a misconception. There's an issue I'd like to raise here about the international context, the cultural and political contexts of global communications technology. It's widely available in the West, but is largely produced or serviced by 'Third World' countries. Who is economically and technologically sophisticated enough to communicate with us?

ROZ: That's exactly the kind of critical engagement with the technology we should be introducing.

ALISTAIR: I want to make one more point. It goes back to the tool, or rather *behind* the tool. The screen, the interface, is what we always see – it's the part you're supposed to engage with. But art isn't simple, art is subversive; it wants you to take the back off and look inside, and maybe stick something in there or change its shape to make the screen obvious not oblivious. Much of the photography work of the 1970s and 1980s, was about examining its cultural and conceptual roles – how photography had been used in a social capacity to construct meanings, to portray people historically or to classify them scientifically. We were re-examining that, looking at our bodies, at representations of the 'other', of homosexuality, or issues like Aids. Computers are going to have to be examined by similar criteria if we don't want them to be completely mediated or controlled by the industries producing them.

ROZ: There's a general assumption right now that everyone under twenty is in their bedroom all the time, playing on the computer. It's just not the case. It's still a small, privileged minority that has access to digital technology. Most of the research done in this area seems to focus on a minority of young people with privileged and sustained access. For me it's really important to work with young people who *don't* have that sort of access and the results of the kind of research I've just referred to are directly contradicted by what I've observed. When the young people I've worked with use the internet, for example, they don't use it to gather information off the web: they use the IRC ('Chat Rooms'), because they know they'll get value for money. Basically, they spend an hour talking to other young people around the country.

There is a strong element of technological determinism, not least in education, which insists that because the technology could be utilised in a certain way, then that's how it *will* be used. But the parameters for how we use digital technologies are still very fluid, very transient. I think the longer we can sustain that fluidity to explore the potential of the medium and push those boundaries as far as possible, developing more meaningful uses, the better. There are far too many debates in this area which focus on what is likely to happen in the future, which I think is a complete nonsense. What is likely to happen in the future is going to be at least partly determined by how people are using the technology today. It makes no sense to say, 'Oh, this is going to happen, this is how it will be; therefore we have to prepare for it.' That's not how things come about.

REBECCA: That's a great place to stop. Thank you. (End.)

Some concluding points

While the participants acknowledged that they have quite different perspectives, there seemed to be a common interest in their concern for where young people figure in the institutional agendas for art education – particularly in the evaluation practices which concern, but don't always involve them, and the power relationships which exist in those contexts. In his 1990 study of young people's cultural habits, Paul Willis observed that galleries and institutionally sanctioned arts have little or no relevance in their lives (Willis 1990: 9). But as Selwood *et al.* (1995) noted, while Willis's findings tell us about young people's cultural consumption they reveal little as to how they actually perceive art and its exhibition spaces. In the post-war period galleries have often been seen as irrelevant by artists who, instead, choose to make site-specific work in public spaces, in the sites of commerce or industry and now of course, in virtual space. Since Willis published his study, the increasing profile of art in the media, through the Turner Prize and the rise of the Young British Artist's has meant that contemporary art has a more visible and, apparently, more youth-orientated appeal. If young people were asked the same questions about the role and value of art in 1999 as they were ten years ago, would they respond in the same way?

It's people who make culture; and community arts has sought to broaden the spectrum of people whose cultural production is seen and valued. Contemporary art, through its translation of myriad cultural forms, trawling the vaults of popular culture and palaces of fine art, re-appropriating histories and sampling from world religions, recycling the refuse from a commodity culture and employing the tricks of the marketing trade, has sought to make everything relevant – fair game for use or comment. Within this context, there is less reason for young people to feel that art 'is not for the likes of us'. Indeed, there is now a recognised cultural capital associated with young consumers which has been exploited by the music and games industries and seems unlikely to be left untouched by the art industry. They might be busy with other things, but it would be hard to argue that there is no entry point, unless in the name of education, and that young people are being led to art by such a tortuous route that they lose interest.

> Two of the most effective ways of avoiding orthodoxy and stereotypical responses are to vary the starting points and methodologies used in delivering an educational programme and to use the stimulus and ideas generated by exposure to contemporary artists, exhibitions and collections.
>
> (Binch and Kennedy 1994: 26)

Throughout the discussion references were made to young people's cultural experiences and how these can, and should, inform the creative practices of formal education in order to give them a voice and a sense of ownership, as well as to trigger a critical engagement within this process. This echoes a number of similar published arguments (see Buckingham and Sefton-Green 1994; Richards 1998; Walton 1995). Roz Hall argues for opportunities where young people can be engaged with a creative process 'on their own terms'. She describes a recent project, where digital equipment was installed on location, with a transient and diverse group of young people, whose common ground was their relationship, through work or recreation, to the Bull Ring shopping centre in Birmingham:

> Young people working, shopping and meeting at the Bull Ring were approached and invited to make images about how they feel about the Bull Ring and their relationship to it, in light of the imminent redevelopment (see figure 8.8). The resultant images are as diverse in concept and construction as were the experiences utilised in making them . . . The project had a non-prescriptive approach so they were able to use it quite differently, some working for an hour – making an image and leaving – others returning regularly, making many images and developing a creative process.

She goes on to question how we might discuss this work, informed as it is by disparate perceptions, experiences and agendas:

> Do we need to frame them in critical discourse? Would this act necessarily validate them within a framework of criteria as defined by a dominant cultural discourse? This issue impacts on young people's lives as work developed in informal contexts is not appropriately 'validated' which undermines the potential for such engagement to be built upon through formal education.

This points to a missed opportunity, where the value of these kinds of informal engagements with creative practice are reduced to a positive experience, but not developed in terms of their learning or critical understanding in the spaces where most art education still takes place, namely, in school. But embedded within this are arguments for some creative activities to remain outside the formal education system, as long as school retains its place within a cultural and social establishment. This is borne out by further research (e.g., Kelly, Wodjat and Khan 1997; Paley 1995).

Alistair Raphael, who has range of experiences working on artist-in-school projects, highlights what he sees as another missed opportunity of institutional collaborations:

> As an artist I have often resisted the opportunity to become an employee of any one institution, choosing instead the autonomy of working freelance which allows the fluidity of art-practice to be the deciding criteria

Figure 8.8 James Harrison. The Bull Ring

for judging varying degrees of success and, or, enjoyment. To me, artists' projects should be as much a learning curve for all the staff (the accountants, the curators, the secretaries and teachers) as for the maker and participants. Too often in an evaluation, the institution scrutinises everyone but itself in terms of how the experience of working with an artist has had an effect. In this way the 'opportunity' of an artist in school is a missed opportunity because even if the young people have had a positive experience, the institution has not really engaged with the artist's presence and what it could mean in relation to its own working practices and structures.'

Ideally, as all the participants would agree, the sorts of collaborations advocated should act as a two-way learning process, but teachers sometimes feel patronised by other art professionals and artists often resent helping to 'deliver' the curriculum. A Tate Gallery Liverpool education project, got pupils to discuss what (and who) galleries are for as a way of introducing them to the collection and the contexts of meaning for the work (Binch and Robertson 1994). This sort of contextual deconstruction is one commonly used by gallery educators and by artists in their own work. While teachers might also apply it to the work of artists through critical studies, how often would it be applied to young people's own production in schools? The ideologies of schooling, the history of art education and the place of professional artists in relation to student producers, are all rarely examined by the students and teachers *together*, as part of the process.

The differences in approach and even philosophy between the individuals in collaborative projects is often cited as an area of possible tension, but in many ways this could be seen as productive. It is precisely these differences which make the residency a valuable learning experience, not only for the insights it affords the young people, but equally for the perspective it can give the teachers and the wider school community. It throws into relief some of the institutional ideologies which can become invisible from inside the system. Structural issues like time-tabling and the organisation of subjects can be, and should be, re-examined in the presence of a practice which develops over time (not in neatly broken into 50 minute segments) and quite possibly across a number of disciplines. As Binch and Kennedy (1994) suggest, there are opportunities afforded by contact with these other agencies through their varied cultural and ideological perspectives.

This is not to suggest that all current schools art practice is stagnant or hamstrung by the constraints of statutory 'guidelines'. As Steve Herne stresses, there is a lot of good and innovative practice which, despite unhelpful time-tabling, through a process of development and a negotiated relationship between teacher and student, produces innovative high quality work with a clear personal investment for the makers.

> In this discussion, I found that I acted as an advocate for the good practice I had seen in schools, while accepting that there is a spectrum of practice and quality. It is important to acknowledge the variety of paradigms of art education in schools which range from a traditional focus on technical and representational skills, through forms which draw on modernism, privileging aesthetics and visual language to contemporary practice in which content is at least as important as form, drawing on diverse personal, social and cultural sources, issues and new media. There is also a principle in formal art education of moving students

towards 'self direction' or autonomy, through gradually increasing the range of choice available in project work in relation to ability to cope.

But there is concern throughout the profession about the relevance of the current art curriculum and there have been several key voices calling for a reconceptualisation, at all levels, from the content and ideological approaches, to teacher training, resourcing and assessment (Hughes 1998; Steers and Swift 1998). This inevitably includes strengthening the relationships between the various sites of young peoples' creative production, and re-examining the way collaborations are evaluated. That the relationship between sectors continues to be slightly prickly is not, however, necessarily a bad thing, since argument can lead to productive developments – and consensus decisions rarely produce interesting art.

References

Binch, N. and Clive, S. (1994) *Close Collaborations – Art in Schools and the Wider Environment*, London: Arts Council of Great Britain.

Binch, N. and Kennedy, M. (1994) *Art, Feat and Mystery – Links Between Schools, Galleries, Museums and Artists*, London: London Arts Board.

Binch, N. and Roberston, L. (1994) *Resourcing and Assessing Art, Craft and Design*, Corsham: National Society for Education in Art and Design.

Buckingham, D. and Sefton-Green, J. (1994) *Cultural Studies Goes to School: Reading and Teaching Popular Media*, London: Taylor & Francis.

Gulbenkian Foundation (1982) *The Arts in Schools*, London: Gulbenkian Foundation.

Dahl, D. (1990) *Residencies in Education*, Sunderland: AN Publications.

Dickson, M. (1995) *Art with People*, Sunderland: AN Publications.

Hughes, A. (1998) 'Reconceptualising the art curriculum', *Journal of Art and Design Education* vol. 17, no.1, pp. 41–9.

Kelly, O., Wodjat, E. and Khan, N. (1997) *The Creative Bits: The Social Impact of Arts Using Digital Technology*, Stroud: Comedia.

Maypole Lesbian and Gay Youth Group (1999) 'Young, queer and safe', *Young People Now* 1999, pp. 26–7.

McDonald, I. (1987) *Arts Centres, Education and Community*, London: Greater London Arts.

Paley, N. (1995) *Finding Art's Place: Experiments in Contemporary Education and Culture*, London: Routledge.

Raney, K. (1997) *Visual Literacy, Issues and Debates*, London: Middlesex University with The Arts Council of England.

Richards, C. (1998) *Teen Spirits: Music and Identity in Media Education*, London: UCL Press.

Selwood, S., Clive, S. and Irving, D. (1995) *An Enquiry into Young People and Art Galleries*, London: Art & Society.

Sharp, C. and Dust, K. (1997) *Artists in Schools*, Berkshire: National Foundation for Educational Research.

Steers, J. (1994) 'Art and Design: assessment and public examinations', *Journal of Art and Design Education* vol.13, no. 3, pp. 287–97.

Steers, J. and Swift, J. (1998) 'Draft Manifesto for Arts Education' unpublished but available at http://www.nsead.org.uk.

TGAT (1987) *National Curriculum Task Group on Assessment and Testing: A Report*, London: Deptartment of Education and Science.

Walton, K. (1995) *Picture My World*, London: Arts Council of England.

Webster, M. (ed.) (1997) *Finding Voices, Making Choices: Creativity for Social Change*, Nottingham: Educational Heretics Press.

Willis, P. (1990) *Moving Culture: An Enquiry into the Cultural Activities of Young People*, London: Gulbenkian Foundation.

9 Making multimedia
Evaluating young people's creative multimedia production

Rebecca Sinker

It is a world in which the creative imagination of the artist is now needed by the men who handle the computers.

(McLuhan 1958: 295)

Multimedia is a term now in common use, even though an understanding of what we mean by it is not always shared. It has in the past indicated anything from an audio-visual slide presentation or a two-dimensional text and image piece (indeed medieval illuminated manuscripts are sometimes cited as the earliest examples of 'multimedia') to the whole range of disciplinary permutations in mixed media arts (see Lanham 1993). Within education, the term now seems to include the digital combination of some, or all, of the following media: photography, illustration, video, animation, graphics, text and audio. Viewed on a computer screen, played from a CD-ROM or sometimes via the internet, multimedia is still largely seen as a consumer technology. The vast majority of what is termed educational multimedia is in the form of 'reactive' learning resources or digital encyclopaedias. The visual and conceptual metaphors for these might range from quite conventional book formats through libraries, schools and museum collections, to funfairs, science labs and spaceships, but they all work on a similar structure, offering a range of linear and non-linear routes. There are several products which use a gaming model – slightly more exploratory but not truly interactive – where the choices are still, at some level, predetermined. Finally, there are a handful of software packages, designed for multimedia authoring (for example *Hyperstudio*, *Genesis*, and *Illuminatus*, as well as some professional multimedia and web design packages like *Macromedia Director*, *Claris Homepage* and *Microsoft Frontpage*), which are beginning to be used for student productions in schools. The uses of educational CD-ROMs have been explored to some extent elsewhere (see, for example, Collins, Hammond and Wellington 1997) and the focus of this chapter will be on creative digital media production by young people.

Since this sort of work is still in its relative infancy, I will not be attempting to draw any definitive conclusions here. Moreover the projects discussed are not representative in that they were all produced under quite particular collaborative art education conditions. But at this point in time, it seems relevant to recount these examples because they do throw up a number of important issues and signal some possible ways forward. I would argue that the work made with multimedia here could be viewed as inherently cross-curricular in that the social, historical and cultural themes explored have relevance across a range of subjects, while being expressed in a form which exercises visual, linguistic and technological skills. Multimedia, with its branching structure, its convergence of media, its hypertext connections and multiple levels, makes it unlike single media forms and, I suggest, creates routes out of subject-specific channels. Outside school, young people will be familiar with a media environment and media texts which are constantly cross-referencing, quoting, sampling, linking and mixing visual, verbal and cultural references. The 'reading' and cognitive skills which these multi-modal texts require, while not new to humanity, are nonetheless different to those which are practised in, for instance, the conventional activities of print literacy education found in The National Literacy Strategy.

The traditional tools for image production, like pencils and paint and the newer communication media of photography and video, have been extended by, or in some cases synthesised into, this new area of digital technologies. In this way, perhaps multimedia should be considered a 'meta-media'. But, precisely because of the relative newness as well as the hybrid nature of multimedia, questions have been raised about how we might approach the evaluation of such work. What are the values we are considering in this multi-modal form and whose values are they? This chapter will consider multimedia production in a group of case study projects from primary and secondary schools, in particular examining its use in the creation of student-authored, issue-based work. Although underpinned by arts practice, the piece will go beyond a subject specific focus to look at some of the broader implications for learning-through-making using digital technologies.

The development and uses of 'new technologies' in schools

Information technology (IT) began having an impact in schools in the early 1980s (for an account of the history of computers in schools and the devel-opment of IT as a subject see Wellington 1989). Initially, there was a strong vocational emphasis aimed at equipping pupils (the future workforce) with the necessary computer skills for working in the 'information age'. Kenneth Baker, then Minister of Information Technology, said in 1981 'I want to try and ensure that the kids of today are trained with the skills that gave their fathers and grandfathers jobs . . . I want youngsters, boys and girls leaving school at sixteen, to actually be able to operate a computer' (Wellington 1989: 15). Less than twenty years on that now seems a remarkably low expectation, given that the skills of the fathers, to which he refers, have become largely redundant and many children of primary age can 'actually operate a computer'. Moreover, those school-leavers now working at computerised MacDonalds' cash registers are not generally considered high achievers. The focus of computers in schools has moved away from the lunchtime computer clubs of two decades ago, which were largely a male activity, to a more integrated curriculum approach where boys and girls are more equally involved (see Spender 1995). However, the political ethos behind ICT (Information Communication Technology), as it is now known, has not changed much. In launching the Government's consultation paper on the National Grid for Learning, Tony Blair declared:

> Education is the Government's number one priority. It is key to helping our businesses to compete and giving opportunities to all. . . . Technology has revolutionised the way we work and is now set to transform education. Children cannot be effective in tomorrow's world if they are trained in yesterday's skills. . . . By 2002, all schools will be connected to the superhighway free of charge; half a million teachers will be trained; and our children will be leaving school IT-literate.
>
> (DfEE 1997)

Obviously this raises questions about training and resourcing – questions the teaching profession have been quick to voice and the Teacher Training Agency (TTA) have begun to address – but it is clearly the applied social and economic uses of computers which drive the rhetoric, rather than the cultural and aesthetic ones.

Computers now have a visible presence in schools, though not necessarily in every area, and ICT is a required component throughout the National Curriculum. The document for Art states that 'Pupils should be given the opportunities, where appropriate, to apply and develop their information technology capability in their study of art, craft and design' (DfEE 1995: 1). But despite this, many teachers still don't make regular use of computers in the classroom. In 1995 the DfEE reported that only 35 per cent of secondary teachers and 25 per cent of primary teachers said that IT had made a significant contribution to their teaching.[1] Kevin Mathieson, who was the Art and IT officer at the National Council for Educational Technology (NCET), found that many art teachers lack the confidence and skills to use IT. Even new generations of student teachers can be initially reticent or nervous about approaching creative production on computers in a way that they are not with paint or clay. Obviously, this is partly to do with a lack of training, hence unfamiliarity with this media.

At the same time, computers are not generally viewed in the same way as traditional art media, that is, as just another tool. For many teachers there seems to be a perception that computers boil down to little more than keyboard skills, data-handling, and curriculum management, since these are actually the values most frequently emphasised in education literature. In general, Computer Studies or IT Literacy, is usually defined in terms of skills, and rarely in relation to theoretical or critical understanding: it almost never includes the creative manipulation of digital data, except perhaps in the form of DTP or graphic design. That artists and musicians have been experimenting in intriguing ways with these technologies for more than three decades seems to be irrelevant or unknown. While Mathieson commented that the lack of confidence among teachers was often accompanied by a strong desire to get involved in IT, there is also a residual suspicion about the place of technology in Art, particularly where the notion of art production is founded on a belief in developing craft-skills. There is a feeling that it is the machine, rather than the person, which is doing the work. In this sense computers have replaced photography as the technology in the dock, accused of inhibiting, rather than enhancing creativity.

These feelings belong in part to traditional ideas about authorship and the authenticity of the work of art. But the belief that a work of art is the singular product of a creative genius has, to an extent, been replaced by arguments about the social and cultural meanings of art and its dialectical position in relation to viewer and maker (see, for example, Barthes 1977, Benjamin 1992, Berger 1972.) If a medium is capable of synthesis and infinite duplication, its products are unlikely to accord with theories of fine art which privilege the value of a uniquely crafted object, and in this way, it is true that digital products have no investment in such values. Paul Brown observed in 1989 '. . . complaints mainly concern the lack of tangibility of the artwork – that it can't be framed, revered or monetarised. Computer art is not concerned with the production of artefact' (Brown 1990: 236). A decade later, Ewan Morrison cited Heidegger's opposition between art and technology as still being highly influential in why (he claims) the art world hates digital art: 'Although very few contemporary artists would support Heidegger's philosophy and its endorsement of the notion of the autonomous individual, the ethically existing subject and the expression of inner truth, the art world continues to distrust technology' (Morrison 1998: 25). Paradoxically, there are many artists now working across a range of media forms (old and new) who would question the recently delineated category of 'digital art', seeing it as falsely homogenous and also medium-specific when art has ceased to classify itself that way. At this point it might be important to say that digital art and multimedia are not synonymous. Digital art is, to some extent, a qualitative term, incorporating anything that is made using digital technology and that is also considered art. Multimedia is more of a technical description and is taken to mean, as described above, a confluence of media into one form, their combination being made possible by the digitisation of all the individual elements. Multimedia could be digital art but it might just as likely be a computer game or an encyclopaedia. Digital art does not necessarily involve multiple media (both, incidentally, have an equal capacity to disappoint.)

Most sources agree that ICT use in the art room is still taking its first steps and in a fairly piecemeal way, dependent on the commitment and enthusiasm of individual art teachers. Probably the largest survey was that undertaken by Kevin Mathieson, for the NCET. He discovered significant discrepancies in provision and resourcing, which ranged from state of the art equipment, down to outdated machines, and some art rooms with no digital technology at all. Judging by the work published in *Fusion*, as a result of this survey, (NCET 1998) most ICT applications in art are using the computer, or more specifically 'paint package' software, to replicate the kinds of formalist approaches to art-making (exploring line, tone and colour, etc.) which have traditionally been used. Alternative applications which examine the technology's ability to replicate and manipulate imagery, interrogating notions of authenticity and representation, were barely evident. Any work of a critical or contextual nature was the result of an artist-in-school project and there was almost nothing which could be termed multimedia. Although some work had been exhibited on the internet, it did not appear to have exploited the communicative or collaborative potential of the medium. There are instances of school practice which go beyond the work cited here but clearly this survey raised questions about appropriate uses of ICT and about a very low-risk strategy towards students' digital production.

The development and uses of 'new technologies' in arts practice

As Philip Hayward points out, the original use of the word technology referred to any practical means or apparatus in science, industry and the arts (Hayward 1990: 1). It was only during the industrial revolution and the years that followed that the definition shrunk back to just the practices of science and industry. But science and art, have had a long-standing relationship, symbolised perhaps by Leonardo da Vinci himself. Karen Raney has noted that the digital revolution has produced some interesting exchanges between different sectors, which serve corporate and non-corporate interests. 'Bill Gates of Microsoft bought the Leonardo Codex and hired an art historian (Martin Kemp) to make it into a CD-ROM which is then used for scholarly and educational purposes' (Raney 1998). The science–art–industry relationship is also evident in the various mechanical apparatuses which have been developed to aid the production of art, the most significant of these being the camera. Photography has sat uncomfortably at the art table for most of its one hundred and fifty year life and perhaps it is only with the emergence of digital art that it is finally being accepted: 'Each new technology creates an environment that is itself regarded as corrupt and degrading yet the new one turns its predecessor into an artform' (McLuhan 1964: 273).

The relationship between digital imaging – the manipulation of the individual pixels of digital information – and photography is an intriguing and contradictory one which has been explored at length elsewhere (see Ritchin 1990; Wombell 1991; Mitchell 1992; Lister 1995). There are a series of well-trodden arguments around authenticity and the image, as well as debate about the new aesthetic emerging through the synthesising culture of digital photography. Comparisons have been made between the digital photographer and the genetic engineer who, it is claimed, also works not in a 'creative' but in a 'perfectionist' model.[2] There are also issues about the place and value of the image as it becomes freed from the anchor of context and referent and is set adrift as floating currency in the global communications market. Kress and van Leeuwen reiterate McLuhan's most famous aphorism when they declare '. . . technology enters fundamentally into the semiotic process: through the kinds of meaning which it facilitates or favours, and through the differential access to the means of production and reception which it provides' (Kress and van Leeuwen 1996: 233). In general, the preoccupations of digital practitioners could perhaps be summarised as: the body (technology versus corporeality, human versus cyborg); space (local, global, inner, outer and virtual); power (surveillance, control, access); interactivity (the relationship between artist, work and audience); and identity (individual, cultural, digital). There are numerous published texts which investigate these themes individually or as a whole (see also Cubitt 1998; Morley and Robins 1995; Plant 1997; Keen 1998).

Identity, interactivity and synthesis

> Kempadoo's techniques, those of fragmentation and layering in Photoshop, are very appropriate mirrors for our collective Western experience at the end of the century. The black artists' use of investigative scraps of history as image and text in their work seem to be a convergence of intentionality and inevitability in their search for a space free of cultural baggage, a space in which they can operate as artists and photographers.
>
> (Gupta 1998: 44)

This issue of 'identity' is one of the central questions of art and culture in the postmodern age. It has been explored in a variety of media, very often lens-based, particularly by those 'others' who were invisible within, or perceived themselves as being outside, mainstream culture and history. The first wave of Black British artists worked with photography to re-examine and re-appropriate their representations because this was the technology which had most often been used to portray or define them (see Bailey and Hall 1992; also Willis 1994 for an African-American perspective). More recently, some of these artists (for example, Keith Piper, Joy Gregory, Pervaiz Khan) have been using digital imaging and multimedia forms to extend and complicate their visual arguments, the hybrid nature of the media seeming to mirror cross-currents they wished to explore culturally, the spaces of creation and exhibition echoing their shifting locations of self. As Kobena Mercer argues:

> Technology is not a monolith, it's meaning is its use. In thinking about

the historical importance of technologies across the experience of Diaspora, not limited to the African or Caribbean Diaspora, but generically
in terms of living through multiple attachments and belonging to more
than one geographical space, the importance of technology is seen in the
literal transportation that creates Diaspora; iconographically, the ship
features very prominently in Keith [Piper]'s work and the metaphor of
the train is similarly realised in African American Blues.

(Mercer 1997)

Susan Collins, who is a media artist and Head of the Slade Centre for Electronic Media, has produced work in a number of public spaces using a range
of electronic and digital media. She emphasises the role of the viewer in
giving meaning to her work, thus forcing a re-examination of the terms artist
and author. She also notes that 'all of this work is of a hybrid, cross-
disciplinary nature, threading together hitherto unexamined and uncon-
nected issues surrounding interactivity, art and technology, public art and
intervention' (Collins in NCET 1996: 51). Collins remarks that for her, computers should be used as a means to an end. 'The problem is not learning the
software but making, doing the art.' Pauline van Mourik Broekman, co-
editor of MUTE, the journal of digital media and theory, recalled the work
of an artist who creates composite images with Photoshop, but in a very
different way to that usually employed by the software:

> He doesn't montage together existing photographs, he makes faces of
> mainly adolescent looking boys that never existed, but they look com-
> pletely like boys. And they end up looking extremely sinister. He builds
> the faces completely out of skin effects, and small samples of textures
> that he then uses like a paintbrush. So in his work, drawing is incredibly
> important. He starts with drawing. He has to make them realistic so that
> they can be as believable as a photograph. And in the end he comes up
> with an image that's very, very compelling, because you know there is no
> original photograph to refer to, not even six different ones. It's made up
> completely out of pixels.[3]

Clearly this sort of synthesis, using a software tool designed to enhance
photographs (which have a trace of the original referent), to create an image
which mimics reality but is pure illusion, is a kind of conjuring trick playing
with perception, memory and truth.

Artists have a relative freedom to experiment with materials, ideas, roles
and spaces. They might be in a position to stretch the boundaries of what it is
possible to do with new technologies in a way that schools aren't, for reasons
that are economic and political. But schools *are* in a position to critically
explore the ways these technologies impact on how and why they are making
work in art classrooms, and the on the changing nature of art practices. All
the examples cited address complex philosophical, political and aesthetic

questions, and clearly present a considerable challenge to classroom practice. But they also speak of issues and experiences which, are in many cases, familiar to and relevant for young people (see Rutherford 1998). It is here, at the point of student experience, where educators might start to import the issues, debates and work of this recent group of art practitioners.

Evaluation

My central argument here is that multimedia work in schools is at the intersection of the cultural project outlined in the previous section and of some of the evaluative approaches in the subjects, Art and Media Studies. I will recap some of these subject models, as well as briefly mentioning other uses of practical multimedia in education before moving onto my case studies.

Chapter two considered the history of Art education outlining competing models of its philosophy. The liberal view considers art for art's sake and values creativity and knowledge in, and of, the arts as part of a holistic education. A utilitarian approach looks at art knowledge from a craft-skills perspective. By contrast, the radical approach considers how art can question social values and conventions, while a conformist approach, conversely, aims to educate in order to produce better citizens. There are overlaps between each of these perspectives and the current National Curriculum contains shades of all – though perhaps the least identifiable is the radical approach. In fact it is probably the first two which underpin most current art education practice.

Arts education is still, for the most part, based on the work of individuals and the development of a unique aesthetic 'voice' – what Ross calls a 'pedagogy of attunement'. He suggests that 'students relish the arts not because "free expression" is a license for self-indulgence and anarchy but because it allows them to exercise a large measure of personal control and self-determination over their work' (Ross and Kamba 1998: 198). Students of art are engaged in the process of discovering and defining selfhood, through their production, and in relation to a wider culture, a process which, in educational as well as personal terms, is highly valued.

Media education, as Chapter seven showed, springs largely from a theoretical approach, examining the socio-economic, cultural and political structures which produce media texts and their meanings. As a subject, it has tended to be much less comfortable with practical work, rarely accommodating the student demand for production experience and training within its own critical agenda. Evaluation in this area would concentrate less on technical skills or visual flair and more on how a student production demonstrated a critical understanding of the chosen media, its signs and conventions.

When multimedia is used in the investigation of topics at primary school, the children's understanding of the key concepts and facts, as demonstrated by the work produced and their ability to communicate such through discussion, is probably the rubric for assessment. Other issues like how well they worked collaboratively, what they contributed individually and what visual and technical skills have been demonstrated might all play a part (see Lachs 1999) .

The National Education Multimedia Awards (NEMA), which accept work from any subject discipline at all ages, use criteria for evaluating multimedia largely based on the technical and communicative aspects of the media itself, in addition to pre-defined benchmarks of quality. In many ways, these are entirely comparable to the sort of criteria which might be applied to a professional production. Work which fulfilled these criteria would demonstrate an understanding of multimedia navigation and design conventions, as well as a high level of technical expertise. However, from an educational perspective, it is significant that there is no reference in the competition criteria made to any critical understanding of the media and certain assumptions are made about shared standards of subjective notions like entertainment and originality. Nor is there any way of evaluating the research and development or the production *process*. These criteria suggest that the production should be largely factual and informative in approach, which of course the vast majority of commercial CD-ROMS are (see Ordidge 1999).

Young people encounter and inhabit a landscape of knowledge created by a range of new media and a pattern of cultural connections far richer and more complex than those enshrined in the traditional curriculum. The multimedia terrain, with its strata of meanings, its combination of media, its compilation of data and its branching, tangential connections would seem the ideal tool for this 'postmodern' age. But its chameleon character – a tool for writing, reading, talking and listening, a tool for drawing and looking, a tool for animating and viewing and a tool for gaming, interacting and consuming – makes it less easy to gauge in evaluative terms. In some ways the very fact that there is no overall model for evaluating multimedia work, since it appeals to any one of the range of subject-specific production paradigms described in this book, makes it a liberating experience for the young people involved in the making. Not because they have some natural inclination towards this way of working, or even, as is sometimes implied, a preternatural affinity with computer technology (see Sefton-Green 1998). It is much more to do with expectations, or the lack of them. By the time they reach secondary school most young people will already have an idea of (or have been told) what they are 'good' at. Many who feel that they 'can't draw' or are 'no good at' spelling will have no such stigma attached to making multimedia where you can contribute to a production in any or all of the forms listed above. This was one of the most significant findings in the following case studies. It is not simply a lazy correlation between computers, young people and motivation. There was a realisation that to have this other valid form of expression, which was not judged in the same way as writing or drawing, produced confidence and a real sense of achievement.

Case studies

The projects I will be discussing all took place during a three-year Arts Council (Visual Arts Dept) Teacher Development post at Middlesex University, with The Photographers' Gallery and ARTEC (Arts Technology Centre), where I was researching the uses of photography and media education in the curriculum (1994–1998). A number of papers and articles giving accounts of these projects have already been published (see Sinker 1996; 1997; 1999).

As I have already suggested, the theme of 'identity' is one of a number of issues which has preoccupied art practice for almost two decades. Consequently, it is increasingly being examined through an issues-based approach to arts and media education, very often involving the intervention of professional practitioners in schools. Much of this practice has used non-traditional art room materials such as photography, video and more recently, digital media. This work has been well documented (see Chapter one; Brake 1997; Kennedy 1995; Walton 1995 etc.) and I will not offer a full examination of these projects here, but will expand upon some aspects of them as they relate to the theme of this chapter.

The George Orwell Media Progression Project grew out of an idea developed by Kathy Stonier (the school's Head of Art) and Kate Kelly (the Arts Education Co-ordinator for the London Borough of Islington). The aim of this work was to investigate progression in media education through Key Stages 3 and 4 of the Art and Design curriculum. It built on a previous media education initiative, established in collaboration with ARTEC and The National Portrait Gallery, which grew from the school's own refugee project. Starting in year 8, the project was designed by Kathy to develop over three years, gradually pulling in different media technologies as well as more traditional art and design media. The broad theme was personal and cultural identities, which was particularly relevant for this school. Based in Islington, George Orwell has an extremely diverse ethnic population with 60 per cent of its pupils speaking a language other than English, and more than a third having refugee status. Over the three years, six different media artists, with a variety of cultural perspectives, were invited into the school to work with the two target classes.

The primary aim was to work progressively over three years, introducing some of the theoretical base from media education, in order to extend the young people's critical experience of making.[4] By introducing a range of media artists, the intention was to make the art curriculum broader, in both critical and cultural terms, more inquiring and above all, relevant to a group of young people whose experience of culture is through the media rather than art galleries, who have an extremely mixed cultural heritage and an interest in, but little access to, media technologies.

The Rosendale Odyssey took place from October 1995 to December 1996 as a collaboration between Rosendale Infants School and The Photographers'

Gallery. The school, in Lambeth, South London had a population of 320 children, from four to seven years old, drawn from a culturally diverse local community. There were twenty-two different languages spoken within the school by children (and staff) of African, Caribbean, Asian, Latin American, Chinese and European descent. Lens-based artists Dave Lewis and Shona Illingworth worked in residence for one school year, along with the gallery's project co-ordinator, Fiona Bailey and myself. In the final term, Fiona worked with internet artist, Julie Myers, to develop the work into a website: http://www.artec.org.uk/rosendale/.

The project was designed to be cross-curricula and to involve the whole school, marking the moment of its centenary by celebrating the histories, experiences and journeys of its current population. Using photography, video, drawing, digital imaging, sound and text the media were brought together into multimedia stories by the children, working with the artists, in *Hyperstudio*. One of the main aims was to give young children and teachers in early years education access to digital technologies as *producers*, and through the internet, to encourage links with other schools. Another aim was to ensure that this access and the impetus to use new technologies didn't end with the project, and my evaluation continued beyond the production period, until July 1997.

De@fsite at Blanche Nevile school, in North London, was a three month artists' residency (March–June 1998) which developed out of a larger Deaf multimedia initiative at The Photographers' Gallery. This initiative had enabled five deaf and partially hearing artists to explore their personal histories, languages and cultures through digital arts, producing a unique and diverse collection of Deaf identities. Two of these artists, Niall McCormick and Damien Robinson then worked with a group of six profoundly deaf young people, helping them create their own multimedia work in response to the artists' CD, a selection of which is now on the website: http://www.artec.org.uk/de@fsite. For all these young people, English is a second or even third language.

Some of the aims for this project were similar to those above, in terms of giving access to technologies and encouraging their creative uses. However, there were also specific aims related to Deaf issues, namely: that the artists and their work would provide role models for these young people who, like 90 per cent of deaf children, have hearing families; that the project be conducted through British Sign Language (BSL) by native signers; and that the work these young people made might be seen, via the internet, by a wide audience (deaf and hearing), thus creating a learning exchange.

Evaluative strategies

All three of these projects had external funding for extra resourcing, all had artists in school and work was not produced as exam material – although the George Orwell work was finished in the first year of Key Stage 4 and was subject to 'end of key stage' evaluations. But there was an evaluative requirement to the work, and there is an inevitable pressure to justify work of this kind; it relies heavily on external funding and can sometimes be viewed as a disruption to the standard curriculum.

In evaluating any piece of work or activity the evaluator must be aware of the general context in which the work is being produced, as well as any particularities of the situation. As an outsider, one might be able to adopt an apparently objective position from which to view a project but, equally, one might be prejudiced by not having enough insight into, say, a specific student's abilities or the traditions of a particular art department. In many ways I have had a peculiar advantage in these projects, in that I grew to know the students quite well, just as they became used to my questioning. This doesn't make me more or less objective (no evaluation is truly objective), but I think it has informed and enriched my overall view. To a large extent the evaluation focussed on what the young people themselves gained from this work, from their own perspectives as well as from the perspectives of those adults involved. The evaluation was based on observation, small group discussions, one-to-one interviews and students' written comments. It also involved the work itself and to some extent, immediate audience response (that is parents, peers, other teachers) and email responses from a wider public.

Getting young people to be critical thinkers, initially from the point of their own work, and then in appraising the work of other artists, means involving them in the process of evaluation and at George Orwell particularly I was able to do this: a number of them interviewed each other during the final residency. At the start of this project none of the students found it very easy to articulate responses to their own and each other's work beyond saying they did or didn't like it. Many were unconfident about voicing an opinion or unable to explain why a picture made them respond favourably (or not). And of course, some of them spoke very little English. Later in the project, for those who were reluctant to give verbal responses, I thought individual written pieces might give them an opportunity to put down their thoughts in relative privacy (although again, for the pupils who have difficulty with English, writing can be a problem). In fact, those pupils who were most responsive in class or group discussions were the same ones who found it easiest to express their thoughts in the written evaluation, indicating a strong link between the two activities. By the end of three years, discussion and debate around their work had become much more integrated into the process of working. As Ross *et al.* argue:

> The advantage we see in the use of conversational talk to explore and elicit aesthetic understanding is that it furnishes the appraisers (both teacher and pupil) with relevant, subjective, yet public evidence upon which to base reasoned judgements.
>
> (Ross *et al.* 1993: 66)

At Rosendale the *development* of the project, prior to actually working in multimedia, was seen as crucial. Ideas were explored with the artists, through photography, writing, talking and drawing and this greatly enhanced the final work because issues were already becoming familiar. In a sense, a form of reflective practice was being fostered as ideas were discussed, demonstrated, tried out, discussed again and then translated into digital work. Multimedia facilitated this reflexive and flexible working process, whereby work made early on in the project could be incorporated and then built on, by the same or different children, in the final interactive piece. But it was actually the artists who built in this practice, right from the start, enabling cross-year and cross-curricular links to happen. Another working principle was that talking was fundamental to the project (see Figure 9.1). When a small group of children were working with one of the artists at the computer it was seen as paramount that in order to develop the children's storytelling abilities, they should be able to converse or recount freely, while the adult typed. Shona commented that 'This kind of storytelling, imaginative description that conjures up images for other people, is very sophisticated . . . and this environment was particularly conducive to getting children to create pictures, images in other children's minds of places or whatever.'

As well as the text, there was the possibility of adding voices. Indeed, the multi-modal format allowed children to experiment with and layer a whole range of linguistic conventions within the vocal and textual forms used. These ranged from commentary, explanation, critique, conversation and

Figure 9.1 Rosendale Infants School: photographer Dave Lewis with a year one group discussing their photographs

interview to songs, captions, storytelling (fact and fiction), oral history and jokes. With these different forms of language, the children were able to extend or re-enforce or even disrupt the meaning of the images. Susan Sharpe, the IT co-ordinator talking about the *Hyperstudio* work she went on to do with Year 3, observed that the work was like a message to someone:

> The pictures that they are *drawing* are their representations, and usually you get them to write a label because you can't understand the picture! But *here* you are actually talking about real photographs that in fact you don't need to explain. You don't need to say 'oh, she's wearing a blue dress', or 'I'm going into the park', because that is all evident from the photograph, so you're extending it. . . . Also you can put in a sound, somebody saying something, so if you've got a button that says, you know, 'This is our classroom in school', you don't then need to write that. What you can write about is the other things that you can't see in the picture, that you can't hear, the things that people don't know about.

In control

Ironically, when the work of contemporary digital artists was divesting itself of editorial control, foregrounding the viewers' interpretations, it was the authorial control afforded to these children and young people that gave them such pleasure and motivation. Their ability to create, or gather, the original material, to manipulate the images, to make design decisions, to edit, decide when the work was finished and then present it to an audience was immensely enjoyable. At George Orwell it was sometimes accompanied by a pretty steep learning curve, but the realisation that they had learnt something was also valuable:

AYESHA: I learned this you know – it's better to work with your friends than on your own. I don't enjoy working on my own. It's nice whenever I work with my friends.

SAMMY: I think if we'd had more time to do more work on the slides we could have improved it (the tape/slide), made it look better. We could have watched it the first time, the way it moved through. So the second time we would have known what to do, where to put things . . . improved it by getting more stuff, more pictures and realistic sounds to go with the pictures . . .

GERARD: When you see things on TV it does seem like it's easy but when we do it ourselves, the amount of hard work that goes into it, I mean like, you get a better understanding.

ALOM: It's more fun making it than just seeing it. It's better going through the process.

NASEEMA: When you get used to it (the computer), it can be easy, but it

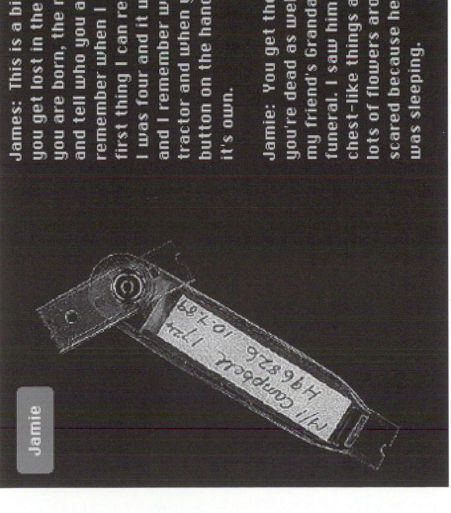

Jamie

James: This is a birth tag so that if you get lost in the hospital, when you are born, the nurses can read it and tell who you are. I can't remember when I was born. The first thing I can remember is when I was four and it was my birthday and I remember what I got. I got a tractor and when you press the button on the handle it moves on it's own.

Jamie: You get those tags when you're dead as well. I saw one on my friend's Grandad. I went to his funeral. I saw him in one of those chest-like things and there were lots of flowers around. I wasn't scared because he looked like he was sleeping.

Figure 9.2 Rosendale Infants School: James and Jamie on the mysteries of life and death

doesn't print colour properly . . . and it's difficult to cut pictures out properly.

ASMA: On the computer you can do some things you can't do in art. You can do different sort of graphics . . . it's good for quite a lot of things: writing and doing different textures of writing and drawing out different layouts. And it's much easier to change if you make a mistake.

It is worth noting that there was a strong perception that this project wasn't like 'art' – Art is about drawing and painting and if you're not good at that you're no good at art. The fact that art is overwhelmingly still viewed as a practical (usually observational) subject using traditional media is significant. But a number of the students commented on how this project actually broadened their idea of 'what art is' and how, freed from the skill-based requirements of drawing and painting, they were able to express themselves and realise their ideas through photography and multimedia:

ANNELISE: I think it's good because sometimes you just tend to think that art is just about drawing but you can actually do 3D stuff and you can do things on the computer. I didn't know that before . . . just like some people are good at drawing but some people ain't so it's going to help. They might have different skills so they can show what they are capable of doing without a pencil.

FAIZA: I just make stuff. At first I thought art was all about drawing, just drawing, but it can be computer work or anything you want you know. This year I'm making something out of clay and last year I was making animation on the computer and the year before it was photography . . .

EZE: It's better than using a pencil I reckon. It's easier. You can put more things onto a computer than you can onto a piece of paper. You've got more options. You can experiment.

The computer work wasn't indiscriminately preferred over all the other techniques used. For instance, an original group photo of three boys was liked better than the 'Photoshop-ed' version which was felt to be messy and cluttered. But on the whole, the aesthetic parity between the look of students' digital work and professional work did mean they felt proud of what they had done. The computer was felt to offer more possibilities and flexibility than other media and the ability to alter or erase things was particularly popular.

At Rosendale Joey felt that there were advantages to traditional and digital media:

With my drawing, you can change the paint, add water or add colour and do the clouds. You can move the brush to get it darker or lighter. If you use a pen you have to scribble for ages to fill it in. But in the computer you just get the bucket and fill it in. It's really easy but it's flat.

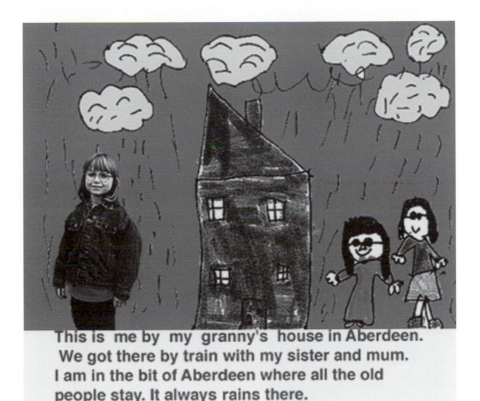

This is me by my granny's house in Aberdeen.
We got there by train with my sister and mum.
I am in the bit of Aberdeen where all the old
people stay. It always rains there.

Figure 9.3 Rosendale Infants School: 'It always rains in Aberdeen' by Joey

The themes of these projects provided an opportunity for all the pupils to use their own personal experiences in making work. No one style or cultural experience was privileged and the fact that the artists who worked with them came from different cultural backgrounds served to emphasise the value of difference. At Rosendale, collaboration was central to the process and all the children were involved, to some extent, in the production. They were able to recognise their work as both isolated elements on a screen and as part of a whole. Use of family photos, interviews, oral histories and images of personal significance, plus parental involvement and links to home, all helped to motivate the children and foster an interest in each other. Shona noted:

> It was very interesting to see how the project worked towards giving children a greater understanding and allowed them to develop an interest in each other's (cultural) experiences and also, at that age, to see a kind of pleasure in diversity appearing. In a sense their first audience was each other.

Figure 9.4 George Orwell School: 'My adorable darling', screenshot from an animation by Faiza, Naseema and Jahanara

The classroom context and beyond

At Blanche Nevile – where the videoed interviews were conducted in sign language, then transcribed, so inevitably losing some things in translation – the communal aspects of sharing ideas and helping each other were also highly valued:

ISAAC: I think all of us know we really learned a lot, with the computer. We all sign together in a group, talk about our ideas, about what we wanted to do.

SEVAL: We also learned words that we didn't know – about the computer – you know all the words (vocabulary) that it uses. Then when it was finished we'd learned all these new words, I thought that was really interesting.

GASPARE: Like with Niall, he would tell us all the different things you could do with the tools and how to use the different menus, like getting different colours, making it lighter and darker, how to smudge things, how to layer one image on top of another, all those sort of different effects. With art you're just sort of drawing, by yourself, and its boring, but this was great. You know when you've got the photo from the digital camera you can cut bits out and then use the different tools to make different effects and draw things on the screen, maybe move things, change the image, change the size.

SPIRO: Yes, composition, we learned all that. You could use all the different facilities within the computer to get different effects, we learned how to bring down different menus and use the different techniques. It's like in a shop, you know, when they serve you, you can see what's for sale, what's available, and then you can use it.

This last comment was wonderful to see signed because in recounting what he had done through sign language Spiro was demonstrating in a most graphic way, what he had learned. If he had to write an account he probably wouldn't have got past the first sentence. In many ways this sums up for me, the value of multi-modal communications. It provides alternative means of expression for people whose cultures don't accord with dominant or standardised forms.

At George Orwell the public nature of a whole class discussion or presentation proved very revealing at an age when who you like and what you look like are so important. Mehmet's text piece was liked for the colour and graphic qualities (font choice and layering effects), regardless of what the Turkish text actually meant (see Figure 9.6). But it was, nevertheless, publicly translated as a clandestine love letter, much to the embarrassment of the object of his desires! One girl commented on a portrait which Danijah had helped her take six months earlier (when she had brought in her favourite clothes) that, the skirt and top were ok but 'the tights have to go!'. So, even

Figure 9.5 Blanche Nevile School: Spiro and Gaspare's digital imaging

when they have control over their images, the pleasure they get from the activity may not be reflected in their response to the final picture. When dealing with issues related to image and identity it's important to realise that these are shifting concepts rather than fixed positions.

When we broached the subject of audience at Blanche Nevile, in preparation for their presentation in the mainstream school, there was a mixed response.

SPIRO: No I don't want to.
HILAL: Oh I do, I want to.
DAVINIA: I want to as well.
SPIRO: No I think it's private. Deaf People can come and see it, but it should be just for deaf people. Hearing people are just being nosy. It's for deaf people.
ISAAC: Any people can come and see it if they're interested. They're not being nosy.
SPIRO: No they might laugh at the facial expressions, hearing people are like that. No, just for deaf people, for a Deaf audience, in BSL. I don't want to show it to a hearing audience.
GASPARE: When I was showing some work to Niall some (hearing) boys were watching and laughing at our expressions.
HILAL: No hold on, I want to say something. If hearing people see our art project they might be interested. They might ask us how we did it and then we can explain, you know, so they could see . . . they never mix with deaf people so maybe they wouldn't criticise us . . . they'd actually be gobsmacked with the work we've done.

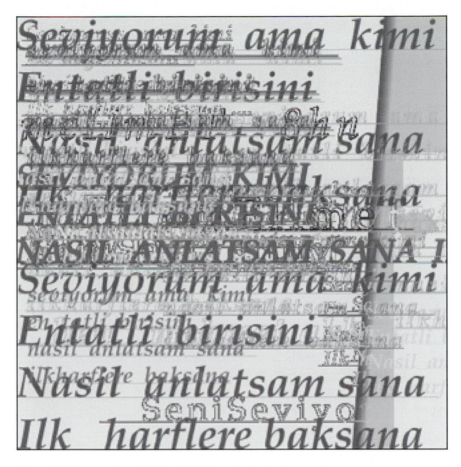

Figure 9.6 George Orwell School: Mehmet's photoshop work

It was in the context of discussing audience that the most vocal opinions (for and against showing work) were expressed and it is precisely this which potentially makes digital technology different. Through the internet, this school art work can virtually be seen by anyone.

Pleasure

What these observations suggest is an open and flexible approach to student production and its evaluation which takes its lead, at least in part, from the desires, expectations and values of those young people who are making the work. 'Teachers are rightly uncomfortable about assessing those aspects of children's art which are concerned with meaning, values and attitudes' (Buchanan 1994: 6). What we tried to do was address the makers' 'meaning, values and attitudes' first, rather than simply applying our own. In my own experience, and in the majority of accounts which I have read, work of this kind seems to provide motivation for young people (see Sefton-Green 1998). What is less clear is where exactly the motivation lies. I have already suggested one reason, namely the possibility of making a creative contribution which is not measured by the seemingly unattainable standards of conventional practice. Making multimedia allows for a form of creative expression which is not usually judged by the same criteria as drawing or writing, but can, nevertheless, display imaginative composition, technical prowess, narrative understanding, a wide range of cultural influences, ironic comment and visual invention. It can also exhibit critique through a sophisticated understanding of structure and conventions, parody and humour. Young people are very familiar with the constant remaking, remodelling and recycling of visual and aural forms, none of which are judged harshly, simply *because* they borrow or quote. Other possible motivating factors might be one or a combination of the following: the possibility for collaborative work, the opportunity to work with artists, the autobiographical nature of the content or the pleasure of interacting with the technology itself. This last point is one I want to emphasise because in education, this sometimes seems like a dirty secret.

The idea (originally proposed by Hume) that art is chiefly valued by the degree to which it gives pleasure or enjoyment is still commonly shared, but it does not seem to be one of the criteria for valuing art made by young people in schools, especially at secondary level. Here, the idea of pleasure as a response, is largely absent. Instead school art is meant to exhibit craft skill, aesthetic understanding, formal sophistication and possibly conceptual rigour. But making something well can give a great deal of pleasure, both in terms of realising an idea and mastering a technique. In assessment terms these achievements might not be apparent, but they may be of paramount importance to the maker. The values of play and pleasure in creative work have almost been lost in the scramble to meet attainment targets, but for young people they might just be the main reason they turn up for the lesson, as Graham suggests:

> Few people find it improper for schools and universities to encourage their students to devote themselves to intensive study of the arts (though some may query the content of the curriculum) . . . But they might well object if they were told that in teaching art, schools aimed to *amuse* their pupils.
>
> (Graham 1997: 7)

Enjoyment – in evaluative terms – says almost nothing. In relation to art practice surely we need to examine what produces pleasure from an object or event? That art gives pleasure or enjoyment may be true but if this is all it does, is that enough for it to be judged good art? In a sense there is always the unspoken idea that good art *transcends* this and affects us spiritually, as well as emotionally, or at least affords us a more serious sort of pleasure than mere amusement. However, this argument seems to brings us back to the conflict where high culture opposes low culture, where an ideological affirmation of one type of art as opposed to another serves to confirm a social structure of dominance. But if a viewer and a maker are able to articulate, or at least speculate what is pleasurable about the work, what makes it visually or emotionally or intellectually satisfying, then shouldn't this too be part of the value system we apply?

When it comes to the judgement of the multimedia work I have described, there is no doubt that someone assessing a finished piece from the outside would be most unlikely to understand the production process. In addition, the piece is as likely to be penalised for merely mimicking popular media forms as for falling short of professional standards. But I think the most difficult issue for many teachers of art is what did the pupil do as opposed to what the machine did? This question simply does not arise in the tactile manipulation of traditional art media where mark-making is obviously the product of the student. But this search for 'the mark of the child' is not as complex as it seems if teachers have at least a cursory understanding of how these programs work. In a typical computer paint package, while there is no direct manipulation of paint to produce the exact colour shade and texture – by mixing, diluting and brush sweep – there are equivalent decisions with regard to picking from a colour chart, changing density or opacity, using a variety of tools or applying an effect. In each case the student will be considering a range of options, making a decision, trying it out and possibly undoing it and trying something new. In essence, there is no problem applying many of the same criteria relating to the formal properties of a piece once we have become familiar with what the 'tool' can do. Similarly, if work is assessed as a traditional piece of collage or photomontage, there should be no problem in evaluating the digital version. The fact that the digital version is smoother and perhaps more 'polished' is merely the digital aesthetic, just as the way the textural layering of a paper collage has its own aesthetic. The fact that young people are using a computer (as opposed to paint or print materials) to generate and manipulate images, should have no bearing on the value of the work produced. Nevertheless, there are qualities which I see as specific to digital media and which do need to be considered, not only in a critical appraisal, but perhaps more crucially in regard to the media's place in education.

Evaluating multimedia

As I have suggested, the difficulty in evaluation does not lie solely in an unfamiliarity with the technology, though this might cause an initial distraction. In their publication, *Fusion*, the NCET suggests that 'the goal in using IT in Art is the development of manipulative skills in a range of computer processes and an increased knowledge and understanding of the visual and tactile elements related to pupil's own ideas' (NCET 1998: 27). As this book-let goes on to explain, the assessment of this kind of activity is not so different from that of work produced using other art processes. But I would argue strongly that there are other broader objectives for using digital media production within and beyond art which are conceptually more challenging and aesthetically less conventional.

The first of these objectives relates to how multimedia facilitates students' conceptual development:

> I regularly visit art schools either to give lectures or as an external examiner and in recent years there has been a recurrent crisis over the assessment of a certain kind of art practice. It is usually photo-text, scripto-visual or some such form; it is often sustained by reference to a body of cultural theories; it generally handles the question of gender, representation, sexuality. The students offering such work are often well thought of intellectually and produce theoretically developed work in complementary studies and art history. Most of the resident staff do not like this work and cannot assess it. (They still try to do so nonetheless.) To an art historian involved with a decade and a half of conceptual art, as well as the diverse and substantial feminist practices of that period, such work, if not brilliant, is recognisable in terms of what it is address-ing, what frames of reference are suggested, what the work is trying to do. It is, by any criteria, certainly assessable.
>
> (Pollock G. 1985: 50)

Pollock articulates the key difficulty with issue-based, multi-disciplinary, multimedia practice, namely the unfamiliar concepts which are interrogated and the new modes of production which are made possible by the technol-ogy – exactly these attributes have drawn artists like Piper, Prophet, Kempadoo and Pope to experiment with it. It is a technology which lends itself to refiguring, remaking and recombining – a digital bricolage of images and styles and a plurality of ideas. While it is possible that this might be done for purely aesthetic reasons, the meanings which emerge from such constructions are often surprising and ambiguous. They raise questions and debate rather than statements and facts and this, as I have said elsewhere (Sinker 1996), can mean such work does not sit easily in the curriculum. As Pollock suggests, this sort of work does emerge out of a substantial body of theory and practice and the practice continues a dialogue with the theory. Such work is closely connected to arguments which occurred not only in the art of the period, but in politics and cultural studies.

One pitfall with the inclusion of issue-based work into an otherwise orthodox art curriculum is that it can sometimes become 'cultural-politics-lite', a sort of watered down critical approach to image-making which uses the framework of inquiry, without any deep or informed investigation. Rec-ognition of bias or stereotype within a history of visual representation is the first stage of critical understanding, but unless the production of students' work, in response, is also the subject of critical reflection then I would argue that the process is incomplete. 'Work does not automatically gain depth or power because it supports an issue' and there is often a gulf between having an idea and having the 'visual eloquence' to create and communicate it (Buchanan 1994: 4). An artist's work can engage critically with a subject and/or a medium. It does not have to advance a doctrine or wear an issue on its sleeve to exhibit a contextual understanding. Mona Hatoum's work, which is formally and materially rigorous and often site-specific, suggests and implies certain conditions through its being, without being 'about' an issue.

It has been suggested that there is a problem with evaluating work of a personal nature in the sense that a large part of what is apparently being judged is the producer herself; her ideas, values, culture and morals. And if this is the case who is in any position to critique any one else?

> In evaluating pupils' work one confronts work which contains personal, individual feelings, perceptions, values and attitudes. It is necessary to consider how to gain access to such meaning in order to decode and 'read' the work as it was intended.
>
> (Buchanan 1994: 7)

In order to avoid either imposing one's own cultural and aesthetic values, or those which are statutorily sanctioned (assuming these are not one and the same), it is necessary to examine these values and allow young people to offer up their own so that the existence of different *value systems* is apparent. Chambers suggests that until we examine our beliefs, values and prejudices, we will continue to promote our own particular world-view and possibly marginalise others as a result (Chambers 1996: 69). As individuals in a society which encourages the notion of individuality, we have all been formed by a multiplicity of values and influences and the same is no less true of the young people we teach – but these values will not necessarily be the same ones. Teaching involves making evaluative decisions. So does making. The key thing is for these to be transparent and negotiated and to be included in a process of production which also involves, research, observation, experimentation, reflection, practice, dialogue, argument, and imagination. I would also argue that successful making and good teaching both involve risk. But risk-taking is not a popular methodology in schools right now because its potential consequence – failure – is not well-handled and tends to be viewed as an end rather than part of a process.

Conclusion

As complex constructions of aesthetic, symbolic and narrative conventions, multimedia technologies cry out for a joint approach to teaching and learning by art and media education, which threads through all the subjects. I am aware that this is not an original proposition and that this call to collaborate has been previously advocated by many when the common technology was identified as photography (Hornsby 1987; Isherwood and Stanley 1994; Phillips 1991; Walton1995). This current call emphasises the position of multimedia as a core communications technology within ICT, and it already has an interdisciplinary mandate. Radnor has identified that in the context of the National Curriculum, the term 'curriculum' is 'virtually synonymous with subject' (Radnor 1994: 3). But she gives a very clear rationale, including evaluation guidelines, for the value of cross-curricular work at all levels, even within the present structure. Her book was written before the full impact of digital technologies could be gauged. Nevertheless, there is one entry by an IT advisory teacher which argues for a cross-curricular approach. 'I am trying to raise people's eyes above the trench as it were to look at the bigger picture ... If you take one of these cross-curricular themes it can flow from one subject area to another and by using IT as the recording process you can then have some sense of where it is going' (Radnor 1994:106).

Multimedia and the internet put the student and the teacher in much more immediate contact with the sorts of issues and ideas which are quite easily closed off or left unaddressed by a traditional curriculum and its resources. The politics of pleasure and the politics of difference can be uncomfortable. As Stuart Hall has noted, 'Multiculturalism is not an easy option. Living with difference is troubling not restful ...', but as he goes to say, 'It's the price of our survival' (Hall 1997: 5). It has been suggested that the power relationships between teacher and learners are being shifted by the introduction of digital technologies, through the questions of expertise – away from the teacher as the repository of skill and knowledge towards the student – and the opening up of schools to an external audience. Time will reveal how radical these shifts might actually be – whether they are more perceived than real – but it will depend, in part, on how much educationalists welcome them.

The McLuhan statement which fronts this piece was chosen deliberately as much to provoke as for its visionary sense. Computer operators and producers are now just as likely to be women and children, not just men as he suggests, and the creative imagination is not the exclusive domain of artists. At the closing of this century we are bombarded with predictions for the next, many concerning the effects of digital technology on society and culture. Indeed, both the countdown to the millennium and the technological revolution provide rich pickings for futurologists, and the year 2000 bug is a veritable godsend. But one thing which computer uses have signalled, particularly in the areas of multimedia and web-distribution, is the need to think laterally rather than lineally. That means realising that creative production can happen outside the art room and that art can exist anywhere. The fact that art constitutes a discrete 'subject' within the context of the National Curriculum reflects a historical fight for recognition, but I would question the continuing relevance of this separatism. Multimedia production could allow formal and critical theories of the visual and an understanding of the way different media construct, inform and transform meaning – a much wider definition of visual literacy than that defined in the National Curriculum – to bleed into any discipline. Professional artists, designers, musicians and media producers have all moved on, retaining some traditional values while adopting or inventing new ones, giving them a wider system of histories, styles and beliefs on which to draw. Pencils and clay can be used along with digital cameras and synthesisers. Line and form and Van Gogh's sunflowers can be considered as seriously as identity or ecology or virtual space. Hybridity needs essentialism and contemporary art needs Brian Sewell! If multimedia production serves to help the curriculum make the leap to cyberspace then it will have earned its place.

Acknowledgement

Thanks to all the staff, pupils and artists involved with the projects at George Orwell School, Rosendale Infants School and Blanche Nevile School.

Notes

1 These percentages were only slightly higher (5 per cent each, respectively), for the contribution IT had made to pupils' learning. These figures were quoted by Annie Grant of the TTA at the Art and IT conference (NCET 1996: 67).
2 Notes from a presentation by Mark Little (Northumberland University) on 'The Digital Aesthetic', Liverpool, *ISEA'98*.
3 Pauline van Mourik Broekman (26 July, 1996), from an unpublished interview with Karen Raney
4 As suggested in the BFI curriculum statement for Secondary Media Education

> Media education enhances art education in its understanding of how a text's form defines its likely conventions. It also informs art about patronage and social productions of art, describing practice as less the preserve of 'geniuses' or in a limited range of forms, e.g., drawing or painting, but more about each child's ability to make meaning in a wide variety of cultural forms and media products.
>
> (Bazalgette 1989: 74–75)

References

Barthes, R. (1977) 'The death of the author' in *Image, Music, Text*, London: Fontana Press.
Bailey, D. and Hall, S. (eds) (1992) *Critical Decade: Black British Photography in the 80s* London: Ten·8.
Bazalgette, C. (ed.) (1989) *Primary Media Education: A Curriculum Statement*, London: British Film Institute.
Benjamin, W. (1992) 'The work of art in the age of mechanical reproduction' in *Illuminations*, London: Fontana Press.
Berger, J. (1972) *Ways of Seeing*, London: BBC and Penguin Books.

Brake, J. (1997) *Changing Images: Photography, Education and Young People*, Salford: Viewpoint Photography Gallery.

Brown, P. (1990) 'Metamedia and cyberspace: advanced computers and the future of art' in Hayward, P. (ed.) *Culture, Technology and Creativity*, London: Arts Council of Great Britain with John Libbey.

Buchanan, M. (1994) *Children Making Art: Teachers' Attitudes and Approaches* Notebook series, London: Institute of Education: University of London.

Chambers, F. (1996) *Celebrating Pluralism: Art, Education and Cultural Diversity*, LA: The Getty Education Institute for the Arts.

Collins, J., Hammond, M. and Wellington, J. (1997) *Teaching and Learning with Multimedia*, London: Routledge.

Cubitt, S. (1998) *Digital Aesthetics*, London: Sage Publications Ltd.

DfEE (1995) *Art in the National Curriculum*, London: HMSO.

DfEE (1997) *Connecting the Learning Society*, London: Department for Education and Employment.

Graham, G. (1997) *Philosophy of the Arts*, London: Routledge.

Gupta, S. (July 1998) Review of Roshini Kempadoo's work *Sweetness and Light*. http://www.omnibus-eye.rtvf.nwu.edu/Homestead in *Creative Camera* no. 352, p. 44.

Hall, S. (1997) 'The Tebbit test and other tribal games and races', *The Guardian* 11 October.

Hayward, P. (ed.) (1990) *Culture, Technology and Creativity*, London: Arts Council of Great Britain with John Libbey.

Hornsby, J. (1987) *Photography, Art and Media Education*, Brighton: South East Arts/ East Sussex County Council.

Isherwood, S. and Stanley, N. (1994) *Creating Vision: Photography and the National Curriculum*, Manchester: The Arts Council/Cornerhouse Publications.

Keen, M. (ed.) (1998) *Frequencies: Investigations into Culture, History and Technology*, London: inIVA.

Kennedy, M. (1995) 'Issue-based work at Key Stage Four: Crofton School – a case study', *Journal of Art and Design Education*, vol. 14, no. 1. pp. 7–20.

Kress, G. and van Leeuwen, T. (1996) *Reading Images: The Grammar of Visual Design*, London: Routledge.

Lachs, V. (1999) 'The moving picture science show: working with multimedia in the classroom' in Sefton-Green, J. (ed.) *Creativity, Young People and New Technologies: the Challenge of Digital Arts*, London: Routledge.

Lanham, R. (1993) *The Electronic Word: Democracy, Technology and the Arts*, Chicago: University of Chicago Press.

Lister, M. (ed.) (1995) *The Photographic Image in Digital Culture*, London: Routledge.

McLuhan, M. (1958 and 1964) in McLuhan, E. and Zingrone, F. (ed.) (1995) *Essential McLuhan*, London: Routledge.

Mercer, K. (1997) from *In the Cut-and-Mix: Possibilities in Collage, Multimedia and Digital Technologies*, a panel discussion with Gary Stewart and Keith Piper, Royal College of Art. London 5 August 1997 http://www.iniva.org/cut_mix/cutmix1.html.

Mitchell, W. J. (1992) *The Reconfigured Eye: Visual Truth in the Post-Photographic Era*, Cambridge, Mass.: MIT Press.

Morley, D. and Robins, K. (1995) *Spaces of Identity: Global Media, Electronic Landscapes and Cultural Boundaries*, London: Routledge.

Morrison, E. (1998) 'Ten reasons why the art world hates digital art', *MUTE*, no. 11, p. 25.

NCET (1996) *Art and Information Technology – Conference Report*, Coventry: National Council for Educational Technology.

NCET (1998) *Fusion: Art and IT in Practice*, Coventry: National Council for Educational Technology.

Ordidge, I. (1999) 'The NEMA experience' in Sefton-Green, J. (ed.) *Creativity, Young People and New Technologies: the Challenge of Digital Arts*, London: Routledge.

Phillips, M. (1991) 'Media education and art and design: other ways of seeing', *Journal of Art and Design Education* vol. 10, no. 1, pp. 23–30.

Plant, S. (1997) *Zeros and Ones: Digital Women and the New Technoculture*, London: Fourth Estate.

Pollock, G. (1985) 'Art, art school, culture' in The BLOCK editorial board (ed.) *The Block Reader in Visual Culture'* (1996), London: Routledge.

Radnor H. (1994) *Across the Curriculum*, London: Cassell.

Raney, K. (1998) 'Digital matters' in 'Show and tell' an unpublished manuscript.

Ritchen, F. (1990) *In Our Own Image: The Coming Revolution in Photography*, New York: Aperture.

Ross, M., Radnor, H., Mitchell, S. and Bierton, C. (1993) *Assessing Achievement in the Arts*, Buckingham: Open University Press.

Ross, M. and Kamba, M. 1998: 'The state of the arts – principal research findings', *Journal for Art and Design Education* vol. 17, no. 2, pp. 197–200.

Rutherford, J. (1998), *Young Britain: Politics, Pleasures and Predicaments*, London: Lawrence & Wishart.

Sefton-Green, J. (ed.) (1998) *Digital Diversions: Youth Culture in the Age of Multimedia*, London: UCL Press.

Sinker, R. (1996) 'Work in progress: some issues around research into evaluation and progression within photography and media education', *Journal of Art and Design Education* vol. 15, no. 1, pp. 59–71.

Sinker, R. (1997) 'The Rosendale Odyssey' in Morgan, M. and Robinson, G. (eds) *Developing Art Experience 4–13*, Oxford: Nash Pollock Publishing.

Sinker, R. (1999) 'The Rosendale Odyssey: multimedia memoires and digital journeys' in Sefton-Green, J. (ed.) *Creativity, Young People and New Technologies: The Challenge of Digital Arts*, London: Routledge.

Spender, D. (1995) *Nattering on The Net: Women, Power and Cyber space*, Melbourne: Spinifex Press.

Walton, K. (1995) *Picture My World – Photography in Primary Education*, London: Arts Council of England.

Wellington J. (1989) *Education for Employment: The Place of IT*, Windsor: NFER-Nelson.

Willis, D. (1994) *Picturing Us*, New York: New Press.

Wombell, P. (1991) *Photovideo: Photography in the Age of the Computer*, London: Rivers Oram Press.

10   From creativity to cultural production

Shared perspectives

Julian Sefton-Green

This chapter is organised in two parts. The first section tries to extrapolate some of the common arguments from the previous chapters, offering a series of perspectives *evaluating evaluation*. The final sections of the chapter argue that we need to explore other models of *cultural production* if we want to change how we value creative work by young people in schools today.

Evaluating evaluation

The limits of evaluation

The contributors to this book have all concentrated their discussion on the theory and practice of evaluation within their subject disciplines. There has been a considerable amount of common ground, not least because the larger context, the changes in assessment procedures in relation to the implementation of the National Curriculum in the UK, has direct bearing on young people's experience of schooling and the values of their education. There are also important differences between the subjects – or at least between the traditions emphasised by the authors collected here – and I shall return to these later. I want to begin the discussion here by paying attention to some of the similarities across the different subjects. The most obvious point of agreement is the unstated one: that evaluation is central to both the discipline of the art form and the pedagogy, the teaching and learning, of each subject.

From this point of view, discussion about evaluation has clearly moved on from some of the arts educationalists of the 1970s, discussed in the introduction, where debate focused not just on how to evaluate progress in the arts, but whether it could, or even should, be done at all. Although several of the contributors here want to be cautious about the evaluation process, for example Garvey and Quinlan explore the potential negative effects of evaluation on children's self-esteem and the difficulty of developing an open culture of criticism in the social environment of the classroom, none of these writers consider dispensing with evaluation as a whole. So what is the point of evaluation?

There seem to be two common arguments here. The first is that in the disciplines discussed here, practitioners are distinguished by their capacities to *self-evaluate* as part of the creative process, or even the experience of production. In other words, whether you are an artist, writer, designer or musician, unless you learn how to stand outside your work and judge its quality, you are unlikely to get very far. There are obviously debates about what constitutes quality and differences in emphasis about how the 'maker' gets feedback about the product, but nevertheless, a key theme is that evaluation is central to the creative process. This is not necessarily an original argument, it is at the heart of most general theories of learning (e.g., Bruner 1996) and creativity in the arts (e.g., White 1993), but it is clearly important to build into the curriculum. From a pedagogic point of view this principle also means that evaluation is not just something teachers do to students, but something that teachers need to be able to get students to do for themselves. This has important ramifications for the power relation between the assessor and the assessed and perhaps is one of the key points of difference between assessment and evaluation.

The second argument follows on from this point. When teachers evaluate there is a tendency to conflate an attention to a student's product with the desire to record the student's *learning*. The learning may be social (negotiating a group situation), it may be cognitive, skills focused or even to do with specific subjects or general knowledge, but its concern is the development of the student and not the value of the product. Somers' discussion of Drama in Chapter six particularly identified this dilemma. As he and a number of contributors suggest, this is not an absolute distinction: sometimes the learning is *implicit* in the product, sometimes explicit in the accompanying talk or writing, sometimes the work itself may have little or no interest in itself, whilst in others, it may be the sole focus of attention. Nevertheless, for different reasons in the development of different subjects, evaluation tends to oscillate between these twin foci. Undoubtedly this leads to some confusion for the pragmatic reason, alluded to in the introduction, that evaluation is, perforce, used for many things at the same time – a sort of double accounting – without a precise attention to the teachers' mixture of motives.

However, what underpins all of the perspectives collected in this volume is the realisation that evaluation (both for the student and by the teacher) is most useful when most explicit. Indeed, it is striking how much common ground there is between the subjects in this respect. The 'response protocols' of English, the 'logs' in Media Studies, the 'talk' in Art, Green's three-part model for Music and so on are all attempts to find mechanisms which facilitate an openness and a common ground. This works at both levels identified above: it helps makers understand how their product is 'read' by, or interacts with, its audience; and it establishes a common purpose and shared agenda for the students' learning (see Edwards and Mercer 1987). Yet this idea, that being explicit gets us beyond the hidden cultural assumptions about artistic value, judgement and taste, can also be an illusion.

There is the suggestion that being explicit equals being distanced and objective, but this is not necessarily true. Having explicit criteria for judging a piece of work is obviously better, most contributors suggest, than having implicit value coded in the culture and language of tradition, but it does not mean we have reached a situation where we can leave behind ideas about taste and absolute value. What explicitness does is put the student and the teacher into a situation where the criteria for evaluation are shared and themselves evaluated. In other words, being explicit can make a difference when it allows for a discussion of the criteria themselves. If it merely reifies set and externally imposed values it may not be that different from relying on the scary teacher judgement – the teacher who knows what he or she likes but can't or won't say why.

This tension between the need to continually justify and re-assess evaluative criteria is going to be different in different circumstances. The multimedia discussed by Sinker in Chapter nine, is at an advantage here, in that *avant garde* practice always has to make up its own rules: though as Buckingham *et al.*'s discussion of early Media Studies examiners (Chapter seven) also proves, we all tend to use established criteria to make sense of new subjects and work. Sinker's chapter also points to a kind of 'cultural convergence', where new media is part of the range of influences re-fashioning traditional subject boundaries, and certainly in the school context, multimedia as a new practice poses fundamental questions about why we evaluate in the first place. Ultimately, despite the argument for explicit dialogue and transparent evaluation procedures there is, as was argued in the introduction, a theoretical tension between the desire to make judgements and the ability to justify those values in an environment, like the school, whose whole *raison d'être* is the making of judgements about individuals. As I argued in Chapter one, this tension is most acute if we try to rationalise macro-sociological perspectives about the role of the school with a micro-focus on how individual judgements get made within the classroom. The language of transcendence, frequently employed by arts educators (Abbs 1994) does try to make grandiose claims to get beyond this tension, but this is substituting rhetoric for reality. All the discussion in this book, and the wider debates about evaluation, accept that evaluation is the exercise of power, sometimes gentle, sometimes cruel, but nevertheless, involving some kind of judgement over others. However hard the talk in Art or response protocols in English try, they cannot escape this structural inequality and, from this point of view, it is important not to pretend that modern evaluation procedures in some way evade the centrality of the power relationship, both in the fields of the arts and the subjects discussed in this book. This then is a limit to evaluation: it may be absolutely necessary to the process of cultural production, it may be more effective when explicit and carried out in a non-hierarchical fashion, but nevertheless, it is part of the exercise of power carried out by schools over young people (see Ball 1990).

The contradictions of evaluation

One helpful way of exploring the differences both between the authors collected here and within their own subject-based discussions is to identify some of the key oppositions that have emerged in the preceding chapters. This is not to suggest that any of these authors have been particularly partial in their work – quite the opposite, in fact – but that in order for us to move forward we have to be clear about the kinds of tensions that continue to vex practitioners and educators alike.

First of all, it is clear that in a variety of subjects there is still a history of opposing critical abilities with creative ones, of implying that the skills of making stand against those of judging. Some of the rationale for these distinctions is presumed to be psychological, some cultural. This particular opposition is often supported by activities that further separate both kinds of practice. Thus, for example, students frequently write critical essays about great painters or musicians, but fail to connect their work in such writing with practical activities. It is quite possible that underlying this particular opposition is a key point of social difference in Western societies; the distinction between manual and mental labour. Paradoxically, creative or making kind of work (especially in the plastic arts) is seen as manual and often involves physical dexterity, whereas critical work is conceptualised as the disinterested play of mind. This divide is particularly pronounced in the subjects of English, Media Studies and Art, though not perhaps in Music.

Further key oppositions relate to the kinds of judgements made about art works. Thus, there is, despite Somers' arguments, a distinction between form and content; between technical skills and self-expression (whatever the need of the former to realise the latter); between empty, lifeless products and those full of meaning and individuality. Here, the paradox of genre comes into play. Student's work is regularly praised and vilified for the same reason: it can either be too imitative and therefore not original, or so idiosyncratic that it doesn't follow a recognised pattern (see Buckingham *et al.* 1995 ch. 6). Sometimes the aim of creative activities is to teach students to work in genres, in others, as Robinson and Ellis argue, they are criticised for not being imaginative enough. In Music and Drama there tends to be a tension between performance and composition, or acting/playing and writing. This again replays an imaginary opposition between creative inspiration (writers/ composers/painters) and actors/players in which, in a further paradox, at its best (great actors, actresses and virtuoso performers) can be described as original, creative and inspired but at its more mundane (jobbing actors, fourth violins, hack portrait painters) is seen very much as second best – as shadows of the original.

Final dualities explored in the preceding chapters relate directly to the process of evaluation itself. Thus, attention has swayed between product and process, although more subtle writers always try to acknowledge the implicit process in the product and the role of product in the assessment of process. I have already touched on the tension between evaluating the product, making a value judgement, and evaluating students' learning. There is also a potential conflict between teaching students to evaluate, and conducting evaluations ourselves – including, in a further twist, of the students' capacity to evaluate *themselves* and their own work.

In very broad terms, many of these oppositions can be traced to a clash of paradigms underpinning how we conceptualise creative work: that is, between a romantic and a cultural model of creativity. The former views creativity as an attribute of special individuals and tends to value qualities of originality and imagination; the latter makes sense of creative production in terms of broader social actions and tends to value the social and *dialogic* nature of genre as well as the input of the maker's reflexive critical understanding to the creative process. The strength of emphasis the different traditions of evaluation pay to process and product tend to reflect the paradigms of creativity used by different educational movements. An attention to process tends to reflect a cultural model of creativity, while a single-minded concern with product stems from the romantic paradigm. However, this is an over-simplification, although I do return to some of these points in the section on a social theory of creativity below, my argument here is to note how *schematic* much of the debate is, and to point to the ways in which the authors represented in this volume try to move beyond these rather constricting binary oppositions.

Thus in Art, Raney and Hollands suggest that dialogue crosses the divide between criticism and making; and a similar role for writing as part of the reflective process, is suggested in the chapter on Media Studies. Green suggests a holistic model to describe Music; and in English the challenge is to incorporate the positive aspects of the recent return to basic skills with a broader sense of the value of children's writing. In Design, Garvey and Quinlan try to integrate ambitious ideas about evaluation into the heart of the making process; and in Drama, Somers tries to suggest a multi-dimensional approach incorporating a range of perspectives. The informal arts educators do not want to be assigned to single perspectives and digital arts are in a position to write new rules for evaluation fully developing the partial perspectives criticised across the full range of subject disciplines.

Given such agreement about the complex and multi-dimensional nature of the evaluation process why, it must be asked, do these authors feel they need to make such a case, simply, in many examples, just to be a little bit more complicated than the current system seems to allow? Are debates about evaluation just another example of the emperor's new clothes, with everybody not wanting to point out that we might not disagree as much as we think. Part of the answer here relates to the fact that evaluation, as is practised, is always much more crude than theorists, even those grounded in practice, want to acknowledge. By definition, what happens in the day-to-day hurly-burly cannot be as subtle as we would like. However, I would also point to the argument raised in my introduction, that the active disempowerment of teachers from the process of educational change, especially that of involvement in assessment procedures, has excluded the perspectives of this book from curriculum reform. Thus, if one of the main arguments of this collection is that we need to allow for greater complexity in the evaluation process rather than simple measurements of fake singularities, this is not just because academics love to complicate for its own sake. It is because there is a genuine belief, that to improve arts education we need to allocate the proper resources, especially teacher-time, to allow for a meaningful understanding of making and creating within the school system.

Evaluation and postmodernity

As the chapter on Music particularly suggests, one key reason why evaluation seems to be such a cause for concern at the moment is because we are living through an era which seems to celebrate diversity, pluralism and relativism in the field of culture. Sometimes going under the name of postmodernism, it is suggested that the cultural domain has lost the boundaries and distinctions characterising the strict traditional hierarchies of cultural taste and instead values forms of popular culture – especially validating cultural activities which transgress conventional disciplines. I am not going to discuss this argument in detail here. There is considerable debate about the characteristics of this new aesthetic (see, for example, Collins 1989; Goodwin 1992), how deep-rooted such changes might be (Harvey 1989), and its significance in terms of wider changes in society (McRobbie 1994). Indeed, to an extent, Green's discussion of the effect of postmodernism in the field of Music, is relevant to all the subjects included in this volume; a point also made clear by the arts educators in Chapter eight.

The effect of postmodernism has been most acute in the academy where fierce argument over cultural value is so excessive and vituperative that it is often reported in the press. Madonna was the icon for this furore in the early 1990s (see Schwichtenberg 1993). To briefly summarise this debate: at a sociological level Madonna was celebrated as force for a liberation – an early representative of 'Girl Power' or vilified as model of patriarchal repression; and on a cultural level her videos and performances were analysed as critiques of dominant forms of the representation of woman and sexuality. On the other hand, studies of this kind were seen as evidence of a failure of cultural value – that the academy had so lost its way in that it considered pop videos subjects of serious study.

Whatever one's position on the Madonna debate, she stands as an image for a more general anxiety in the study of culture, and in this respect the overall effect of postmodernism has been to unsettle criteria for evaluation in the arts in two ways – the neo-conservative backlash and cultural relativism. First of all, as Green discusses in detail, and as the chapters on Art and English imply, the National Curriculum Orders in these three subjects suffered from the backlash effect. Both on this side of the Atlantic, and in the

States (see Hughes 1993; Jones 1992), there is evidence of a concerted attempt to return to a nostalgic and conservative view of culture where making judgements about what is good or pleasing is a question of return to a lost world of high culture. On the other hand, it is suggested that all cultural activities have equal value and we can judge them according to their social impact (for a critique of this view, see Frith 1996 ch. 2).

These debates about cultural value obviously impact on subjects at school level in a number of different ways, not all of which are directly relevant here. Indeed, many subjects make an artificial distinction between the critical study of 'great Art' and the practical activities undertaken by students, and do not actively suggest that the same criteria used for discussion of the former should be applied to the latter. As I have already discussed, the peda- gogical perspective – looking at what students learn – often excludes study of what they make. However, as Buckingham *et al.* discuss in Chapter seven, when teachers are placed in an evaluator's role they will supply criteria for evaluation from other discourses and disciplines. In other words, if one effect of postmodernism is to throw open what constitutes cultural value, teachers' responses are not likely to welcome the opportunity to define and debate what criteria they should be employing for the differing circum- stances of their students' work. On the contrary, as I have suggested above, evaluation is the exercise of power and requires the making of judgements and ranking distinctions. There is a logical inconsistency here. On the one hand we have the questioning of what constitutes cultural value, on the other the need to make judgements, and both tensions held in play by very definite histories relating to particular subjects and the individual students con- cerned. The clear difference of opinion between the arts educators in Chapter eight proves that this is a complex picture.

From this perspective, it is going to take some time to assess the effects of postmodernism on evaluation in the arts. Simon Frith's (1996) study of the question of value in popular music is applicable to many of the other art forms discussed in this book. He suggests a way of integrating popular crit- ical discourse with more academic traditions and of using personal feelings and responses to music in concert with the distance provided by sociological analyses. He argues that personal taste has a role to play in determining value as long as it can be something which is both produced by and produces response to the aesthetic experience. As a model of evaluation it is subtle and complex and again, time consuming: it is not a simple system of measure- ment. However, like the comments on the value of being explicit above, if cultural value can be negotiated by teacher and students in a relevant histor- ical and personal context, then making judgements will have salience for all concerned. Again, my argument and that of this book, is that for evaluation to be meaningful, it needs to be the subject of reflection itself by teachers and students alike.

The language of evaluation

If evaluation is to move away from something which is done to others to a position where it is incorporated into the day-to-day structure of teaching and learning it has to address the problem that in some circumstances, the process of evaluation might need to move beyond conventional language. In the chapters on Art and Music particularly, there is a continual questioning of the fact that the *visual* and the *aural* are domains, if not beyond, then co-existent with the *linguistic*. As the main methods of evaluation discussed in this book primarily involve the use of language in talk or writing, I want to discuss the implications of the non-verbal – the idea that the aesthetic experience might be unmeasurable simply, as it were, for technical reasons.

As Raney and Hollands discuss in their chapter, the idea of language has advantages and disadvantages. The main issue here is with the longstanding assumption that language is in some way inseparable from how we con-ceptualise thought. In general, it is argued that not only do we live in a society which values words as the primary means of expression, but which identifies the fundamental act of thinking as being in some way a linguistic process. Again, this is to simplify a complex body of enquiry and skates over recent attacks on the linguistic as the primary domain of meaning (e.g., Derrida 1977). In education, the influence of the social psychologists, Lev Vygotsky (e.g. 1962) and Jerome Bruner (e.g. 1996), has been immense, and as Robinson and Ellis suggest in their chapter on English, this has led to a position where English – as the subject concerned with the development of language abil-ities – is regarded as a more central subject for students than some others. In general, Vygotsky argues that our understanding of concepts is mediated by linguistic ability (see Barnes *et al.* 1969). The implication for education is that teaching has to pay attention to the acquisition and development of language if it is to develop conceptual understanding in students.

It is quite clear that the model of evaluation I have been developing in this chapter, which emphasises explicitness and a shared discourse, derives from this paradigm of language and learning. Indeed, as I have suggested, the commonality of approaches across all subject chapters only serves to re-enforce how much we are all drawing on the same ideas explaining how learning works. However, as I suggested in the introduction, recent study of multiple intelligences (Gardner 1983), coupled with ideological critiques of Western 'logocentrism', the primacy of language, might suggest we need to rethink some aspects of this approach (see also Eisner 1985 ch. 14). While Raney and Hollands show very clearly how not using words can act as a form of cultural exclusion, and intimating communication beyond language has a long tradition in the discourse of transcendence, in particular in relation to the apprehension of religious and aesthetic experience, this is not to say that non-verbal domains might not have any place in our evaluative procedures. Roz Hall, particularly, argues this point in Chapter eight and Herne, Raney and Hollands all refer to the use of sketchbooks as part of process-based evaluative procedures. There is, nevertheless, a contradiction between any attempt to introduce other modalities into the process and an appeal to implicit shared values – a return to the position that, if you don't understand a piece of art, you are in some way, inadequate.

Some of the strategies suggested by Raney and Holland's' case studies, by the arts educators in Chapter eight, or in the chapter on Media Studies do suggest that oblique methods of evaluation can be effective. In particular, these chapters stress what we might call, the 'translation effect', where moving across domains helps the learner become explicit about the making process. What is more, this translation does not always operate in one direction – towards linguistic transparency – sometimes it is suggested students benefit from viewing their work and teacher's evaluations of it through other perspectives (see Wolf 1989). The contributors to this book do not, by definition, have any simple models of this process, nor do they offer single methodological solutions. They do suggest that we need to find a way of including 'translation' strategies and honest and fair use of the non-verbal in our evaluative procedures. How this squares with the primacy of verbal language within the teaching and learning process needs, perhaps, to be the subject of further research.

Cultural production

A *social theory of creativity*

At several points in this chapter I have referred to an underlying tension between competing models of creativity. As I suggested in the introduction to this book, the term creativity is not exclusive or peculiar to the arts and we should not privilege artistic production above other forms of creative work within the education system in general. Nevertheless, it is impossible to discuss the evaluation of creative arts-based activities by young people without addressing what we might mean by creativity in the first place. At a number of points in the preceding chapters, contributors use terms like 'imagination' or even 'inspiration', and traditionally, these processes these have been seen as crucial to creative activity. However, what is more striking about the authors collected here is that they frequently characterise the creative process as a kind of dialogue. In virtually all the chapters the making process is described as a collective activity, often involving group work. Even in those subjects which stress individual achievements, the author in English or the composer in Music, the contributors have identified the social nature of the creative process as being of paramount importance.

This is not to say that in other circumstances the contributors might have emphasised work by individuals, but it is significant that in a culture which rewards the achievements of gifted individuals, attention to individuals has not occupied the preceding pages. I think there are three reasons for this shared approach. First, the pedagogic perspective emphasises that creativity employs skills and that these have to be learnt. Second, even gifted individuals learn within the social environment of the school and their development is not an entirely individualistic matter. Finally, I suggest that these authors are all working with a model of making which emphasises how products relate to the immediate and wider social influences surrounding their production. This is not, I would emphasise, any attempt to impose a crude model of Marxist economic determinism, but it does show how creativity is now conceptualised as a complex social process and not simply as an attribute of special individuals.

This shift in emphasis is significant for two reasons. First, at a general level, it shows how the romantic model of the creative artist, with its origins in the myth of divine inspiration, has to an extent been replaced with an understanding of the creative process as a complex, socially embedded multi-dimensional affair (see Kearney 1988). This is partly the result of post-structuralist theories of writing (e.g., Barthes 1977), and partly the growth of art-forms, especially multimedia, as Sinker argues, which are the result of collaborative activity. The models and ideas about genre and dialogue which occupy Art and English derive from much of the theory here. Secondly, it is very difficult for educationalists to make much use of the romantic theory of creativity because such ideas frequently suggest that gifted individuals are born rather than made – thus leaving little space for the influence of teachers. While some teachers may feel this is sometimes the case, the theory of romantic creativity and gifted individuals offers little insight into how such individuals develop and it does not explain the importance and value of creative activities for all those young people, for whom production, in one form or another, may be as valuable for the learning process as for the outcome of the creative activity.

If there is a shift in emphasis within education towards a social, rather than a romantic, theory of creativity then it poses a number of challenges. First of all, many of the contributors stress dialogue and interaction, with a premium being placed on the teacher as mediator of the creative process. This is not easy to assess and it is not easy to allocate marks to individuals within schemes where individuals are compared against one another. Indeed, the competitive nature of the examination system is frequently in conflict with teachers' abilities to even address the complexity of the making process, especially as Buckingham *et al.* describe, where making may be the result of a group activity. This conflict is both practical and ideological in that, to return again to macro-sociological perspectives, one aim of the examination system is to individuate students through differentiation from their peers, and the romantic model of creativity which rewards the creative individual, is the appropriate paradigm for this kind of differentiation.

Finally, in this section I want to suggest that a social model of creativity has greater vocational relevance than the romantic paradigm. As has been noted, creative activities in schools are often valued for their general educational worth, group work, discussion, negotiation etc. rather than their specific arts-based value. For example, Drama is frequently cited as the subject many employers look to find on applicants' CV's for precisely these kinds of reasons – that Drama gives students confidence in presenting themselves and ideas and that these are the kinds of skills valued in the workplace. Leaving aside the question of whether Drama can fulfil this kind of training function, it is important to note that working collaboratively in teams to set briefs is precisely the kind of contemporary labour skills allegedly in short supply (see Bentley 1998 ch. 8; for a critique of flexible labour see Cohen 1990). The kind of process described in a Drama, Media or Design classroom with an emphasis on peer and self-evaluation is exactly this kind of practical or 'useful' education despite its exclusion from National Curriculum Orders. The critical dialogue emphasised in Art or even Music suggests qualities of self-criticism and reflexivity: again qualities allegedly in demand by employers. I am not suggesting that creative activities in the curriculum be solely tailored to the demands of employers, or even that arts activities have to be validated by their vocational relevance. However, given that most students will derive *transferable* rather than subject specific value from creative activities at school, it is important that we pay attention to a process of evaluation which credits the social nature of production rather than solely values the gifts of unique individuals.

The sphere of cultural production

While a social theory of creativity may offer a broader approach with which we can make sense of the making process, it does not necessarily help us gain insight into how we evaluate the products of students' creative activities. Here I want to consider a number of arguments which develop a way of valuing students' expressive work in terms of their publication, or presentation, to real audiences; of what it might mean to think of young people as 'real' producers in the cultural sphere.

The key point of principle here is how we distinguish between evaluating students' work in educational terms – what it tells us or them about their progress in any discipline – and how we, and they, value creative work for its personal meaning or expressive salience. In the preceding chapters, authors have been concerned to value both what students are learning, but also to, as it were, respect, arts activities which allow students to make meaning for themselves. In particular, all the subjects considered in this book argue that 'making' gives students the opportunity to communicate and express themselves. These are not simple terms and to an extent they too, like the paradigms of creativity considered above, derive from a set of underlying assumptions. However, the preceding chapters all suggest that creative work is valued by students and teachers alike because of the personal investment made in such projects and the apparently 'meaningful', often emotional, value ascribed to arts activities.

On the whole, I would suggest that those teachers and arts educators who ascribe value to creative activities are, in effect, valuing their students as people who have something to say. On the other hand, an exclusive attention to what students are learning suggests that young people have not quite attained that status – they are 'intermediate beings', on their way to becoming proper people. This potentially contradictory tension essentially arises because of the conflicting ways we value the state of childhood and youth itself. Again, this tension touches on a wider set of arguments that I can not hope to do full justice to here. As a number of writers have noted, young people are defined simultaneously as caught between several definitions: between a state of being or becoming – of existing as entities in themselves and as vessels of change, caught in transition, on their way to becoming somebody else (e.g., Griffin 1993; James 1993). In terms of education, this curious double focus has played itself out over time. Thus, we have the child art movement, stemming from the 1920s which today may look gauche and patronising, but did, at some level, actually try to value what young people made as being of intrinsic interest in itself. On the other hand, young people are considered more in terms of what they *become* or what we, as adults, can make them be. Education here becomes a form of social investment and we as adults need to shape how young people mature in order to fully realise societies prudent husbandry of its precious resources.

Of course, both of these views of childhood can be, and indeed have been, held at the same time. Again, I would suggest that they are not necessarily notions which need to be thought of in opposition, but rather in terms of a continuum. The challenge for us is to realise that the expressive and communicative value we attribute to creative activities does, ultimately, rest on whichever view of young people we hold. If we think that school activities are simply a preparation for the 'real thing', that the curriculum is a series of simulations and exercises training young people for meaningful activities in the future, then it is very difficult to value young people's creative work in education for itself. On the other hand, if we conceptualise young people as being, in some way, independent agents, then we will read and enjoy their work in its own right. As I have already suggested, the common response to this dilemma is to mix and match: we find young peoples' work expressive but in need of support; it may communicate with a limited audience but needs refocusing to reach a broader range of people and so on.

The most fully developed studies of young people's independence as cultural producers is, however, in the field of Youth and Cultural Studies, notably that of Paul Willis (1990). Willis' survey of what he calls 'symbolic creativity' takes into account a huge range of informal educational activities undertaken by young people either in disorganised settings, like friendship groups, or in semi-structured environments such as youth clubs and community arts centres. There are a range of other studies, particularly of aspirant popular musicians (Finnegan 1989: Fornäs *et al.* 1995) again focusing on out-of-school cultural activities which show young people actively making culture either for themselves, their peers, or the wider community.

What is strange about virtually all of these studies is that they exclude the school and arts activities made in the school from this picture of creative youth.

In common with several other cultural studies projects, Willis' target is the elitist establishment of high culture and his study convincingly makes the case that the huge variety of expressive activities undertaken by young people proves how vibrant popular culture is, in contradistinction to the arid exclusiveness of high culture. However, this attack on the credibility of high culture as the privileged site of meaning and expressiveness leads him into a situation where schooling becomes allied with the enemy, and therefore part of the problem. The argument of this book, and others, suggests quite the contrary. While there clearly are a number of tensions in various curriculum areas, the evidence is, that many teachers and young people find school the institution where they are most likely to have access to creative activities and where an audience for their work can most readily be found. In other words, what happens if we consider creative activities made in school, in the same way as Willis conceptualises the forms of 'symbolic culture' he finds in young people's activities at large? And a further question follows on from this: can we consider the school as a proper 'site' for cultural production? After all it creates a community and an audience, and performing and displaying work has resonance for audiences and producers alike in much the same way as culture produced by amateur arts for local or community audiences.

There are two key arguments here. First, the notion of audience and audience response, and second, the status of amateurism. I shall consider each in turn. I have already suggested that the capacity to self-evaluate is prized by practitioners across the range of disciplines represented in this book, but equally the shared valuing of dialogue stresses how important feedback from others is to the creative process. A number of subjects, (especially Music and Drama) discuss the value of live or mediated audiences and the role audience plays in the overall experience of the product. The new media discussed by Sinker in Chapter nine, and the conferencing described by Robinson and Ellis in Chapter four also raises the possibility that digital media, especially the Internet, can provide a genuinely new public arena for young people to meet and share their culture. However, in all the excitement surrounding the communicative prospects of the web, it is important not to forgot the values of old-fashioned community participation, like the school play or concert. In other words, there are a range of public, or even semi-public (like the 'crits' described by Raney and Hollands) arenas which provide real audiences for expressive work. The feedback from the experience of public production is crucial for all forms of cultural production and, again a key theme across all of these chapters, is the need to draw on the real context for pupils' work as part of the evaluative process. From this perspective, teachers in creative subjects have to find ways to involve pupils' peers as audience and help students learn from the experience of display. Indeed, showing work in most of these subjects to an audience is probably the most important way of beginning evaluation.

The second argument about amateurism relates to this. Although the history of amateur arts in this country tends to be blighted by the image of the village 'am-dram', in fact, as Willis' work suggests, there is a huge range of creative activities undertaken on an amateur basis up and down the country (Hutchinson and Feist 1991). Traditionally, much amateur work has suffered from lack of public funding. It would seem as if quite early in its troubled history the Arts Council of England drew lines between professional arts activities and amateur ones (Bartlett 1996). However, the boundaries between the professional and amateur arts are not always that clear: performers, producers and audiences often criss-cross work in both sectors (Casey *et al.* 1996). However, young people are nearly always exempt from these debates and again I would suggest this is a strange exclusion. School and community arts centres frequently stage performances and displays in addition to the quite voluntary 'amateur' medium of the Internet, so why are young people discounted from the sphere of amateurism? As I have already suggested, this is partly because young people are seen as intermediate, as at stages in their development, and partly because much creative work is undertaken as an educational activity and justified for the learning process. However, if arts work in schools could move more into the public or semi-public arena it may be that the status of creative production by young people would begin to change. In turn this would affect how teachers and pupil value its impact and overall this would affect how we evaluate creativity.

Different subjects?

The rationale for this collection was that young people experience a range of creative activities as part of their schooling and that the different histories and traditions of these subjects may establish contradictory expectations for the young people themselves. However, the accounts given by the contributors to this volume do actually suggest a significant amount of common ground. In this sense the volume as a whole makes the case not so much for an original theory of evaluation, but for a shared body of experience across the subjects with their discrete skills and values. There seem then to be two kinds of conclusions: theoretical and policy orientated. For the former I would say that writing about evaluation tends to be a bit like attempts to square the circle, or perhaps, just going round in circles. There are a number of shared practices across subjects and the teachers can work more closely with colleagues to improve these. Teaching students the language to self-evaluate; learning how to evaluate; and how to teach students to do so; developing opportunities for talk and other kinds of reflection are the most important of these. Developing a value for students' work in the real context of the school, and highlighting the impact of audience are also significant.

(And in teaching these, the teacher will inevitably reflect on their work, the art of teaching, and this in turn may act, reflexively, to change educational practice.)

At the policy level, the findings of this collection suggest a need to be able to cope with a series of contractions in creative subjects, not to try to *resolve* conflict but to accept that the evaluation of creative work calls on so many different perspectives that it has to be seen as a complex process. Here, myself and others have stressed that in an era of increased centralisation of the curriculum, teachers need to be given time and authority to be able to resolve these matters in the contexts of their own classrooms and schools – that is the only way for better teaching and learning. We cannot expect evaluation to be simple and straightforward if we want to deal properly with all the implications of getting young people to work creatively in the curriculum.

References

Abbs, P. (1994) *The Educational Imperative: A Defence of Socratic and Aesthetic Learning*, London: The Falmer Press.

Ball, S. (ed.) (1990) *Foucault and Education: Disciplines and Knowledge*, London: Routledge.

Barnes, D., Britton, J. and Rosen, H. (1969) *Language, the Learner and the School*, Harmondsworth: Penguin.

Bartlett, H. (1996) 'Facilitating participation in the arts' unpublished paper presented at A4E consultation at the Arts Council of England.

Barthes, R. (1977) *Image, Music, Text*, London: Fontana Press.

Bentley, T. (1998) *Learning Beyond the Classroom: Education for a Changing World*, London: Routledge.

Bruner, J. (1966) *Towards a Theory of Instruction*, Cambridge, Mass.: Harvard University Press.

Buckingham, D. Grahame, J. and Sefton-Green, J. (1995) *Making Media: Practical Production in Media Education*, London: English and Media Centre.

Casey, B., Dunlop, R. and Selwood, S. (1996) *Culture as Commodity: The Economics of the Arts and Built Heritage in the UK*, London: Policy Studies Institute.

Cohen, P. (1990) 'Teaching enterprise culture: individualism, vocationalism and the new right' in Taylor, I. (ed.) *The Social Effect of Market Policies*, Brighton: Harvester Wheatsheaf.

Collins, J. (1989) *Uncommon Cultures; Popular Culture and Post-Modernism*, London: Routledge.

Derrida, J. (1977) *Of Grammatology*, Baltimore: Johns Hopkins Press.

Edwards, D. and Mercer, N. (1987) *Common Knowledge. The Development of Understanding in the Classroom*, London: Methuen.

Eisner, E. (1985) *The Art of Educational Evaluation*, Brighton: The Falmer Press.

Finnegan, R. (1989) *The Hidden Musicians: Music-making in an English Town*, Cambridge: Cambridge University Press.

Fornäs, J., Lindberg, U. and Sernhede, O. (1995) *In Garageland: Rock, Youth and Modernity* (trans. Teeland, J.), London: Routledge.

Frith, S. (1996) *Performing Rites: On the Value of Popular Music*, Oxford: Oxford University Press.

Gardner, H. (1983) *Frames of Mind: The Theory of Multiple Intelligences*, London: Paladin.

Goodwin, A. (1992) *Dancing in the Distraction Factory*, London: Routledge.

Griffin, C. (1993) *Representations of Youth. The Study of Youth and Adolescence in Britain and America*, Cambridge: Polity Press.

Harvey, D. (1989) *The Condition of Postmodernity: An Enquiry into the Origins of Cultural Change*, Oxford: Basil Blackwell.

Hughes, R. (1993) *Culture of Complaint: The Fraying of America*, Oxford: Oxford University Press.

Hutchinson, R. and Feist, A. (1991) *Amateur Arts in the UK: The PSI Survey of Amateur Arts and Crafts in the UK*, London: Policy Studies Institute.

James, A. (1993) *Childhood Identities*, Edinburgh: Edinburgh University Press.

Jones, K. (ed.) (1992) *English and the National Curriculum: Cox's Revolution?*, London: Kogan Page.

Kearney, R. (1988) *The Wake of Imagination: Ideas of Creativity in Western Culture*, London: Hutchinson.

Kress, G. and van Leeuwen, T. (1996) *Reading Images: The Grammar of Visual Design*, London: Routledge.

McRobbie, A. (1994) *Postmodernism and Popular Culture*, London: Routledge.

Schwichtenberg, C. (ed.) (1993) *The Madonna Connection: Representational Politics, Subcultural Identities, and Cultural Theory*, Boulder, Col.: Westview Press.

Vygotsky, L. (1962) *Thought and Language* (trans. Hanfmann E. and Vakar G.), Cambridge, Mass.: M.I.T. Press.

Willis, P. (1990) *Common Culture*, Milton Keynes: Open University.

White, H. (1993) *Careers and Creativity: Social Forces in the Arts*, Boulder, Col.: Westview Press.

Wolf, D. (1989) 'Artistic learning as conversation' in Hargreaves (ed.) *Children and the Arts*, Buckingham: Open University Press.

Index